Generative AI for Students

STUDENT SUCCESS

Generative AI for Students

The Essential Guide to Using Artificial Intelligence for Study at University

David Meechan

1 Oliver's Yard
55 City Road
London EC1Y 1SP

2455 Teller Road
Thousand Oaks
California 91320

Unit No 323-333, Third Floor, F-Block
International Trade Tower
Nehru Place New Delhi 110 019

8 Marina View Suite 43-053
Asia Square Tower 1
Singapore 018960

Editor: Kate Keers
Editorial assistant: Becky Oliver
Production editor: Imogen Roome
Copyeditor: Ritika Sharma
Proofreader: Girish Sharma
Indexer: TNQ Tech Pvt. Ltd.
Marketing manager: Maria Omena
Cover design: Sheila Tong
Typeset by: TNQ Tech Pvt. Ltd.
Printed in the UK

© David Meechan 2025

Apart from any fair dealing for the purposes of research, private study, or criticism or review, as permitted under the Copyright, Designs and Patents Act, 1988, this publication may not be reproduced, stored or transmitted in any form, or by any means, without the prior permission in writing of the publisher, or in the case of reprographic reproduction, in accordance with the terms of licences issued by the Copyright Licencing Agency. Enquiries concerning reproduction outside those terms should be sent to the publisher.

Library of Congress Control Number: 2024939701

British Library Cataloguing in Publication data

A catalogue record for this book is available from the British Library

ISBN 978-1-5296-8343-1
ISBN 978-1-5296-8342-4 (pbk)

Contents

About the Author xi
Acknowledgements xiii

Introduction 1
Why write a study guide on using Generative Artificial Intelligence at university? 1
How is the book organised? 1
How was Generative Artificial Intelligence used in the writing of this book? 2

Part 1 What You Need to Know About Generative AI 5

1 Navigating the AI Landscape 7
  1.1 Chapter objectives 7
  1.2 Having read this chapter you will… 7
  1.3 Introduction 7
  1.4 How can we understand the concept of 'Artificial Intelligence?' in relation to this book? 8
  1.5 Generative AI: Key terms and jargon 10
  1.6 Historical context and evolution of AI 12
  1.7 Generative AI and the evolution of GPTs by Open AI 12
  1.8 Controversy and limitations in the development of ChatGPT 13
  1.9 The rising sea of AI knowledge, AI application and its interpretation in academia 14
  1.10 Moravec's Paradox and landscape with AI 16
  1.11 How can AI contribute to equity, diversity and inclusion at university? 17
  1.12 Summary of chapter 19

1.13	Chapter hacks	19
1.14	Chapter MCQs	20

2 What Can Generative AI Do for Your Study Skills?   22

2.1	Chapter objectives	22
2.2	Having read this chapter you will…	22
2.3	Introduction	23
2.4	Your study buddy AI assistant	23
2.5	Enhancing learning, comprehension and application independently	25
2.6	Start scenario	27
2.7	Critical thinking and analytical skills	29
2.8	Searching for literature and writing assistance	31
2.9	Time management and studying more efficiently	34
2.10	What will AI-assisted study look like in the (near) future?	35
2.11	Summary of chapter	36
2.12	Chapter hacks	37
2.13	Chapter MCQs	38

3 Academic Integrity and the Ethical Use of Generative AI at University   39

3.1	Chapter objectives	39
3.2	Having read this chapter, you will…	39
3.3	Introduction	40
3.4	Academic Integrity: What is it and why should you care?	40
3.5	How has Artificial Intelligence impacted Academic Integrity and what does this mean for the award gap that university students face?	42
3.6	Promoting academic integrity in relation to Bloom's Taxonomy and AI literacy	44
3.7	Are you allowed to use AI tools, assistants and content?	46
3.8	Protecting your privacy when using AI tools	48
3.9	Future-proof your skillset	49
3.10	Skills to prioritise	50
3.11	Summary of chapter	51
3.12	Chapter hacks	51
3.13	Chapter MCQs	52

Contents

Part 2 How to Support Your Study With Generative AI — 55

4 Getting Started With Generative AI — 57
- 4.1 Chapter objectives — 57
- 4.2 Having read this chapter, you will... — 57
- 4.3 Introduction — 58
- 4.4 To sign-up or not to sign-up? — 59
- 4.5 Free or fee? — 59
- 4.6 Officially vetted vs the wild west? — 61
- 4.7 Novice or pro? — 61
- 4.8 Prompting and prompting frameworks — 62
- 4.9 Unpacking the AI tool kit — 63
- 4.10 AI Writing tools — 64
- 4.11 AI image creation tools — 66
- 4.12 AI presentation/slides tools — 69
- 4.13 AI video creation tools — 72
- 4.14 Summary — 73
- 4.15 Chapter hacks — 73
- 4.16 Chapter MCQs — 74

5 Using Generative AI Tools to Support Your Study — 76
- 5.1 Chapter objectives — 76
- 5.2 Having read this chapter, you will... — 76
- 5.3 Introduction — 76
- 5.4 Traditional approaches to studying — 77
- 5.5 AI-assisted approaches to studying — 79
- 5.6 AI-assisted study notes — 80
- 5.7 Summary — 88
- 5.8 Chapter hacks — 89
- 5.9 Chapter MCQs — 90

Part 3 How to Approach Your Assessments With Generative AI — 91

6 Essays — 93
- 6.1 Chapter objectives — 93
- 6.2 Having read this chapter, you will... — 93
- 6.3 Introduction — 94
- 6.4 What is an essay? — 94

6.5	Why are essays used in the assessment process?	96
6.6	Checklist to begin the assignment: Essay	97
6.7	Understanding the assessment format	99
6.8	Understanding the learning outcomes	101
6.9	Connecting the Learning outcomes with assessment format and taught content	104
6.10	Is the use of GAI permitted in the final assignment?	107
6.11	Time management – When to research and write an essay with AI	109
6.12	Walk-through example: AI-assisted approach to creating an essay	113
6.13	Summary of chapter	119
6.14	Chapter hacks	119
6.15	Chapter MCQs	120

7 Presentations — 122

7.1	Chapter objectives	122
7.2	Having read this chapter, you will…	122
7.3	Introduction	123
7.4	What is a presentation?	123
7.5	Individual or group presentations	124
7.6	Different types of presentation	125
7.7	Why are presentations used in the assessment process and why is feedback from them important?	126
7.8	Checklist to begin the assignment: Presentation	127
7.9	Understanding the assessment format	127
7.10	Understanding the learning outcomes	129
7.11	Is the use of Generative AI permitted in the final assignment?	133
7.12	What could the ethical use of Generative AI in a presentation involve?	133
7.13	Time management – When to create and practice a presentation	133
7.14	Walk-through example: AI-assisted approach to creating a presentation	135
7.15	Summary of chapter	142
7.16	Chapter hacks	143
7.17	Chapter MCQs	143

8 Exams — 145

- 8.1 Chapter objectives — 145
- 8.2 Having read this chapter, you will… — 145
- 8.3 Introduction — 146
- 8.4 What is an exam? — 146
- 8.5 Types of exam — 147
- 8.6 Typical question types in an exam — 148
- 8.7 Why are exams used in the assessment process? — 149
- 8.8 Checklist to begin the assignment: Exam — 150
- 8.9 Understanding the assessment format — 150
- 8.10 Is the use of GAI permitted in the final exam? — 152
- 8.11 What could the ethical use of AI for an exam involve? — 152
- 8.12 Time management: What needs to be done when preparing for an exam? — 154
- 8.13 Familiarisation with the learning outcomes that the exam is based on — 155
- 8.14 Walk-through example: AI-assisted approach to a take-home exam assignment — 156
- 8.15 Summary of chapter — 159
- 8.16 Chapter hacks — 160
- 8.17 Chapter MCQs — 161

9 E-portfolios — 162

- 9.1 Chapter objectives — 162
- 9.2 Having read this chapter, you will… — 162
- 9.3 Introduction — 163
- 9.4 What is an e-portfolio? — 163
- 9.5 Why are e-portfolios used in the assessment process? — 165
- 9.6 Checklist to begin the assignment: E-portfolio — 166
- 9.7 E-portfolio tools and software — 166
- 9.8 Understanding the assessment format — 167
- 9.9 Is the use of GAI permitted in the final assignment? — 169
- 9.10 What could the ethical use of GAI in an e-portfolio involve? — 169
- 9.11 Example learning outcomes from an E-portfolio — 170
- 9.12 Time management – What needs to be done by when for an e-portfolio? — 173
- 9.13 Connecting theory and literature to an e-portfolio entry using an AI assistant — 174

9.14	Summary of chapter	177
9.15	Chapter hacks	178
9.16	Chapter MCQs	179

Part 4 How to Explore Feedback With Generative AI   **181**

10 Grades and Feedback   **183**

10.1	Chapter objectives	183
10.2	Having read this chapter, you will…	183
10.3	Introduction	184
10.4	What are university grades and feedback based on?	185
10.5	Understanding what grades and feedback mean at your university	185
10.6	Types of grades used at universities	186
10.7	Types of summative related feedback used at universities	186
10.8	Why is feedback important?	187
10.9	Using AI assistants to help understand initial assignment feedback	188
10.10	Interpreting feedback across assignments	191
10.11	Summary of chapter	192
10.12	Chapter hacks	192
10.13	Chapter MCQs	193

References	195
Prompt List	199
Index	201

About the Author

David Meechan is the author of *Generative AI for Students: The Essential Guide to Using Artificial Intelligence for Study at University*. He is currently a Senior Lecturer in Education at the University of Northampton.

David has worked in Higher Education in England since 2018, having previously trained and worked in a number of education-related roles predominantly based within Early Childhood or Primary aspects of education. Since entering Higher Education, David has engaged with and supported a wide range of innovative approaches to teaching, learning and assessment. This has led to a natural interest in how technology, and more recently AI, can be utilised in assisting students in the processes of study at university.

Acknowledgements

First, a big thankyou to my students. Your reactions and honesty in relation to the use of Generative AI-based tools were what instigated the process that has led to me writing this book.

A huge thankyou to my colleagues at the University of Northampton, many of whom have played a role in shaping the direction of my evolving engagement with how AI can be used as a force for good within Higher Education. A further specific acknowledgement to those colleagues who shared examples of practice and assessments when I was researching the chapters in Part Three of the book.

Thankyou to my family and friends for the debates on this contemporary subject. These have informed the foundations of why I believe using AI to support students at university will become the norm in the future.

Finally, a very special thankyou to Hortencia, Davi and Manu for their support. They have had many weekends' worth of patience so that I could spend time writing. Thank you.

Introduction

Why write a study guide on using Generative Artificial Intelligence at university?

When I first used Chat GPT in December 2022 I was impressed. I was surprised with its feel as it was different from the typical search and return experiences that I had become so accustomed to. I quickly began to experiment with creating different types of 'prompt' and exploring the results. This, I felt, needed to be shared with work colleagues and the students I taught. But what really surprised me next were people's reactions. They weren't all positive. Many far from it. However, it felt like pandora's box had been opened and was not going to be closed anytime soon. As a respectful disruptor I knew more application, experimentation and reflection were needed. I therefore signed up to every AI newsletter I could find online and dived in headfirst. Not all experiments reaped the results I had hoped. In fact, most did not.

> *If you fail, never give up because F.A.I.L. means "first Attempt In Learning".*
> APJ Abdul Kalam

What the failure quickly taught me was that the AI tools were not as good as I had assumed. Using AI tools also held a mirror up to my role as an academic at a university. My job had not changed, but the tools at my disposal had. What an exciting time to be alive! This book therefore attempts to capture some of the evolving approaches to study and learning that can be utilised as the use of Generative AI becomes more embedded across society.

How is the book organised?

The book has ten chapters which are divided into four parts:

1. What you need to know about Generative AI
2. How to support your study with Generative AI

3. How to approach your assessments with Generative AI
4. How to explore feedback with Generative AI

Part 1- What you need to know about Generative AI

Chapter 1 provides a general overview of the AI landscape at the time of writing, exploring a brief history, some theory and relevant key terms relating to AI. Chapter 2 begins to introduce and unpick what and how Generative AI may be able to help students with their study skills by exploring the use of an AI assistant as a 'study buddy'. Chapter 3 explores the ethical use of Generative AI and specifically considers what is meant by academic integrity and how this should be adhered to when using Generative AI to assist students in their study.

Part 2- How to support your study with Generative AI

Chapter 4 explains some of the basic considerations that should be undertaken when deciding which AI-based tools to engage with, especially relating to the protection of your own private information and identity. Chapter 5 explores how Generative AI and AI assistants can be utilised to capitalise on traditional approaches to study but enhance the efficiency of such approaches.

Part 3- How to approach your assessments with Generative AI

Chapters 6–9 each explore a specific type of assessment: essays; presentations; exams; and e-portfolios. A brief introduction and explanation of each format is provided before considerations of 'how', 'when' and 'if' the use of Generative Artificial Intelligence Tools is allowed.

Part 4- How to explore feedback with Generative AI

Chapter 10 was a late addition to the book and not originally planned for. However, in response to continuing experimentation and how Generative AI can be utilised to support students with understanding their feedback, it provides a worthy final chapter.

How was Generative Artificial Intelligence used in the writing of this book?

It would feel sacrilege to not acknowledge the integral role that Generative AI has played in assisting me to write this book. The first draft of each chapter's structure was generated based on my initial plan and ideas (see Prompt 19 for an insight into developing plans and structures). Chapters often diverged from the generated draft structures as I began writing, but attempts were made to keep the chapters in Part 3 of the book aligned when approaches to essays, presentations, exams and e-portfolios are explored. The main content or sections of each chapter were written first by myself. Once the main sections of a chapter had been completed, Generative AI was used to produce first drafts of:

Chapter Objectives
Having Read this chapter you will...
Introduction to chapter
Summary of chapter
Chapter Hacks
Chapter Multiple Choice Quizzes (MCQs).

Any output from an AI assistant was based on the direct input of content by myself and edited as needed to ensure it aligned with my intentions for the chapter and associated parts, as well as my commitment to promoting an AI-assisted approach to academic work, study and writing.

PART ONE

WHAT YOU NEED TO KNOW ABOUT GENERATIVE AI

1
Navigating the AI Landscape

1.1 Chapter objectives

1. Introduce AI concepts so that they are easier to understand. This will involve some history, theory and key terms relating to AI.
2. Highlight AI's relevance through examples in Higher Education and University life.
3. Introduce the opportunities that AI presents in enhancing teaching, learning and assessment in higher education.
4. Discuss AI's role in promoting equity, diversity and inclusion in educational environments.
5. Highlight continuous learning as a key part of adapting to AI's continued development and evolving capacity in relation to skills.

1.2 Having read this chapter you will...

1. You will be introduced to complex AI concepts in an accessible manner, including historical context, theoretical foundations and key terminology.
2. You will recognise AI's relevance through examples and applications within Higher Education and University.
3. You will understand the opportunities AI provides to enhance teaching, learning experiences and assessment across higher education.
4. You will learn about AI's role in developing further equitable, diverse and inclusive experiences for students at university improving access for all.
5. You will appreciate the importance of continuous learning and adaptation in response to the ongoing development and expanding capabilities of AI in academia.

1.3 Introduction

AI is a disruptive technology, and, as is the case with all such technologies, it creates risks and opportunities.

(Zarbin, 2020)

Artificial Intelligence (AI) is having a huge impact on teaching, learning and research at all levels. As Zarbin (2020) observed, this creates both risk and opportunity. It also challenges traditional ways of doing and thinking about things. In academic speak, this contributes to the world we live in changing and how we conceptualise the impact of such a technology. AI is leading to new possibilities within established frameworks and outside of them. AI is anything but stagnant and therefore avoids a clear definition. It is developing and evolving in many forms and across many applications. AI is not yet able to replicate the cornerstone of human experience – natural intelligence – but, without doubt, it is moving in that direction and will continue to impact our lives for the foreseeable future.

In simplest terms, the type of AI can be defined as narrow/weak AI or strong AI. Narrow/weak AI applications are embedded across our lives and operate internet searches, disease detection, recommender systems and speech detection. These systems have been developed using machine learning and natural language processing – terms that will be explained in more detail later on in this chapter. 'Strong AI' or 'Artificial General Intelligence', however, is the direction of travel developments within AI are heading towards. For example, strong AI is the technology behind autonomous vehicles by Tesla, Uber and Waymo. Strong AI also informs speech recognition and approaches to image processing. With time, strong AI applications will become more prominent. Applications of strong AI are becoming adept at producing original content that the unsuspecting eye may glance over without questioning its authenticity. In terms of higher education, this can range from written assignments to more complex research projects which include data and analysis. As long as it is used ethically, this sort of AI has the potential to support further creativity and innovation across the higher education sector.

With such constant evolution in mind, it is recognised that some of the applications of AI and tools discussed in the book may have already transformed by its date of publication. However, the wider dialogue that this chapter covers is relevant and will contribute to developing AI literacy across higher education and the university experience. This chapter will discuss the historical context of AI, key terms, the evolution of significant models like the GPT series and insight into AI's growing capabilities and potential in higher education. Two key framings on AI by Professor Max Tegmark and Professor Hans Moravec will be explained, before a final snapshot of how AI is informing more equitable, diverse and inclusive approaches across higher education is considered.

1.4 How can we understand the concept of 'Artificial Intelligence?' in relation to this book?

> AI is not really one thing but describes a constellation of methods, approaches and technologies that help systems mimic aspects of natural intelligence.

Originating in the middle of last century, AI is both diverse and constantly evolving and, as such, has far evaded a consistent and agreed upon definition amongst AI scholars.

(Luger, 2023, p. 4)

The above explanation provides a basis for us to begin to conceptualise and think about what AI is and is not in relation to this book. Multiple conceptions of AI have existed in both a historical and contemporary sense as the above quote acknowledges. The second sentence alludes to why this is a problematic area in terms of AI's constant evolution. Indeed, as already stated, during the time spent writing, the author has been very aware that the examples covered may well have evolved by the time of publication due to the rapid developments currently taking place in AI. This fact, however, is also part of the rationale for this book – as it is important to document how students can engage ethically with the use of Generative AI in their studies. If anything, this book is capturing a shift from more traditional digital-based, but transaction-heavy approaches, to AI-assisted approaches that allow for the automation of some tasks. This book will therefore contribute to the current conceptualisations of AI in Higher Education as it stands.

AI is a general term applied across an increasingly wide range of avenues. To date, few technological advancements in human history have impacted us as much as AI is predicted to. Tran (2023) provides us with an analogy worthy of further exploration: AI as the 'new electricity'. The concept of electricity was not new when Benjamin Franklin began experimenting with it in the mid-18th century. Franklin's ability to negotiate the risks with opportunities has led to his cementation in the history books when it comes to electricity. Many other scientists and inventors have since contributed discoveries, experimentation and applications regarding electricity. Such endeavours have allowed electricity's use and integration across everyday life. However, such integration is not universal across the globe. It is estimated that 10% of people do not have access to electricity, hence the United Nation's Sustainable Development Goal 7: Affordable and Clean Energy (UN). Even though the analogy of electricity impacting nearly everyone's daily lives is valid, it is also worth considering the question of access both across and within countries in relation to AI.

The early pioneers of AI, such as Alan Turing, a British mathematician and computer scientist, and John McCarthy, an American computer scientist, enabled foundational research in both theory and application. This created interest in both the risks and the opportunities created, in much the same way as early experimentation with electricity had. AI is now present in mainstream applications across smartphones, internet services and home automation. AI interacts with daily and provides convenience, machine efficiency and enhancements across many tasks. Just as users of electricity do not need to understand electromagnetism to benefit from electric lighting, neither do users of AI-based technologies have to understand machine learning algorithms or neural networks to benefit from it. Furthermore, just as not all people have access to electricity across the globe, many, many more, do not have access to the latest AI-based systems and even in countries where access is higher, there are still discrepancies. For example, a survey of high school students in the USA found that 46% of students surveyed were using AI tools, but that students with higher academic performance were significantly more likely to use AI tools than students with lower academic performance (Kyaw, 2023).

Even without universal access to electricity, electricity dependence is a cornerstone of modern society. It is critical in powering our homes, industry, and infrastructure. Yet the average person who interacts with and depends on this form of energy in their daily life, rarely questions what principles lie behind it. You only need to spend a day in a region where 'load shedding' is common or get caught in a storm-induced power cut, and you will soon realise the hole left by an absence of electricity in our modern lives. The creep of AI into daily life is not a recent phenomenon (Estienne, 2016). AI algorithms power search engines, social media feeds and publicly available Large Language Models. Active experimentation of AI technology within financial, healthcare and military-related systems also exists, although less publicised because of concerns around who is making the decisions. It cannot be denied, however, that with the increasing application of AI-based approaches across our lives, both increased opportunities and risks accompany them.

For the purpose of this skills book then, how can the concept of AI be conceptualised? AI, Generative AI and AI assistants refer to publicly available tools and applications that are based on AI technology. Within the sphere of Higher Education and University, such tools, software and functionality are seen as endeavours to support and enhance human development. Ultimately, they are a force for good. Jane Mills, a Senior Lecturer in Fashion at the University of Northampton, has described the potential of such AI practice best – 'it promotes human creativity, with machine-based efficiency'. Parts 2 and 3 of this book explore this further.

1.5 Generative AI: Key terms and jargon

This section is not aiming to make you an 'AI scientist', but aims to introduce key terms that are commonly used in relation to AI technology. The purpose of this is to increase your exposure to such jargon in the hope that the more they are heard, the less threatening they feel. With decreasing alienation, the terms will become easier to understand as concepts in the wider AI landscape and improve AI literacy, questioning and critique. This will be important as you explore and interact with AI-based tools and technology in the future, especially the tools and assistants that are not yet created! For a more comprehensive introduction to the below terminology, please refer to the work of Luger (2023, pp. 4–9).

Algorithms: These are a set of automated instructions and have been developed by computer scientists for decades. Algorithms range in complexity. The greater the number of steps, rules and calculations within an algorithm, the more complex it is. For algorithms to work, the steps need to be in the correct order. If the different parts of the algorithm are not in the correct order, then it will either fail or produce an unintended outcome. Testing algorithms, their application and their results is essential. Traditionally, humans created and tested algorithms, but AI systems can now do this as well (Hutson, 2023).

Machine Learning: This term was first coined by Arthur Samuel in 1959. It is considered a sub-field of AI and focuses on the creation of learning within machines. Different techniques are used, but the ultimate aim is to deduce a model from the algorithms and data that the machine receives as input. Once an initial model is created, it cannot only change with the addition of more data but the patterns learnt can be applied to predict things in different situations. This application of prior knowledge (or data) to new contexts is the 'learning' aspect.

Deep Learning and Neural Networks: Deep learning is an approach that offers complex and adaptable models of learning based on the detection of complex patterns. Deep learning requires vast amounts of data (text/images/video/audio etc.) to train such models and optimise output. Neural networks consist of an input layer, an output layer and a hidden layer, with deep learning networks consisting of many, many neural networks. This is essentially modelled on the human brain and the vast array of networks that connect within it to make it work.

Generative Adversarial Networks: This includes two models in a learning process. The first model is trying to improve its generation of new and synthetic data based on its training. The ultimate aim is that the second model will not be able to distinguish this new data generated by the first model from the real data that both models have been trained on. This becomes a key part of the learning and mastery of outputs.

Natural Language Processing: This term within the AI field focuses on the technology that enables devices to respond to commands. This may be in the form of speech or text generated by humans with the most widely accessible examples being voice-activated assistants such as Siri, Google, Alexa etc.

Pre-trained models: This type of model is pre-trained on an extensive and diverse range of inputs. This training enables it to establish patterns in the data and therefore respond and create when prompted. An example is a GPT (Generative Pre-Trained Transformer); these excel in predicting the next word in a sentence having been trained on a wide range of language patterns, structures and information. It was the public release of ChatGPT version 3.5 in November 2022, that signalled a new error for pre-trained models.

1.6 Historical context and evolution of AI

'Can machines think?' (Turing, 1950, p. 433) is a key question that continues to drive the AI revolution today. During the time Turing was asking this question, the earliest computers lacked a key prerequisite for intelligence – the ability to store commands, not only execute them. Several years later, Allen Newell, Cliff Shaw and Herbert Simon created a programme called 'Logic Theorist'. This was designed to mimic the problem-solving skills of a human and is considered by many to be the first AI programme which paved the way for the next 20 years of AI research. However, from the late 1970s to the late 1980s, developments in AI fell short of the high expectations that had been set. This period is referred to as 'The AI winter'. Fast forward to 1997 and interest in AI was reignited once more. The world chess champion and a grandmaster at the time, Gary Kasparov, was beaten by IBM's Deep Blue, a chess-playing computer programme. Speech recognition software was also implemented in Microsoft Windows that year as AI-related capacities increased. It was not until 2016, however, that a computer programme was capable of beating the world champion in the board game 'Go' – a strategy game invented in China more than 2,500 years ago.

1.7 Generative AI and the evolution of GPTs by Open AI

Although the concept of Generative AI was not new, it was only after the creation of Generative adversarial networks in 2014 that AI began to create more convincingly authentic images, videos and audio of real people. Fast forward to 2024 and the latest Generative AI programmes are capable of creating content indistinguishable from content created by humans to the unsuspecting eye. This has led to the creation, development and improvement of several GPTs by Open AI. The GPTs it has created have been trained on increasing amounts of data (see Table 1.1) which have improved outputs, mimicking creativity and understanding across multiple subjects and disciplines.

Table 1.1 GPT development

Iteration and release date	Parameters	Capabilities	Examples	Limitations
GPT-1 June 2018	117 Million	Introduced the potential of transformer models in Natural Language Processing (NLP), capable of generating text based on input, and understanding context to a basic extent	Simple text completion, basic question answering	Limited understanding of context, prone to generating irrelevant or nonsensical text beyond simple tasks
GPT-2 February 2019	1.5 Billion	Advanced text generation with more coherent and contextually relevant outputs, enhancing a range of NLP applications	More sophisticated text completion, short story writing, simple translation and basic coding assistance	Still struggled with more complex understanding, maintaining context over longer texts, and sometimes producing biased or incorrect information
GPT-3 June 2020	175 Billion	Significant leap in text generation and understanding, capable of sophisticated writing assistance, advanced conversational AI and more	Advanced story and article writing, comprehensive language translation, complex coding assistance, creative content generation like poetry and dialogue and educational tutoring	Despite vast improvements, limitations include occasional lack of common-sense reasoning, producing factually incorrect information and challenges in truly understanding user intent

1.8 Controversy and limitations in the development of ChatGPT

Identification of the exact financial cost may be much easier to conclude than the human cost. It was reported by Time magazine in January 2023 that 'Open AI used Kenyan workers on less than $2 per hour to make ChatGPT less toxic' (Perrigo, 2023). Whilst such tasks were outsourced by Open AI to other companies, it does show the continued need for human input and potential exploitation in order to develop new models. Strait (2023) comments:

They're impressive, but ChatGPT and other generative models are not magic – they rely on massive supply chains of human labour and scraped data, much of which is unattributed and used without consent. These are serious, foundational problems that I do not see OpenAI addressing.

Ray (2023) also raises the need for ensuring the ethical and responsible development and use of ChatGPT with a focus on data integrity, user safety, fairness and accountability. These are no mean feats for Open AI and other tech companies to achieve going forward in the development of their AI-based tools and services. This is also a core consideration for users of such models in terms of developing their own AI literacy skills.

1.9 The rising sea of AI knowledge, AI application and its interpretation in academia

Max Tegmark, a professor of physics and AI researcher at Massachusetts Institute of Technology, presented the analogy of AI as a 'rising sea' that floods more and more land, with landmarks representing tasks that AI-based technology can or cannot complete. The rising sea engulfs and transforms landscapes. The landscape in this study skills book relates to learning, study and assessment. The rising sea is the increased number of tasks that AI can be drawn on to do, whereas, before the sea rose, these tasks had to be completed independently by humans. The evolving nature of AI and its capacities often means that it is perceived as transformative in its application. Further consideration is cautioned, however, in relation to this assumption. Can AI be both an enhancement and transformative as defined by the SAMR model (Puentedura, 2013)? Are such enhancements and transformative approaches subjective and time-bound? Will the continued evolution of AI logically lead to further enhancements and transformations? Without a doubt, academics and universities have been made to reconsider traditional approaches to common tasks undertaken within and by their institutions. This has meant that the unthinkable is often now 'knowable', and at the very least perceivable, in the flooded landscape of AI capabilities.

1.9.1 AI's role in academia

The 'rising sea' of AI technology has made significant waves in academia, turning what was once considered insurmountable challenges into achievable tasks. This transformation is evident in several key areas especially when considering research and analysis. For the purpose of this study skills book, the focus will be on assignment preparation and creation. AI-powered tools have increased the efficiency of searching for literature by enabling students to see and access connected articles and journals in a split second, compared to the time it would need to complete such tasks pre-AI-based tools. The ability of AI assistants to present visual maps or trees of connection between a key paper and papers it has referenced is a huge enhancement. Before such AI assistants, students would record references of interest before spending much time searching for them and then reading them. A transformative aspect of supercharged AI assistants is their capacity to make links to papers published after the key paper that cite the key paper in question. This enables an increased amount of relevant and contemporary papers to be identified in a vastly reduced amount of time. Furthermore, there are AI assistants that can read, analyse and summarise content in a fraction of the time that it would take a student to do so. Overall, this results in a reduction of cognitive processing and time, which can be spent on validating, critiquing, and creating the output and original content for revision or assessment.

AI assistants are now competent creators of content including text, images, video and presentations. What AI is still to master are the increasingly complex and authentic contexts of university-level work demanded of students as they progress in their studies. Whilst AI assistants can create a first draft for students across a range of formats and subjects, they currently struggle to produce a top-quality final draft based on a single attempt. Significant and further refinement from a knowledgeable person on the matter is needed – primarily this means a person who can draw on specific experiences in relation to the assignment context. The best fit for this person other than a lecturer on the course is a student on the course or programme. Of the Ten steps and three phases identified by the Learning Development team at the University of Northampton in creating a written assignment, all can be attempted by current AI assistants with input from students.

Phase 1: PLANNING – for half or a third of the time:
1. Formulate an idea or title
2. Plan time
3. Research
4. Assemble ideas
5. Plan

Phase 2: WRITING – for a quarter or third of the time:
6. Write draft
7. Edit
8. Write re-draft

Phase 3: CHECKING – for a quarter or third of the time:
9. Proofread
10. Finalise

Whilst the conception of AI in this book has been clearly stated as a force for good for students studying at university, there remains concern. This is partly in relation to students relying on Generative AI and AI assistants in creating their assignments and therefore missing fundamental aspects of the learning process. It is an unethical use of AI tools and assistants if students pass off AI generated work as their own which misrepresents their knowledge, understanding and capability. This will be discussed further in Chapter 3.

1.10 Moravec's Paradox and landscape with AI

Moravec's Paradox is explained by Arora (2023) as 'tasks that are easy for humans to perform (e.g., motor or social skills) are difficult for machines to replicate, whereas tasks that are difficult for humans (e.g., performing mathematical calculations or large-scale data analysis) are relatively easy for machines to accomplish'. The paradox alludes to a potential reason why Generative AI-based assistants can produce a first draft with ease, but not a final draft, as mentioned in the previous section. The key terms and jargon covered previously in this chapter combine to align with the second part of the paradox. Throughout the key terms, you should notice that the 'learning' aspects are presented as input/output and multiplied in a linear fashion, whereas natural learning is far more nuanced, holistic and reflexive in a non-linear fashion.

The consistent and reliable responses to the datasets that GPTs (Generative Pre-Trained Transformers) are trained on are unimaginable for the average and uninitiated human. However, the average, uninitiated human lives in a world that they experience with all their senses and more. This leads to nuance and diversification an experience that cannot be readily replicated and passed off as another's. Each human has a unique dataset that is original. It is an ability to offer a critique between the localised and lived experience with the more general ideas and assumptions of society that demonstrate natural learning and intelligence. It is AI's lack of ability to navigate the day-to-day realm of human experience and understanding that is its biggest limitation.

Moravec's 'landscape of human competence' (Tegmark, 2018) is a metaphorical terrain where elevation represents increased complexity for AI. The lower levels of the landscape represent tasks that are intuitively simple for humans such as social interaction, emotional expression and sensory perception. As the landscape ascends, the terrain becomes increasingly structured and abstract, symbolising mathematical problems and logical puzzles that are built on structure and order, typically easier for AI systems. A core aspect of Moravec's landscape is that the higher and the lower are connected and the relationships evolve. Moravec wrote 'By 2040, I believe, we will finally achieve the original goal of robotics and a thematic mainstay of science fiction: a freely moving machine with the intellectual capabilities of a human being' (Moravec, 2009). The vision that Moravec has for robotics means a total remapping of his landscapes and the potential end of his paradox. It still remains to be seen, whether this will be achieved, but we are further along this path, in 2024, than we were in 2009 when Moravec was writing. Ultimately, if this is to be achieved it would not only have a profound impact on the roles of students and lecturers at universities across the world but also on what it means to be human.

1.11 How can AI contribute to equity, diversity and inclusion at university?

The evolving nature of Generative AI and AI assistants etc. should be seen as an opportunity to capitalise on such developments and contribute to universities becoming more equitable, diverse and inclusive places to work and study. Steps towards creating a more structurally physical and digitally accessible environment in Higher Education in the UK have gathered pace in the last decade but more can still be done. AI-based tools mean more accessible resources and access to assistive tools as a benchmark for students at university. Many accessibility tools and monitoring tools are built on AI-based technology. AI tools can also be utilised to review information and highlight and suggest appropriate mitigation for identified bias. Furthermore, AI tools can be used to design and reflect a wide range of content from a diverse number of perspectives. Such diversification of content allows for a more nuanced and inclusive experience for students. For example, AI assistants can provide valid points for consideration for students, academics and professional services in relation to promoting greater inclusion. Prompt 1.1 is an example of how a neurodiverse student may engage with an AI assistant to create points for consideration in relation to their success at university. Prior to AI assistants, whilst the guidance provided in Prompt 1.1 may have been accessible somewhere on the internet on a website, the use of an AI assistant, allows for further prompting and the personalisation of the input/output (discussion). This exemplifies the rising sea of AI's capabilities.

Prompt 1.1   Guidance for a neurodiverse student to be successful at university

INPUT:

As a neurodiverse university student, what are the key considerations I should reflect on to ensure I am successful at university

(Continued)

Bing.ai:

As a neurodiverse university student, there are several key considerations to keep in mind to ensure your success. Here are some important points:

1. Understanding Your Needs:
   Take time to understand your unique needs related to your neurodiversity. Reflect on how it affects your learning style, communication and overall well-being.
   Consider factors such as academic accommodations, sensory sensitivities, social support and mental health resources relevant to your neurodivergence.
2. Advocacy and Communication:
   Advocate for yourself by communicating your needs to professors, academic advisors and support services.
   Be open about your neurodiversity and any specific requirements you may have. Remember that you have the right to request reasonable accommodations.
3. Flexible Learning Environment:
   Challenge the assumption that everyone learns in a linear and stepwise manner.
   Create a flexible learning environment that caters to your unique needs. This might involve alternative study methods, extended deadlines or personalised support.
4. Social Support:
   Seek out peer support groups or connect with other neurodiverse students. Sharing experiences and strategies can be helpful.
   Build a network of friends, mentors and professors who understand and support your journey.
5. Self-Care and Well-Being:
   Prioritise your mental and physical health. Practice self-care by getting enough rest, managing stress and seeking professional help if needed.
   Understand your limits and learn to balance academic demands with self-care.
6. Time Management and Organisation:
   Develop effective time management skills. Use tools like calendars, reminders and to-do lists to stay organised.
   Break down tasks into smaller steps and create a study schedule that works for you.
7. Accessing Resources:
   Familiarise yourself with the support services available at your university. These may include disability services, counselling and tutoring.
   Utilise assistive technologies, such as speech-to-text software or mind-mapping tools, to enhance your learning experience.
   Remember that every neurodiverse student's experience is unique. Be patient with yourself, seek help when needed and celebrate your achievements along the way. You've got this!

1.12 Summary of chapter

This chapter has provided a broad introduction to AI and several of the key terms and concepts that accompany it. A distinction has been made between 'weak AI' and 'strong AI', recognising the evolving nature of AI. The direction of travel suggests continued advances towards general AI which will mean constant review, refinement and advancement of the conceptions of AI. The example of the ChatGPT series was provided to demonstrate not only the speed of development but also the rapid level of system enhancement that we are currently seeing continue. Whilst such developments will lead to associated risks, opportunities that are offered by such developments should also be explored. This book focuses on such opportunities as they currently stand in relation to higher education and students using AI ethically to support their study and assessments.

The rapid nature of developments in AI, however, means that this book offers a snapshot of the current state of AI tools and practices for university students. The key terms and models discussed in this chapter provide a wider and historical context on the contemporary state of AI. Practical uses of AI in relation to equity, diversity and inclusion are also introduced. This feeds into consideration relating to the skills and processes needed to navigate new and future AI-based tools and systems. Fundamentally, the need for continuous learning and adaptation in how AI is engaged with and applied will enhance students' success both at university and beyond.

1.13 Chapter hacks

1. Understanding AI: Grasp the basics of AI, distinguishing between narrow, general and Generative AI. Recognise AI's evolution from theoretical concepts to practical applications in academia.
2. Historical Context: Delve into AI's historical milestones, from early conceptualisations by Turing and others to the development of transformative models like GPT.
3. AI's Academic Applications: Explore how AI tools like voice assistants and learning platforms are already enhancing study habits, research methodologies and personalised learning experiences.
4. AI in Enhancing Education: Understand AI's potential to revolutionise teaching, learning, and assessment methods, making them more efficient and tailored to individual learning styles.

(Continued)

5. Promoting Inclusivity: Learn about AI's role in creating equitable educational opportunities, helping to bridge gaps in access and learning experiences for diverse student populations.
6. Continuous Adaptation: Acknowledge the necessity of continuous learning to keep pace with AI's rapid advancements and its implications for future academic and professional landscapes.
7. Equity, Diversity and Inclusion: Explore how AI can support broader institutional goals of inclusivity, making learning materials and experiences accessible to all students.
8. Preparing for the Future: Equip yourself with the knowledge and skills to utilise AI effectively, ethically and creatively in your academic journey and beyond.

1.14 Chapter MCQs

1. What distinguishes general AI from narrow AI?
   A) General AI can perform any intellectual task that a human being can
   B) Narrow AI is designed for specific tasks like playing chess or language translation
   C) General AI has not yet been fully achieved
   D) All of the above
2. Which AI model series is known for its significant contributions to the advancement of Generative AI?
   A) IBM Watson
   B) GPT series
   C) Deep Blue
   D) AlexNet
3. According to Max Tegmark's 'Rising Sea' analogy, how does the advancement of AI capabilities impact academic challenges?
   A) It makes all academic challenges obsolete
   B) It increases the complexity of academic challenges
   C) It makes previously insurmountable academic challenges more accessible by AI
   D) It has no significant impact on academic challenges
4. What does Moravec's Paradox suggest about the capabilities of AI?
   A) AI can perform tasks that require human intelligence, such as emotional understanding
   B) Tasks that are easy for humans are often difficult for AI and vice versa
   C) AI can replace human intelligence in all aspects
   D) AI is incapable of learning from data
5. What role does continuous learning play in adapting to AI's development?
   A) It is unnecessary since AI tools are user-friendly
   B) It helps individuals keep pace with rapid technological advancements

C) It is only important for AI developers, not users
D) Continuous learning is less important than hardware updates

Correct answers:

1. Correct answer D
2. Correct answer B
3. Correct answer C
4. Correct answer B
5. Correct answer B

2

What Can Generative AI Do for Your Study Skills?

2.1 Chapter objectives

1. To explore the fundamentals of using Generative AI as a study buddy/assistant
2. Recognise the capacity of Generative AI to promote personalised learning
3. Utilise AI tools and assistants to improve efficiency in research and writing
4. Appreciate the role of Generative AI in promoting critical thinking and analytical skills
5. Evaluate the ethical implications and practical considerations of integrating Generative AI into your study practices

2.2 Having read this chapter you will...

1. **Be Introduced to the Generative AI Basics**: You will grasp the core concepts of Generative AI and discover how to use these tools to make your studying more effective and efficient, giving you a solid base to enhance your academic performance.
2. **Personalised Study Support**: Learn how Generative AI can adapt to your unique way of learning, offering customised assistance that matches your study habits, preferences and goals, making your study sessions more fruitful.
3. **Enhance Research and Writing Skills**: Find out how Generative AI can simplify and improve your research and writing tasks, saving you time and boosting the quality of your essays and projects.
4. **Develop Critical Thinking**: See how Generative AI encourages you to think more critically and analytically, presenting you with various viewpoints and complex issues that deepen your understanding of your subjects.
5. **Understand Ethical Use**: Reflect on the ethical side of using generative AI in your studies, including how to maintain academic honesty, protect your privacy and

strike a balance between using AI tools and relying on your own critical thinking skills.
6. **Look Ahead to AI's Educational Potential**: Imagine the future possibilities with Generative AI in your education, thinking about how upcoming innovations might offer even more personalised learning experiences while still valuing the irreplaceable aspects of human teaching and guidance.

2.3 Introduction

Generative AI represents an evolutionary step in academic support as it offers to contribute to and enhance existing approaches to study. This technology acts as a catalyst for more efficient and personalised learning, reshaping traditional approaches and practices to study. Generative AI and AI assistants do not replace the foundational skills and techniques students need to develop and master, but it does allow for augmentation and refinement, making the learning process more adaptable to individual needs and preferences. This is especially advantageous for both non-neurotypical students and neuro-typical students, as content cannot only be created and curated but reinterpreted and presented based on a student's needs and preferences.

This chapter explores the multifaceted role of Generative AI for students at university and considers its potential to enhance and streamline study practices. It unpacks how AI can serve as a dynamic study assistant, offering customised support and a deeper understanding of complex subjects by simplifying their delivery. By navigating through various applications of AI, from literature searches and writing assistance to the development of critical thinking and analytical skills, the chapter provides an overview of how this technology can be integrated into the university experience. The chapter also highlights ethical considerations with regard to the moderation of technological assistance and human intellectual engagement in terms of AI-assisted study.

2.4 Your study buddy AI assistant

Beginning university and studying in general can be a daunting task. Although AI cannot do your course for you, it can become a go-to study buddy for times when it is needed! AI assistants can offer a more personalised experience but will need some information from you first. Here is an example from when Google's AI assistant Gemini was asked what it needed to know if it was to help a university student study better:

About your learning:
1. What are your biggest challenges when it comes to studying (e.g., staying focused, retaining information and managing time)?
2. What study techniques have you tried in the past? What worked well for you, and what didn't?
3. What is your preferred style of learning?
4. How do you usually take notes during lectures or readings?
5. Do you typically study alone or with others?

About your goals:
6. What are your academic goals for this semester/year?
7. Are there any specific courses or subjects you're struggling with more than others?
8. How much time do you typically dedicate to studying each day/week?
9. What motivates you to learn?
10. What rewards do you set for yourself when you achieve your goals?

Additional questions:
11. Do you have any distractions that interfere with your studying (e.g., social media and phone notifications)?
12. How do you manage stress and anxiety around exams?
13. Do you have access to any academic support services offered by your university?
14. Are there any specific skills you'd like to improve, such as time management, critical thinking or reading comprehension?
15. Are there any accessibility needs I should be aware of?

Open-ended questions:
16. What do you think would make studying more enjoyable or effective for you?
17. Is there anything else you think I should know about your learning process?
18. What questions do you have for me about studying better?

The above set of questions is a great starting place with or without an AI study buddy! They cover a wide range of factors and prompt you to consider what works for you and be honest about where you are currently in terms of your study experience. This will be different for different people, so the above questions are trying to gauge that. It is also excellent to see that Gemini included a question about accessibility. As long as a student is comfortable with doing so, details of specific needs or disability can be shared with an AI assistant. Remember that your personal information should not be. Sharing specific information on needs, disabilities or preferences will allow an AI assistant to tailor its response in relation to this information. Table 2.1 provides an overview of the sort of needs that can impact on study and how they may be supported. Please note that the suggestions are further reaching than AI assistance.

Table 2.1 Needs and studying

	Potential impact on studying	Support suggestions
Vision impairments	Difficulty in reading printed materials and accessing visual aids	Audio recordings, Braille materials, screen readers and accessible learning platforms
Mobility impairments	Difficulty accessing physical study spaces and taking notes	Accessible study spaces, note-taking assistance, flexible scheduling and virtual learning options
Chronic pain or fatigue	Limited stamina and difficulty in focusing for extended periods	Pacing strategies, ergonomic setups, breaks as needed and resources for managing chronic health in academia
Dyslexia	Difficulty with reading fluency, spelling and writing	Assistive technologies for reading/writing (text-to-speech and grammar checkers), alternative note-taking methods and dyslexia-friendly resources
Dyscalculia	Difficulty with math concepts and calculations	Math manipulatives, visual aids, step-by-step problem-solving, real-world examples and specialised tutoring/assistive software
Attention Deficit Disorder	Inattention, hyperactivity and impulsivity	Strategies for managing these symptoms (see previous discussion), ADHD-specific resources and support groups
Anxiety or depression	Difficulty concentrating, low motivation and fatigue	Stress management techniques, mindful exercises, self-care strategies and information on mental health resources
Autistic Spectrum Disorder	Sensory sensitivities and social interaction challenges	Quiet study spaces, noise-cancelling headphones, clear instructions and predictable routines
Hearing impairments	Difficulty hearing lectures and accessing audio information	Transcripts of lectures, captions for videos, assistive listening devices, note-taking assistance and visual learning materials
Invisible disabilities	Unseen challenges that may impact learning	Sensitivity and understanding, open communication about individual needs and appropriate accommodations

2.5 Enhancing learning, comprehension and application independently

Generative AI and AI-based assistants have a foundational role to play in providing learners with round-the-clock, accessible input. Nowhere should this be more impactful than for a student's increased capacity to learn and extend their comprehension independently. Of course, this is not a new phenomenon. Independent study is an essential part of both undergraduate and postgraduate study. What is a significant development, however, is Generative AI's ability to tailor responses to specific prompts around the clock (providing you access to the AI assistant). How does this work then?

Cognitive science has revealed that human memory involves multiple systems, notably conscious and unconscious memory systems (Squire & Dede, 2015). Generative AI can support students in utilising both of these systems in the learning process. As an example, an AI assistant could be used to customise learning materials that are input by creating output in a different format: e.g., flashcard summaries or quizzes (see Prompt 2.1). AI assistants are also capable of asking questions and formulating the next question in relation to the previous answer. This can also be utilised in a Socratic style of questions and follow-up questions in response to given answers on a chosen subject or area (see Prompt 2.2). This is a particularly useful approach when developing understanding in a chosen area as it avoids being given direct answers or solutions and still requires thought on the part of the student. Such dialogue can encourage short-term memories to enter the longer-term memory, a core element of learning!

Prompt 2.1 Study buddy/coach prompt

Role: You are to act as an expert teacher in [enter subject]. You are going to be my study coach.

Task: You are to review the following input [text/document/image etc.] and summarise key points.

Format: Produce a series of resources as [Flashcards/Quizzes] that will aid in learning the content.

Prompt 2.2 Socratic study coach prompt

Role: You are an expert teacher in [enter subject]. You are going to be a Socratic study coach.

Task: Your goal is to review the following input [text/document/image etc.] and then engage in a Socratic dialogue with me. You need to ask probing questions, encourage critical thinking and guide me towards understanding the content deeply.

Format: Engage in a back-and-forth conversation, asking questions and providing explanations as needed.

Building on back-and-forth interactions with an AI assistant also allows for simulations to be created. For example, the AI assistant may be asked to create a simulation and role-play for a specific event. These could involve scenarios relating to inclusive education, social inequality, the digital learning divide, cultural diversity in society, behaviour management in schools, sustainability policy and practice etc. The possibilities are literally endless. The below example was created using ChatGPT and asked for a safeguarding scenario specific to a primary school based in England. Once a scenario has been created, the AI assistant can then be asked to play a role, for example, the child's parent, and respond to the questions that you ask. This will enable you to explore the types of questions and consider relevant responses in said scenario.

2.6 Start scenario

2.6.1 Scenario: Safeguarding concerns for Jamie

Jamie is a 7-year-old student in Year 3 at Oakwood Primary School in England. Jamie has always been a quiet child but has recently become more withdrawn and less engaged in class activities. Jamie's teacher, Mrs. Smith, has also noticed unexplained bruises on Jamie's arms and legs on several occasions. Additionally, Jamie seems to be wearing the same clothes multiple days in a row, which appear to be unwashed. When asked about the bruises or clothing, Jamie becomes visibly upset but does not provide an explanation.

Mrs. Smith recalls the school's safeguarding training and recognises these signs could indicate potential neglect or abuse. She knows it is critical to act but is unsure how to proceed without causing further distress to Jamie.

Created using ChatGPT: You are going to create a scenario that includes several safeguarding concerns for a child who attends a primary school. This scenario is to be used for training purposes.

2.6.2 End scenario

Attention is a finite resource, so using an AI assistant to present and ask questions regarding specific information in a back-and-forth manner is deemed to be more interactive than traditional approaches to independent study. This reduces cognitive overload and ensures that learning content is processed more effectively. This increased engagement or focus is what is ultimately needed when learning and revising. As well as simulations or role-playing with different scenarios, AI assistants are also capable of creating visualisations and overviews of topics. For example, if you are studying sociology and want to recap the main theorists, an AI assistant could create a table of theorists and their contributions in seconds (see Prompt 2.3). Not only this, but the AI assistant also could then create a Multiple Choice Quiz based on the table and ask you questions to test your understanding.

Prompt 2.3 Study prompt example

INPUT:

I need to revise for an exam on key sociological thinkers and their theories. Can you create a table with the key information that I will need to get started?

Claude.ai output:

Sociologist	Key Theories	Summary
Karl Marx	Conflict theory	Society is based on conflicts between social classes driven by economic factors. Lower classes are oppressed by elite upper classes who control production
Max Weber	Rationalisation Theory	Society is increasingly rationalised through formal rules and bureaucracy. This leads to disenchantment and loss of meaning
Emile Durkheim	Functionalism	Society is a system of interconnected parts that function together to maintain stability. Deviance threatens this
W.E.B Du Bois	Double consciousness	African Americans experience a divided self-identity due to racism and marginalisation by the dominant white culture
Harriet Martineau	Feminist theory	Women are systematically disadvantaged due to patriarchal social structures. Advocated for women's education, suffrage and equality
Erving Goffman	Dramaturgical theory	People's social interactions and self-presentation resemble theatrical performances

---

Prompt 2.4 Explain it to me like I am a 5-year-old

INPUT:

Explain [enter subject, concept, text, document etc.] to me like I am a [enter age] years old.

The Cognitive Load Theory was coined by John Sweller in 1988 and highlights the limitations of working memory and the need for educational content to be designed in a way that does not overwhelm it.

As already shown in this section, AI assistants can promptly produce content for learning and revision. However, what happens if the student does not understand it? A tried and tested prompt is asking for information to be explained in a way that a 5/8/10/12-year-old would understand it. You choose the age (see Prompt 2.4). At university level study, students are expected to do more than just recall theory or facts. This leads to analysis, synthesis and development of a critique of theory involving similarities, differences, reflections and application to real-world scenarios or experiences.

2.7 Critical thinking and analytical skills

AI assistants can also be used by students to assist in the development of critical thinking and analytical skills. A primary skill that needs to be developed is analysis. Students should engage with the following opportunities in order to develop their analysis:

Read, and read critically – Do not accept information at face value. Question who wrote it and why?
Apply theory to real-world issues – Consider the concepts and theories that are covered in your subject and how these can be applied to your own or other's experience.
Question your own thinking and the reasons behind it – Why do you think what you think? What information do you base it on? What has made you change your thinking? Or helped to develop it?
Engage in academic discourse – Maximise the university experience, attend classes, see guest speakers, attend events outside of your course, utilise the university's resources.
Take your time – Patience can often lead to insight or an increased understanding of a subject or matter.
Ensure reflection becomes a cornerstone of your approach to your study and work – The more you reflect, the more you analyse. Ensure your reflections are grounded in experience, but connect with theory, literature and logic.

Developing such an analytical approach to study, assignments and university life are the foundations of critical thinking and analytical skills. Such skills are not content-bound, but applicable across a wide range of scenarios, not least to say the use of AI at university. This skills book is focused on promoting the ethical use of AI as a force for good by university students, but incorporating AI into learning brings several ethical questions to the forefront. Privacy, consent and reservations around the datafication of the human experience are becoming central to the debate about AI's role across all levels of education. Such contemplation regarding the broader societal impacts of technology offers current students firsthand experiences on the debate of AI's evolving role. Furthermore, this lived experience allows for critical thinking and analysis in response to it. For example, should a university ban the use of AI assistants across all of its courses and programmes? If so, would students at this university then be disadvantaged when they enter the job market? Or worse still, use AI assistants without declaring them and risk the termination of their studies if found out?

AI assistants can be utilised to present a diverse range of viewpoints or approaches to a given topic. An exploration of an 'alternative way' in the face of the 'dominant way' forms the bedrock of critical thinking and analysis. For instance, when discussing access to and costs of Higher Education in England, AI can generate articles from different perspectives allowing students to analyse and compare such viewpoints (see Prompt 2.5). This exercise would teach students to evaluate the sources, identify biases and appreciate the complexity of real-world issues, exemplifying the skills needed to navigate their studies at university. A fundamental skill that graduates should possess is the ability to independently think and critique information from a range of sources, especially in terms of AI-generated content.

Prompt 2.5 Developing critical analysis

INPUT:

Develop a critical analysis of the debate on [enter subject/theme/content here]. Ensure that your arguments make links to theory and connect with real-world examples. Include links to all sources that inform the analysis.

Generative AI can also transform passive learning into an interactive experience. For example, AI can create custom scenarios of increasing complexity which are adapted to student's interests and needs. Such an approach means that students now have an accessible resource that can be used to create, adapt and refine teaching materials to suit their specific interests more efficiently. This should contribute to increasing relevance, allow for active participation and enable students to share their experiences and thoughts. Being able to articulate and discuss key debates, arguments and ideas is a crucial skill that will assist students in both writing and presenting ideas in their studies and beyond.

> **Prompt 2.6   Developing a critique based on student interests**
>
> INPUT:
>
> I am interested in [insert contemporary interest]. Present an analysis and critique of how this relates to [insert relevant theory/scholar/concept etc.].

2.8 Searching for literature and writing assistance

Generative AI models and assistants can support students with both finding literature, understanding it and writing in an appropriate style. They are a great resource for combatting procrastination, as the initial thought of 'where' and 'how' to start can be asked of the AI assistant (see prompt 2.7). Starting from scratch is also mitigated by the use of an AI assistant in terms of what to search for or how to start your writing. This section will provide a brief exploration of approaches and tips for harnessing AI in academic contexts.

> **Prompt 2.7   Starting an assignment**
>
> INPUT:
>
> I am a university student and have a [enter type of assignment] to start. Break down, step by step, where I should begin and what I need to do in order to complete it successfully.

> **Prompt 2.8   Generating key search terms**
>
> INPUT:
>
> I am a university student and need suggestions for the top ten key terms to search in relation to [enter topic/subject/assignment focus].

Generative AI can streamline any literature search making it more efficient and effective. AI assistants can provide students with ideas for search terms and queries (see Prompt 2.8). AI assistants can be prompted to ask students questions about their assignment so that the format/title/Learning Outcomes etc., are shared before consideration is given to what sort of literature needs reviewing.

This provides the AI assistant with a logical interpretation of a student's needs and enables the AI assistant to draw on its pre-trained database to specifically respond to the information that has been entered. This will then enable the AI assistant to provide detailed and precise search terms for the student to explore as they wish. However, should the AI assistant produce a term or concept that the student is not familiar with, then the student can ask for this to be explained further (see Prompt 2.4).

Once relevant literature has been found and identified, AI tools that allow for files/documents to be uploaded to them can then provide detailed summaries of the source information; however, students should enquire with their university in terms of what content can be uploaded or shared to external platforms. Once you have confirmed that you are able to upload a document to an AI assistant, ensure that you skim-read the document in full first. This is part of developing your AI literacy, as it will help you to infer whether the summaries or responses of the AI assistant match your initial interpretations of the article that you have uploaded. This type of critique is fundamental to developing your AI literacy skills alongside your analytical skills. AI assistants are adept at highlighting key findings, methodologies and conclusions (see Prompt 2.9). This enables students to determine the relevance of each source without reading the entire document – a painstaking affair for undergraduates new to reading academic journals! This is also an enhancement of traditional skim reading and note-taking approaches which allow for similar results with significantly less requirement on your cognitive load. Furthermore, depending on your level of study, you may wish to use a reference manager. See your university's guidance for which reference manager they recommend, but a freely available reference manager is Zotero. Reference managers are capable of creating references in the chosen style that you need – this is a huge time saver when writing and researching.

Prompt 2.9 Document or text analysis prompt

Action: Upload a document or copy and paste in the text for analysis.

INPUT:

Review the document/text and provide an analysis of the input in relation to:

Who is the author?
When was it published?
Where was it published?
What are the key findings?
What were the methods used (if stated)

What are the key theories or literature drawn on?

How to begin writing is explored in more detail in Part Three, but we will provide a brief introduction here. AI assistants can be used to create structures and writing frames for assignments based on content and word count. This is particularly useful if you are not sure what to start researching – although assignment guidance should also be given in your taught sessions as well. Once a plan has been generated and the initial research of relevant literature completed, AI assistants can provide sentence starters for each section you have outlined (see Prompt 2.10). This is really useful as they will often model an appropriate academic style and tone. However, remember to critique this if the language suggested is not appropriate, ask it to rewrite it until you are happy with it or rewrite it yourself!

Prompt 2.10   Sentence starters

INPUT:

I am a university student writing an assignment on [insert topic/subject/title here]. Can you suggest a number of sentence starters for the introduction, main body and conclusion?

One step further along the AI-assisted to AI-generated spectrum would involve AI assistants providing first drafts of sections for you to then revise and edit, making them more appropriate for the assignment based on your knowledge and experiences and the course content. Although this can be useful, it is not an approach suggested for new or struggling students. This is because AI assistants can often produce writing in an academic style at a higher level than new or struggling students are capable of. This may then become a debilitating exercise as a student ponders what they can do to improve it. It would also be considered academic misconduct, should the student submit work that is at a higher level than they are capable of. On this basis, until a student has completed several assignments and begun to develop their academic style, using first drafts produced by an AI assistant should be avoided. Furthermore, guidance and support in relation to this should always be sought from the programme and module teams who are teaching the student. It should be noted though that AI assistants are superb at reviewing first attempts by students at academic writing and can offer feedback. This is a great place to start in terms of student shaving a go themselves, before using an AI assistant to assist them in improving their work. As always though check what guidance has been provided by your university or course on using AI in such a way. And always check that any redrafted versions by an AI assistant still capture your voice, ideas and opinions from the first draft. Sometimes, AI can generalise and neutralise content, or interpret an aspect wrongly altogether. Whilst remaining objective is a key aspect of academic work, academic work should not be soulless!

Combining AI tools to aid in researching literature, and then the processes of writing and editing, should essentially act as a third teacher or helper. Not only this, but as long as you have a suitable device and connection, it is accessible twenty-four hours a day, seven days a week. For students who have worked in more traditional ways previously, the use of AI may feel transformative in this manner. For students who are familiar with using AI to assist in tasks, this may feel more like an enhancement and honing of AI-based skills and tools to support your research and work. For those already using AI tools across a range of tasks as standard, it may be incomprehensible how study, research and writing were undertaken before!

2.9 Time management and studying more efficiently

Generative AI can provide personalised study schedules based on students' preferences and in response to upcoming commitments. Whilst this can be completed manually with paper or digital calendars, an AI assistant can ask and prompt questions regarding a study schedule that you may not have considered. For example, it may ask for previous feedback and grades to identify areas of priority or seek further information on when you feel most productive or a time you are most able to commit to. In relation to assignment management, an AI assistant can break down what you need to do when to remain on task and meet a submission date. Task prioritisation is also a worthy skill to hone if you want to be successful. AI tools can assist with this by understanding the urgency and importance of assignments, alongside the student's personal goals and submission dates (see Prompt 2.11). AI can suggest an order of tasks that optimises study outcomes and prioritises assignments with closer deadlines or greater impact on the overall grade, ensuring that students focus their efforts where they will receive maximum recognition for it.

Prompt 2.11   Time management prompt

INPUT:

I am a university student preparing for an assignment titled [enter title here]. It is due on [enter due date]. The date today is [enter today's date]. Please talk me through a step-by-step process that will enable me to manage my time efficiently.

AI assistants can contribute to more efficient study in several ways. For example, adaptive learning paths can respond to student performance on AI-created quizzes. Depending on the student's previous performance, feedback and grades, an AI assistant may provide recommendations on areas to study further, especially if there are misunderstandings in relation to key or core theoretical underpinnings. An AI tool's ability to also summarise lengthy texts, extract key points from lectures and generate concise notes can make study materials more accessible and reduce the time spent on revising these (see Chapters 2 and 5). By generating practice questions and tests in a required format, AI can provide students with targeted practice opportunities and experience, enhancing their readiness for certain assessment types, e.g., exams.

AI assistants are becoming increasingly integrated with existing tools and platforms, providing a potentially seamless experience for students across traditional software programs or applications. This can include syncing with digital calendars to update study schedules in real-time, integrating with learning management systems (LMS) to pull in assignment deadlines and materials or working alongside productivity apps to track tasks and study habits. AI assistants can also learn from student feedback and performance data with the aim of reviewing previous approaches and scheduling in relation to the progress being made. This iterative process ensures that the AI assistant's recommendations become more aligned with the student's needs as the process plays out, but it does mean the AI assistant is reliant on input. Students need to be continuously mindful of what information they are sharing and are prepared to share with an AI assistant, as well as where that information is then stored and how it is used by the AI assistant.

2.10 What will AI-assisted study look like in the (near) future?

Without a doubt, during the writing of this book and hopefully during its publication, the rise of Generative AI's capabilities and AI assistants will mean that there is an undeniable future and place for AI in all things study-related at university. AI's ability to create, reinterpret and present insight into the input it receives has felt revolutionary. Exactly what this revolution looks like and how it is experienced will be different for different people across the higher education sector. However, there are several aspects that you should continue to seek out and explore in relation to developing your own study buddy assistant as described in the first section of this chapter.

1. What AI assistants do you have access to through your university and how can they be personalised to offer you the information or input needed, as and when you require it? If your university does not officially sanction the use of Generative AI or AI assistants, then do not be afraid to seek out what other students may be using. Just be very aware of what information is shared with third-party tools and ensure you abide by your university's IT and account policy etc. to avoid any breaches on your part.
2. Using the same AI assistant will enable you to pick up from where you left off. The previous dialogue often remains visible and accessible. This is particularly useful when

undertaking an assignment over a number of days, as when you return to an AI assistant, the first prompt that should be entered is 'recap on what we have discussed so far'. To not use such a function or tool is a missed opportunity when it comes to studying. Furthermore, it is predicted that big tech companies will fully integrate their AI assistants across their platforms. This will mean an AI assistant will be your first point of contact for tasks and reminders.

3. AI assistants will continue to increase their capabilities and be able to offer students simulations of real-world scenarios and problem-solving opportunities in an interactive nature. Whereas the inclusion of case studies and then related questions in textbooks has long been commonplace, AI assistants will be able to create related questions and respond to answers offering support as needed.

4. Desktop and portable devices are still the norm for using AI assistants, but it is predicted that this will change as there is a shift to more 'wearable' AI assistants, as well as improvements in using AI assistants across virtual, augmented and extended reality scenarios. However, such tech will no doubt come with a heavy price tag to begin with, so it is yet to be seen how such technology may become more mainstream and used by universities.

2.11 Summary of chapter

The integration of Generative AI into academic settings presents a contemporary approach to learning, offering both enhancements and challenges to traditional study methodologies. This chapter has considered various dimensions of AI-assisted learning, from personalised study assistance to critical thinking and ethical considerations, underscoring its potential to transform its application across Higher Education. Generative AI, as a non-transformative but significantly augmentative tool, redefines study practices by providing customised learning experiences. It can act as a personalised study buddy, adept at tailoring its assistance to individual preferences and challenges. This bespoke approach facilitates a deeper understanding of the subject matter, enabling students to engage with content more interactively and effectively.

AI's role in searching for literature and writing assistance is particularly notable. It streamlines the research process, offering efficient strategies for finding relevant literature and extracting key insights. This capability not only saves time but also enhances students' ability to engage with academic materials critically. Furthermore, AI's feedback on academic writing can significantly improve the quality and clarity of students' work, fostering better communication skills. Students, however, need to be aware of the risk of over-reliance on AI, the potential for academic dishonesty, and the need for critical engagement with AI-generated content. Students should be cautious if they find themselves substituting AI's capabilities for their own critical thinking and analytical skills. Instead, AI should be used by students as a complementary tool that enhances, rather than replaces, their intellect and creativity.

The future of AI in education appears promising, with advancements in technology potentially leading to more immersive and personalised learning experiences. This chapter advocates for a hybrid model that synergises AI's efficiency and adaptability with the irreplaceable nuances of human teaching and learning dynamics. To conclude, Generative AI is reshaping academic study practices. Its capacity to personalise learning, enhance engagement and streamline research processes presents a significant boost for students. Nonetheless, this technological embrace must be tempered with critical reflection on ethical implications, the importance of human oversight, and the indispensable value of critical thinking skills.

2.12 Chapter hacks

1. **Start with Self-Reflection**: Before diving into the AI tools and applications, take a moment to reflect on your current study habits, challenges, and goals. Understanding your starting point makes it easier to identify how Generative AI can best serve your needs.
2. **Customise Your AI Study Buddy**: Engage with AI tools that allow personalisation. Input details about your study preferences, goals, and challenges to tailor the AI's support to your unique needs.
3. **Leverage AI for Efficient Research**: Use AI-powered tools to streamline your literature searches and source gathering. These tools can help you find relevant research faster, leaving you more time to focus on analysis and study.
4. **Enhance Writing with AI**: Experiment with AI writing assistants to improve the structure, clarity and coherence of your academic writing. These tools can provide suggestions for improvement and even help with grammar and style.
5. **Develop Critical Thinking with AI Simulations**: Engage with AI-generated simulations and scenarios to challenge your understanding and encourage deeper learning. These interactive experiences can be a fun and effective way to enhance critical thinking and analytical skills.
6. **Stay Ethical and Authentic**: While leveraging AI for study assistance, remain vigilant about maintaining academic integrity. Use AI as a tool for enhancement, not as a substitute for your own critical thinking and creativity.
7. **Prepare for the AI-Assisted Future**: Stay informed about the latest developments in AI and education. Being adaptable and open to new tools and methods will ensure you remain at the forefront of learning innovations.
8. **Balance AI Use with Self-Care**: While AI can significantly enhance study efficiency, it's essential to balance technology use with regular breaks, physical activity and social interactions to maintain overall well-being.

2.13 Chapter MCQs

1. How does Generative AI primarily assist students in their academic studies?
   A) By replacing traditional study methods entirely
   B) By introducing entirely new study skills never seen before
   C) By enhancing existing study skills with new approaches
   D) By diminishing the role of instructors and professors
2. What is one of the key benefits of using Generative AI as a study assistant?
   A) It requires minimal input from the user to be effective
   B) It offers a personalised learning experience based on individual needs
   C) It guarantees improved grades without the need for studying
   D) It eliminates the need for any other study resources or materials
3. In what way can Generative AI aid in the process of literature search and academic writing?
   A) By conducting all necessary research autonomously
   B) By writing entire research papers without student input
   C) By making the research process more efficient and improving output quality
   D) By replacing the need for peer-reviewed sources
4. Generative AI can foster critical thinking and analytical skills by:
   A) Providing direct answers to all student queries
   B) Presenting diverse perspectives and encouraging engagement with complex topics
   C) Discouraging independent research and thought
   D) Limiting exposure to challenging material
5. What ethical consideration is associated with using Generative AI in academic settings?
   A) The potential for decreased technology use in other areas
   B) The unequivocal acceptance of AI-generated content as academically valid
   C) Issues related to academic integrity, data privacy and maintaining a balance between AI assistance and independent thought
   D) The guaranteed improvement of interpersonal skills through AI interaction

Correct answers:

1. Correct answer C
2. Correct answer B
3. Correct answer C
4. Correct answer B
5. Correct answer C

3

Academic Integrity and the Ethical Use of Generative AI at University

3.1 Chapter objectives

1. To introduce and explore the fundamentals of academic integrity in relation to the use of generative artificial intelligence
2. Explore AI's impact on academic practices and assessments
3. Foster AI literacy and ethical engagement
4. Address privacy and security concerns
5. Consider what future-proof skills in an AI-impacted environment involve

3.2 Having read this chapter, you will...

1. **Be Introduced to Academic Integrity**: Recognise the deeper significance of academic integrity beyond avoiding plagiarism, understanding it as a foundational principle that upholds the credibility and trustworthiness of academic endeavours.
2. **Navigate AI Tools Responsibly**: Be signposted to the guidelines for ethical AI use in various assessment contexts, recognising when and how AI tools can be employed to support learning without compromising the integrity of your academic work.
3. **Enhance AI Literacy**: Develop the ability to critically engage with AI-generated content, identifying biases, questioning validity and applying a refined understanding of AI's capabilities and limitations to your academic work.
4. **Safeguard Privacy and Security**: Be conscious of the importance of data privacy and security in the use of AI tools, adopting best practices to protect personal information in digital academic environments.

5. **Future-Proof Your Skills**: Prepare for the evolving academic and professional landscapes influenced by AI, cultivating a skill set that includes digital literacy, ethical awareness, adaptability and a commitment to continuous learning and critical engagement with technology.

3.3 Introduction

Ethics and academic integrity are foundational aspects for any university student, academic or researcher. This is to ensure the authenticity and credibility of all work conducted within and by the university. Embedding principles of honesty, fairness and responsibility guides academic conduct and establishes a culture of trust. Integrity in all forms of academic work, from research and writing to examinations and collaborative projects, shapes the academic experience for students and has relevance both in and beyond their world of study. Amidst such rapidly advancing technologies, innovative and publicly available AI-based tools and capacities have prompted a reconceptualisation of what it means to maintain academic integrity. As students and lecturers navigate this period, the challenge lies in harmonising the principles of honesty, fairness and responsibility with the opportunities presented by AI. Such aspirations are leading to a range of approaches that straddle both the pragmatic and restrictive use of AI-generated content.

This chapter explores the ethical considerations surrounding the use of Generative AI technologies within Higher Education in the UK. It systematically unpacks the multifaceted implications of integrating AI tools into practice, beginning with a critical examination of how these technologies intersect with traditional notions of academic integrity. The discourse progresses to explore the opportunities and challenges that AI presents in reshaping academic norms, emphasising the need for a balanced approach that upholds ethical standards. Through a series of thematic sections, the chapter provides a roadmap for navigating the ethical quandaries posed by AI, offering practical guidelines for its responsible use in assessments, strategies for enhancing AI literacy among the academic community, and reflections on the broader ethical and privacy concerns that accompany the adoption of AI. The chapter aims to equip students and lecturers alike with the insight and tools necessary to consider the ethical use of Generative AI in their role whilst maintaining academic integrity.

3.4 Academic Integrity: What is it and why should you care?

If you have not already, you will at some point in your studies come across the term 'academic integrity', or possibly its opposite, 'academic misconduct'. Academic integrity is important for universities and indeed, all levels of education, as trust and the consideration of ethics are core components. These permeate the level of every operation within a university from taught lectures to assignments to research projects. Most, if not all, agree that trust and ethics are important if universities are to be valued places of study, work and research. However, the first time a student may come into contact with such terms is if they are suspected of not having adhered to them. In an attempt to clarify key aspects of academic integrity further, the International Centre for Academic Integrity (ICAI, 2021) has defined six key values that academic integrity consists of honesty, trust, fairness, respect, responsibility and courage. These values are more than just avoiding cheating, as academic misconduct can sometimes be simplified as; they are about sustaining a community of shared values where everyone's work is acknowledged and credible.

Imagine a university where everyone, from your peers in class to your lecturers, respects these values. Everyone's ideas and efforts are taken seriously, and why shouldn't your ideas be taken seriously? But it is more than just talk and lip service. These values guide how decisions are made, big and small, leading to a more ethical, respectful community within the university. Whilst the reality may not be as clear cut, the values of academic integrity are a constant and can provide a place to check in relating to the decisions that are being made. This is especially important when the pressure is on and assignment deadlines or exams are looming. It is also about being fair and promoting an equitable experience for all students at university. Furthermore, graduating from university is an important milestone and achievement, and it remains this way because of the academic integrity that all university programmes are based on. If you want to know more about academic integrity in relation to your programme or course, seek guidance from your university. Furthermore, you could explore it using an AI assistant (see Prompt 3.1), but be aware that this will lead to a more general interpretation than what your course/university will offer.

Prompt 3.1 What is academic integrity and how is AI impacting it for my course?

Input 1:

I am a university student studying for [insert full title of programme as well as the level of study]. Can you explain to me what academic integrity is, how it is relevant to my course and an example of good practice?

Input 2:

In response to the above output (from input 1), can you explain how AI is impacting my chosen course of study? Please provide examples to illustrate this further.

3.5 How has Artificial Intelligence impacted Academic Integrity and what does this mean for the award gap that university students face?

Whilst the answer to the above question could be several books long in itself and constantly evolving, both the positive and less positive points will be considered here. AI developments have been used to improve digital plagiarism tools such as Turnitin to become better at what their main function is to ensure honest, transparent and original work is submitted by students. AI tools are also allowing researchers to conduct and analyse data more efficiently with transparency about the steps in such a process. This is contributing to wider academic debate and practice. AI-informed systems are being used to monitor student activities, for example, to ensure test conditions are adhered to, maintaining fairness and integrity in online assessments. AI assistants can also be used to support students in developing their understanding of academic integrity and ensuring that they follow appropriate processes and that their work meets the required standards. AI assistants can also assist you if you are wrongly accused of academic misconduct and support you through the process (see Prompt 3.2), although you should always seek guidance from your university services on this matter first.

Prompt 3.2   How to respond to a wrongful accusation of academic misconduct?

INPUT:

I am a university student and have been wrongly accused of academic misconduct. Please provide a step-by-step guide that will support me to challenge this.

Just as AI has enabled enhanced practices of academic integrity, it has also enhanced opportunities for academic misconduct. As has already been discussed in the previous chapters, one of the biggest initial concerns of academic institutions is the temptation for students to submit AI-generated work as their own, thereby undermining academic integrity. The use of AI assistants to create academic content also leads to concerns about true authorship and acknowledgements of source content and ideas. Currently, there is a lack of transparency in relation to AI models, including what data have informed the response and how. Eaton (2021) was aware of this as being a cause for concern before the public release of Large Language Models like ChatGPT in 2022 and revisited their initial response to this in Eaton (2023). Please see Figure 3.1 for a simplified version of this. What is interesting here is that Eaton posits the potential and opportunities of the human–AI dialogue over the

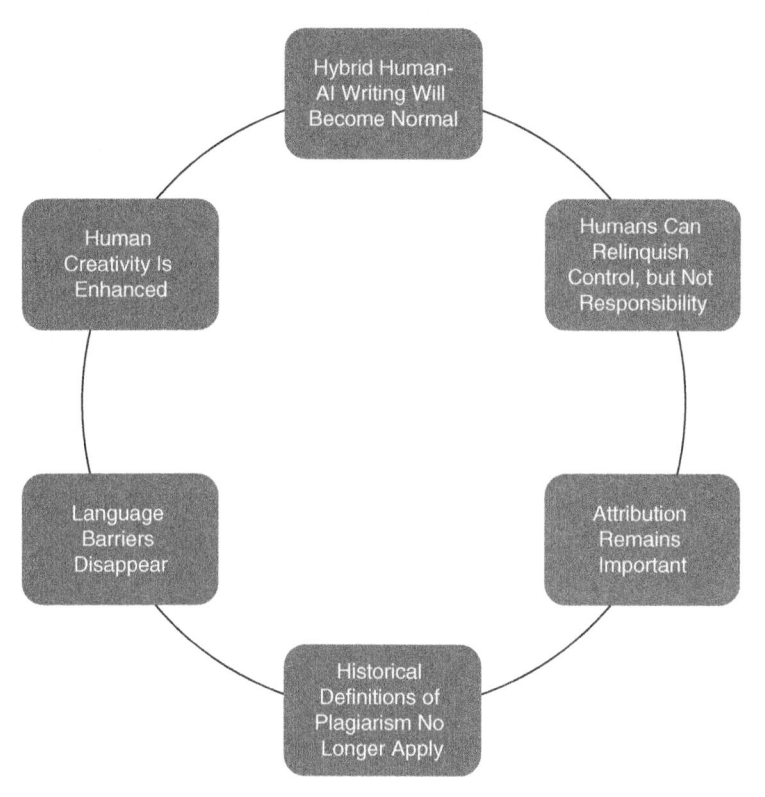

Figure 3.1 Eaton's (2023) 6 Tenets of Postplagiarism: Writing in the Age of Artificial Intelligence.

challenges. It also highlights the shortfall between non-existent or very little guidance in the contemporary context of using AI in an assistive role for student, their study and assignments.

There are also huge concerns regarding the inherent biases that have been shown to exist in some AI models because of the data that they have been trained on and as a result, the outputs are biased. Just recently, the CEO of Google apologised and that the bias was 'completely unacceptable and we got it wrong' in response to Google's Gemini AI image creator which depicts historical figures such as the US Founding Fathers, Popes and Vikings as racially diverse or as different genders (EuroNews, 2024). Left unchecked or questioned, biases can lead to unfair advantages or disadvantages for certain groups and compromise fairness. Concerns have also been raised regarding equitable access to AI tools for students and the impact this may have on the award gap. The award gap is defined by Advance HE as the difference in 'top degrees' – a First or 2:1 classification – awarded to different groups of students. Furthermore, 'there continues to be a considerable gap between the proportion of white British students receiving these degree classifications compared to UK-domiciled students from minority ethnic groups' (Advance HE). However, Fido and Harper (2023) state that academics must put their fears aside and understand how ChatGPT can be utilised to bridge the attainment gap.

Finally, the increasing reliance on AI assistants or tools to complete educational processes for a student may compromise the overall integrity of the course they are studying. This is especially a concern if first-hand, student-led experience and knowledge acquirement is an essential component of the programme of study with the intention of this aspect to then inform practice in the workplace and beyond. Whilst various steps can be taken to address and mitigate many of the concerns around the use of AI, fundamentally, the increasing prevalence of artificial intelligence-based tools and assistants across the sphere of higher education and workplaces will need a reconceptualisation of the core concepts of academic integrity: honesty, trust, fairness, respect, responsibility and courage. Indeed, it is this last concept of courage that should inform academic integrity moving forward. The courage to respond to developing technologies and their impact on student's lives beyond university.

3.6 Promoting academic integrity in relation to Bloom's Taxonomy and AI literacy

Bloom's Taxonomy (Bloom et al., 1956) has been a key educational philosophy for well over half a century with continued iterations and revisitation suggested. It is one of the central ideas concerning how educators at all levels can approach the learning process. It has led to a segregation of lower-order and higher-order thinking skills which are useful to think about in terms of how AI assistants are engaged with. Both types of skill inform many aspects of teaching and assessment with the expectation that students demonstrate all associated cognitive processes whilst learning. However, the familiarity with lower-level skills may be threatened if a response to a prompt can address them instantly. Rivers and Holland (2023) rightly recognise that the dawn of Generative AI and AI assistants has implications for the age-old order of Bloom's Taxonomy – as creation, once the pinnacle of the taxonomy, is now the first step in many respects based on a prompt. Rivers and Hollands' (2023) reconceptualisation of Bloom's Taxonomy allows for academic integrity to be explored with a particular focus on 'creation' first, with a conscious effort needed on the part of the student to develop across the other skills of the taxonomy. Figure 3.2 maps some key considerations that students should consider when using Generative AI in order to maintain academic integrity.

	Honesty	Trust	Fairness	Respect	Responsibility	Courage
Create	Generative AI can assist in generating ideas or content, but it is crucial for students to remain honest about the origin of these ideas. When required, students should distinguish between their own contributions and those generated by AI.	In this context, trust involves using AI as a tool without overdependence, maintaining a balance between AI-generated content and personal input. This ensures the educational process is present.	Fairness means that all students are aware of what AI tools can be used, have access to them and know how to acknowledge them in the process of creating.	Respecting diverse perspectives means critically assessing AI-generated content for inclusivity and bias.	Responsibility is key across all levels of Bloom's Taxonomy when using Generative AI. It includes the responsibility to use AI ethically, to ensure academic integrity by acknowledging AI-assisted work, and to critically assess and refine AI-generated outputs.	Courage involves the willingness to challenge AI-generated content, question its validity, and innovate beyond what AI can generate.
Evaluate	When evaluating or analysing content with AI assistance, honesty involves transparently acknowledging the use of AI tools and critically assessing the AI-generated content for biases or inaccuracies.	Trust also extends to understanding the capabilities and limitations of AI, ensuring that evaluations are subject to human oversight and critical thinking.				It includes the courage to rely on one's analysis and application of knowledge, even when AI provides alternative insights.
Analyse				Respect involves acknowledging the contributions of AI while also respecting the human effort and intellectual property involved in creating original content.		
Apply		Trust in one's abilities to apply concepts and solve problems, while also understanding the reliability and appropriateness of AI-generated solutions when used.	When applying knowledge or understanding concepts with AI's help, fairness involves using AI ethically, ensuring that AI-generated solutions do not disadvantage or unfairly advantage some students over others.	Respect the intellectual property of others by applying knowledge in a way that avoids plagiarism and demonstrates an understanding of how to credit all sources.		Demonstrate the bravery to apply knowledge in innovative ways, challenging conventional solutions, and questioning AI-generated answers when necessary.
Understand	Approach the understanding of concepts with integrity, ensuring that the use of AI to aid comprehension is not overly relied upon.					
Remember	... that AI Literacy is all of the above!					

Figure 3.2 Bloom's Taxonomy meets Academic Integrity.

3.7 Are you allowed to use AI tools, assistants and content?

Guidance on the use of artificial intelligence may differ depending on the higher education institution, faculty or programme you are enrolled on. However, there should be some overall guidance around the use of AI which is then interpreted down to course and potentially module level. It is important that you seek out guidance in relation to each assessment that you undertake. To provide an idea of the different approaches that may be taken in relation to the use of AI within an assessment, we will look at University College London's guidance (UCL, 2023). At the time of writing, UCL had some of the most pragmatic guidance in this area. Hopefully, this will pave the way for how many other universities approach the ethical use of Generative AI:

> *As a general principle, we need to recognise that AI will be used by students at many different stages in their learning process, including preparing for assessments... A key element of such an approach is communication with students so that they are fully aware of the parameters of the assessments, particularly in relation to the use of AI.* ***Therefore, the use of generative AI does not automatically constitute academic misconduct.***
>
> (UCL, 2023)

UCL's guidance for using AI tools in assessment begins with the categorisation of assessment into three types and an explanation under each. Within each category, how AI tools may or may not be used is defined, and examples are given. These categories are useful to explore and reflect on in relation to your own programme and course of study. Is it obvious at first glance which sort of category your assessments would fall under? Or is it more complex? Regardless, the programme team is always the best source to ask first and foremost. However, for now, here are UCL's three categories of assessment:

3.7.1 Category 1: AI tools cannot be used

Certain assessments are deemed unsuitable for AI tool usage due to their focus on assessing basic learning outcomes such as memorisation, comprehension, critical thinking, and the application of fundamental knowledge and skills essential for the entire programme. These assessments aim to support the knowledge and competencies necessary for successful study and future work. Discussion with students will be required to explain the rationale for this category (e.g., pedagogy, employability etc). Some example assessments are:

- In-person unseen examinations
- Class tests

- Some online tests
- Vivas
- Some laboratories and practicals
- Discussion-based assessments

3.7.2 Category 2: AI tools can be used in an assistive role

Students can use AI tools for certain tasks within the assessment to develop specific skill sets as directed by the module team. Such applications may include data analysis or pattern recognition with lecturers providing guidance to ensure a consistent learning experience. However, the integration of AI is not a learning goal in itself, and its use may be deemed unsuitable for certain aspects, e.g., writing the final submission. Some example assessments include:

- Draughting and structure content
- Supporting the writing process in a limited manner
- As a support tutor
- Supporting a particular process such as testing code or translating content
- Giving feedback on content or proofreading content

3.7.3 Category 3: AI has an integral role

AI can be used as an integral tool in the assessment process. The application of AI will enable learners to apply it innovatively to solve complex issues and make sound decisions. The evaluations will highlight the adept and ethical use of AI, with educators playing a crucial role in ensuring a consistent and equitable learning experience through guidance and support in AI utilisation.

- Drafting and structuring content
- Generating ideas
- Comparing content (AI-generated and human-generated)
- Creating content in particular styles
- Producing summaries
- Analysing content
- Reframing content
- Researching and seeking answers
- Creating artwork (images, audio and videos)
- Playing a Socrative role and engaging in a conversational discussion
- Developing code
- Translating content
- Generating initial content to be critiqued by students

3.8 Protecting your privacy when using AI tools

The datafication of the student experience via virtual learning environments, online libraries, attendance apps etc., means that understanding the ethical considerations of privacy, consent and data security should be a core part of a student's induction to university life. Although such areas can be bogged down in long reams of text, that are easier to skip and click agree to, students should have an awareness of them. Admittedly, the reality is that without agreeing to the collection of your data on your user habits, you will not be able to engage with your studies at all. This means that for most universities, when you sign-up to study for them, you are also agreeing to their policies on privacy, consent and security. On the other hand, this is an increasingly important part of a university's provision as Higher Education Institutions are increasingly the focus of both successful and unsuccessful cyberattacks. Official statistics from the Department for Science, Innovation and Technology (2023) in the UK found that six in ten of the Higher Education Institutions that identified any breaches or attacks report losing money or data, or having compromised accounts used for illicit purposes as a result. Universities were also more likely to experience a wider range of attack types, such as impersonation, viruses or other malware, and denial of service attacks.

In terms of AI tools and services, your first priority should be to explore the tools and options that you are guided to by your university and course. Sometimes, these tools will be included within the licensing arrangements that your university already has and therefore sanctioned as legitimate and safe tools to use. Sanctioned tools may use a single sign-on authentication meaning that your university account name and password work for the tool as well. However, it may be that you are recommended a third-party AI tool or want to explore the use of a third-party AI tool as it offers functionality not offered within the university's standard offer. First, it is important to double-check that the tools you want to use are not blacklisted or banned by the university. Second, if a sign-up is required, it is incredibly important not to sign-up to third-party tools with the same username and password as your university account. This is to protect that information. It would also not be advisable to use your personal e-mail and password. This is to minimise the potential of your details and passwords being hacked and then that information being used. It is a good idea to create a secondary e-mail account that you can use to sign-up for third-party tools. This way, your username and password will be protected from any potential leaks or hacks that an AI tool may experience. This is discussed further in Chapter 4. To summarise this section:

Privacy: Think about what you need access to on a daily basis to ensure you can study and partake in your studies. Protect the key information that grants you this, i.e., your university username and password.

Consent: When was the last time you read through a terms-of-service agreement before hitting 'accept'? True consent means understanding how your data is used, whether it is for improving educational tools or something less benign. It is about having the power to say yes or no, knowing exactly what you are signing up for.

Data Security: If a breach was to happen to a third-party tool, what information can potential hackers access and how could it be used? Remember to keep your digital self and data safe.

What You Can Do: Be selective about what you share and where. Question the apps and services you use: what data are they asking for, and why? Do they need access to so much data? Can you limit the access that they have and cancel or delete the account and its associated data if needed?

3.9 Future-proof your skillset

As a university student, you are at the forefront of what appears to be a significant shift in academia- as captured in the electricity analogy used in Chapter 1 to explain the impact of AI on society. The speed of development in terms of AI and its uses will depend on several things: your university's approach to the use of AI; the academics that teach you and their approach to AI; and your own approach to and experimentation with using AI. The one thing that you have full control over is your own approach; however, as you will have gathered from this chapter, using AI tools and approaches ethically is paramount if you are to reap the rewards of such application in the future. Understanding the current changes and those that are on the horizon will equip you with essential skills and attributes for interviews and the workplace beyond study. However, you should take stock of the opportunities that your university programme offers you to fine-tune such skills.

Whilst you will be taught by a number of academics across your course, do not be limited to them as your only sources of input for study. Utilise the other resources that your university offers, gain any additional experiences through your course/university and personalise your study with the use of AI assistants. Once you have grown in confidence and familiarity, use AI assistants to challenge youself and extend your thinking. Furthermore, work with longer-term goals that an AI assistant can regularly remind you of and suggest areas of improvement and advancement (see Prompt 3.3). Action planning can quickly become a forgotten exercise, but AI assistants cannot only talk you through the process, but remind you of its outcomes as well.

> **Prompt 3.3   How to future-proof your skillset**
>
> **INPUT:**
>
> I want to ensure that I am future-proofing my skillset for beyond my studies at university in [enter course here]. Help me identify appropriate short, medium and long-term goals. Then help me develop a step-by-step approach to each, as well as how I can utilise you as an AI assistant to remind me of the goals and check in on my progress each step of the way.

Utilising AI tools across your studies will impact your learning. Capitalise on the efficiencies that AI can provide in terms of mind mapping ideas, structuring assignments, suggesting key aspects, searches etc., and use the saved time to think outside of the box. Such thinking, as long as you are able to relate it to the purposes of your assessments and make relevant connections with your programme of study, will enhance your overall achievement. Furthermore, the utilisation of AI assistants will help you develop your AI literacy skills and be confident in the use of AI tools for future tasks. The ability to plan, prioritise and manage your time well, will serve you long after your university course has finished.

3.10 Skills to prioritise

To navigate the AI landscape and prepare for what the post-AI landscape brings consider investing time and understanding in the following areas:

- **Critical Engagement**: As AI-generated content becomes more prevalent, your ability to critically assess its validity and relevance will be crucial.
- **Self-directed Learning**: AI can guide and assist, but your ability to set goals, seek out resources, and engage deeply with your subject matter will define your success.
- **Ethical Awareness**: With AI's potential to generate content, understand the ethical use of such tools, especially regarding plagiarism, originality and academic integrity.
- **Adaptability**: The AI landscape is constantly evolving. Staying curious, open to new ideas and ready to adapt will be key to leveraging AI effectively in your studies and beyond.

For you as a student, it offers a unique opportunity to engage with your education in a more personalised, interactive and profound way. Embracing these changes, while developing the skills to use AI responsibly and effectively, will not only enhance your academic journey but also prepare you for a future where AI is an integral part of the graduate and professional landscape.

3.11 Summary of chapter

This chapter has offered a thorough examination of the ethical use of Generative AI in universities, concentrating on academic integrity, addressing privacy concerns and adapting to the changing Higher Education Environment as a result of AI. It began by outlining academic integrity and exploring its significance, underscoring the need for honesty, trust, fairness, respect, responsibility and courage. The narrative then moved to the impact of AI on academic integrity, showcasing both the positive – like improved plagiarism detection tools and efficient research analysis – and the negative, such as the risk of academic misconduct with the submission of AI-generated work as one's own. The chapter then considered Bloom's Taxonomy in relation to academic integrity and provided a framework for students to draw on in order to develop their AI literacy. Such AI literacy will foster the ethical usage of and critical interaction with AI-produced content.

It highlighted the critical role of students in developing their own awareness, alongside institutional policies, to protect privacy and security. Illustrated with an example from the UCL, the chapter provided practical advice for considering how AI tools may be used in relation to academic assessments. It divided assessments into three categories, explaining when and how AI could be suitably used, from no AI involvement to AI being a fundamental part of the assessment process. In conclusion, the chapter suggested areas for students to consider in terms of future-proofing their skill set in response to the course or programme they are studying.

3.12 Chapter hacks

1. **Honesty in Creation:** Always acknowledge and reference the use of AI in your work according to the requirements of the course or programme that you are studying. This ensures transparency and maintains the integrity of your academic contributions.
2. **Balanced AI Utilisation:** Employ AI tools as aids without becoming overly dependent on them. This includes using AI for brainstorming or preliminary drafts while ensuring that critical analysis and personal insight are predominantly your own.
3. **Critical Assessment for Bias:** When engaging with AI-generated content, actively look for biases or lack of inclusivity and critically assess the content to ensure it aligns with ethical standards and academic integrity.

(Continued)

4. **Ethical Responsibility:** Across all aspects of your academic work, use AI ethically, acknowledging its assistance where applicable, and refine AI-generated outputs to align with academic standards and personal intellectual contributions.
5. **Innovative Challenge:** Challenge the limitations of AI by questioning its validity, pushing beyond its suggestions and innovating with your own ideas to enhance the depth and originality of your work.
6. **Transparent Evaluation:** In tasks involving evaluation or analysis, transparently acknowledge the role of AI as required, ensuring that your assessments are subject to your critical thinking and not solely reliant on AI-generated conclusions.
7. **Ethical Application:** Apply your knowledge ethically, ensuring AI-generated solutions or contributions do not unfairly advantage or disadvantage any group and demonstrate a clear understanding of crediting all sources to avoid plagiarism.
8. **AI Literacy:** Embrace AI literacy by understanding the functionalities, limitations and ethical implications of AI tools, and use this knowledge to enhance your academic integrity and digital responsibility.
9. **Privacy Protection:** Be cautious about the privacy and security implications of using AI tools, particularly third-party applications. Ensure you understand and adhere to university guidelines regarding AI tool usage to protect your personal information and academic integrity.

3.13 Chapter MCQs

1. What are the fundamental values of academic integrity as defined by the International Center for Academic Integrity (ICAI)?
   A) Creativity, Efficiency, Innovation and Transparency
   B) Honesty, Trust, Fairness, Respect, Responsibility and Courage
   C) Originality, Independence, Compliance and Confidentiality
   D) Accountability, Openness, Professionalism and Reliability
2. How has AI been used positively in relation to academic integrity?
   A) By facilitating more engaging and interactive classroom experiences
   B) By improving digital plagiarism detection tools like Turnitin
   C) By enabling easier access to restricted research materials
   D) By automating the grading process to reduce teacher workload
3. Which of the following is a concern related to the use of AI in creating academic content?
   A) Increased efficiency in research and data analysis
   B) Enhanced personalisation in learning experiences
   C) The temptation for students to submit AI-generated work as their own
   D) The ability of AI to provide real-time feedback to students

4. According to the chapter, how should Bloom's Taxonomy be approached in the context of Generative AI?
   A) By focusing solely on lower-order thinking skills due to AI's limitations
   B) By starting with 'creation' and consciously developing other skills across the taxonomy
   C) By eliminating the need for higher-order thinking skills altogether
   D) By prioritising memorisation and recall over critical thinking and analysis
5. What analogy is used in the chapter to describe the ethical considerations of using AI in education?
   A) AI as a compass guiding students through the wilderness of knowledge
   B) AI as a conductor of a symphony orchestra, enhancing performance without overshadowing human creativity
   C) AI as a builder constructing the foundation of academic integrity
   D) AI as a librarian organising and providing access to information

Correct answers:

1. Correct answer B
2. Correct answer B
3. Correct answer C
4. Correct answer B
5. Correct answer B

PART TWO

HOW TO SUPPORT YOUR STUDY WITH GENERATIVE AI

4

Getting Started With Generative AI

4.1 Chapter objectives

1. Consider the practical steps for safely integrating AI tools into your academic studies
2. Navigate the decision-making process between using free versus paid AI tools
3. Assess the value and limitations of AI tools in relation to academic requirements and personal learning goals
4. Categorise various types of Generative AI tools and their applications in academic work
5. Explore different AI tools and their relevance for writing, image creation, presentations and video creation

4.2 Having read this chapter, you will...

1. Be equipped with knowledge on setting up accounts for AI tool access, with an emphasis on security and privacy
2. Be able to make informed decisions about whether to use free AI tools or invest in premium versions based on your academic needs
3. Understand the support and resources available from your educational institution regarding the use of AI tools
4. Have practical tips for evaluating and using AI tools effectively, including the development of AI prompts for various tasks
5. Receive an introduction to the broad spectrum of AI tools available and how to evaluate their functionality and suitability for specific academic tasks
6. Be prepared to ensure the integrity of your work when using AI-generated content and to articulate the processes and sources behind the generated output

4.3 Introduction

The introduction of Generative AI into the academic sphere marks a shift in the way knowledge is created, shared and consumed as discussed in Chapter 1. This chapter begins by exploring practical considerations when getting started with Generative AI tools. It is designed to serve as a guide offering points for thought and reflection, as well as clear points for direction and action. This will support students in using AI-based tools in their studies. Central to considering any use of AI-based tools should be concerns around maintaining academic integrity and ethical transparency as already discussed in Chapter 3. Understanding the framework and guidance from your university regarding the use of AI tools in your studies is paramount as this will ultimately inform how and when you can use them. The next question that you should also reflect on to develop your own AI literacy is 'why' are you using them? What is it that the tool is 'automating' for you as a student and is this contributing to or taking away from your learning experience?

Generative AI raises important questions about authenticity, intellectual property and the integrity of academic work. We will further examine how these tools align with the ethical standards and the importance of maintaining academic integrity in an era of automated assistance and content generation. The limitations of Generative AI should not be overlooked as the critical role of human oversight and accountability still remains. Technology is an adjunct to, not a replacement for, the critical thinking and analytical skills that are the hallmark of university study. It is essential that users of Generative AI develop their critique of it, ensuring that the output aligns with academic standards and contributes meaningfully to their study. This chapter aims to equip readers with the knowledge and tools necessary to engage with Generative AI in a thoughtful and effective manner. It is a step towards navigating the complex interplay between technology and academia, providing a clear-eyed view of the opportunities there are to integrate AI-based tools into learning and study tasks. This chapter will provide practical advice on how to integrate different types of AI tools into academic practice.

A snapshot of getting started with AI tools
- Prioritise using the AI tools that you have access to through your university
- Before you start signing-up for third-party AI tools, you need to consider if you want to use your personal email account and what information the tool is asking for when creating or syncing a pre-existing account with it
- You may consider setting up a secondary account if you do not already have one. For example, many AI tools allow you to sign in with a Google account. If you already have a personal Gmail account, it is easy to set up and manage a secondary one alongside it, which can then be used for signing-up for third-party AI tools
- Keeping such sign-ins and sharing of your details separate from your personal account information is an added layer of security to consider

- Also, please be aware that many AI tools offer free or limited credits to get you started, or per day-what is called 'Freemium access'. After such credits are used, they will ask you to sign-up for premium accounts
- As a general rule of thumb, do not sign-up for anything that asks for your bank card!

4.4 To sign-up or not to sign-up?

AI tools often have different requirements in terms of providing access to them. Some AI tools are freely accessible and do not require you to sign in to use them – although usage limits are often in place for such tools, e.g., the AI-powered PDF reader tool and Chat PDF. This grants immediate access to the tool and avoids account creation or the sharing of personal user data. However, the norm of signing-up is generally a requirement for you to gain access by creating or linking a pre-existing account to the AI tool. There are both advantages and disadvantages to this process (Table 4.1):

Table 4.1 Advantages and disadvantages of using an account to access an AI tool

Advantages of using an account to access an AI tool	Disadvantages of using an account to access an AI tool
+ Linking to a pre-existing account of yours will streamline the sign-in process + Offer a personalised experience based on your user data + Password and details can be saved for easy retrieval	− Sharing personal data with AI tools raises privacy concerns regarding how your data are used and who else could have access to it − It is not always clear who owns and controls the AI tool itself. Furthermore, the ownership of the tool may change in the future, especially if it is successful

A **solution** to the requirement of linking an account to an AI tool in order to have access to it is to create a second account for this purpose. For example, if you use a Gmail account as your primary email account, create a second Gmail account and use that for signing-up for any AI tools that require an account to be linked to it. The purpose of this is to guard against AI tools having access to your personal data and information. Often there is no time to explore in full an AI tool's ownership or data policy etc., when you primarily want to use the product on offer. Furthermore, the ownership of AI tools may change hands in the future and changes may be made to how your data are used, stored or shared.

4.5 Free or fee?

As a general rule, students should not be encouraged to sign-up for fee-paying AI tools. This is because there is currently an array of AI tools competing for market space, meaning that it is possible to access 'freemium' models of competing tools that do the same thing. For example, the tools Connected Papers and Litmaps, both offer a similar service that aids in researching academic literature. Both offer a freemium model with capped usage. Once a student has reached their usage limits in one tool, instead of paying for access to the premium service, search for an equivalent AI tool that also offers initial free access and use that. There may also be open-source and free tools that provide a similar function in this case. In relation to the two tools mentioned in this paragraph, there is a free, no-sign-up-needed tool called Inciteful, which is also designed to enhance literature searches in a similar way to the tools mentioned.

AI tools that require a sign-up come with varying plans and cost structures, each carrying its own set of merits and drawbacks. A commonly used example of this is the tool Grammarly. The basic version of Grammarly is available for free, offering a no-cost entry point with restricted features. On the flip side, premium versions of fee-paying tools like Grammarly offer a broader range of advanced features on top (Table 4.2).

Table 4.2 Advantages and disadvantages of free access and paid access to an AI tool

Advantages of free access to an AI tool	Disadvantages of free access to an AI tool
– Immediate access without financial commitment – Suitable for casual or infrequent use	– Limited features and capabilities – May lack customer support or updates. – May only be available in the short term (not good for longer research time spans or projects)
Advantages of paid access to an AI tool	**Disadvantages of paid access to an AI tool**
– Access to advanced features and capabilities – Often comes with better customer support	– Requires financial commitment – The cost may be prohibitive for some users

Grammarly also offers 'Freemium' users limited access to premium features to demonstrate the potential value of these. This approach allows users to explore the tool at no cost and only invest as they see value. This is also a clever way of tools offering free usage alongside limited usage of premium features to encourage users to upgrade to its fee-paying premium version. Regardless of the model, it is prudent to understand the cost structure, assess the tool's value proposition in relation to your needs as a student and consider any long-term costs, especially when utilising the tool for academic or professional purposes. Ultimately ask yourself, 'Can I get by with the freemium version?' The author believes that students can in most scenarios.

4.6 Officially vetted vs the wild west?

Primarily, seek advice and support from the institution where you are studying. All universities should offer support relating to research (Librarians), assignment preparation (Learning Development) and technology (Learning Technologists) as part of their service for you undertaking study there, although such support services may have different titles at your institution. A good starting place is to find out which tools are supported by your university for use in your studies and begin there. Many of the digital tools used in teaching and learning now have added AI functions or functionality. The support services at your university will have more in-depth knowledge and be able to provide access to the tools that it has vetted and purchased licences for. When using new tools, you may run into certain challenges or problems in terms of getting the tool to actually do what you want it to. When such problems occur, your university should have guidance and support in place for you. Additionally, you can ask the lecturers from your programme and engage with peers from your course, as well as access any university-sanctioned forums for questions and answers relating to what AI tools are supported. However, universities have budget restrictions and tendering processes that need to be followed in order to enact such subscriptions. It is therefore possible that you may seek out AI tools which are external to the officially vetted tools of your university, which for the purpose of this section is labelled the Wild West of AI tools!

Engaging with a new AI tool can be a daunting prospect especially when you do not know where to start. The dominance of tech companies such as Microsoft, Google and Apple, often means that you are subconsciously accustomed to user interfaces and controls looking or feeling a certain way. Using AI tools that have been developed by startups and tech entrepreneurs can mean that you need to expand your digital skill base in terms of navigation and application. In the longer term, larger tech companies tend to buy up the smaller startups and integrate such tools within their wider offering and align them with their interfaces. However, exploring any new AI tool or feature should mean understanding its purpose and use of it, and how this relates to what you are doing in terms of your study or assignment preparation. For example, if you have extensive notes from seminars and now want to collate and curate these, using an AI tool that is language or text-based to support you in this process would be a logical first step as opposed to using an image-generation-based AI tool. This may sound obvious, but understanding what you can and cannot do with a tool is important if you are to use it effectively. This will be explored further in Chapter 5.

4.7 Novice or pro?

When beginning with an AI tool you may initially feel like a novice. This could be for a number of reasons relating to the 'newness' of experience: new tool, new functionality, new user interface, new applicability etc. A novice approach will often involve accessing the freemium version of the AI tool (if not vetted by your university) and exploring what it has to offer. Review any 'getting started' documentation and introductory tutorials that are on offer to gain an insight into its capabilities and limitations, especially regarding 'freemium' usage. Begin with simple queries/prompts or exploration to see how the tool responds and develop your input in relation to this. Many tools will also offer video tutorials or users may even create their own reviews and guidance for tools which can be accessed through platforms such as YouTube. Just as you are expected to undertake research when completing your university studies, you should also research how to use new AI tools. Some tools may also offer blogs or free webinars, where they offer a walk/talk-through of how to use their tool. These are great starting places for any novice.

The more you engage with AI tools the easier it becomes to navigate new tools as you develop your approach to 'prompting' and refine why you are using a tool and what you want or need from it. Signs that you are no longer a novice with such tools may be that you are increasingly finding new ways to engage with and use the tool or that you are supporting others in their use and access to the tool. Becoming a 'pro' will also mean that you keep up to date with developments in the tool as it releases new features and expands its repertoire in terms of the services it offers. However, if you are a freemium account user, as previously mentioned, this may bring limitations in terms of developing your 'pro-ness'. At times, it may be that you do not feel like a pro yourself, but you are more familiar with a tool than a peer or friend, so they see you as a pro. This can be related to the proverb 'In the land of the blind, the one-eyed man is king' and a common phenomenon for early adopters of new technology and tools.

4.8 Prompting and prompting frameworks

Whilst this topic could easily form the basis of a skills book for students in itself, a brief introduction to and summary of approaches will be provided here. Harvard University (2023) offers some useful guidance on getting started with prompts for text-based Generative AI assistants (see Figure 4.1). Although the focus here is on text-based assistants, the principles discussed in the article can be applicable to image and video-based AI assistants as well.

When prompting you should focus on specificity, clarity and conciseness to enhance output quality. It also suggests giving the AI a specific role, defining the format of its response, considering a specific audience, as well as any examples that can be offered in relation to the intended output. It also advises on iterative improvement, corrects any errors in outputs and asks the AI for assistance with creating further prompts or seeking further information should it be needed to complete the task set. As well as the considerations raised in Figure 4.1, numerous prompt frameworks have been created to aid users with creating effective prompts (see Table 4.3). Both prompting and the use of frameworks to construct prompts are something that needs experimenting with. The more you experiment, the better you will get at constructing prompts and refining the outputs meaning that the process of engaging with an AI assistant becomes more iterative and reciprocal, not input/output and extract.

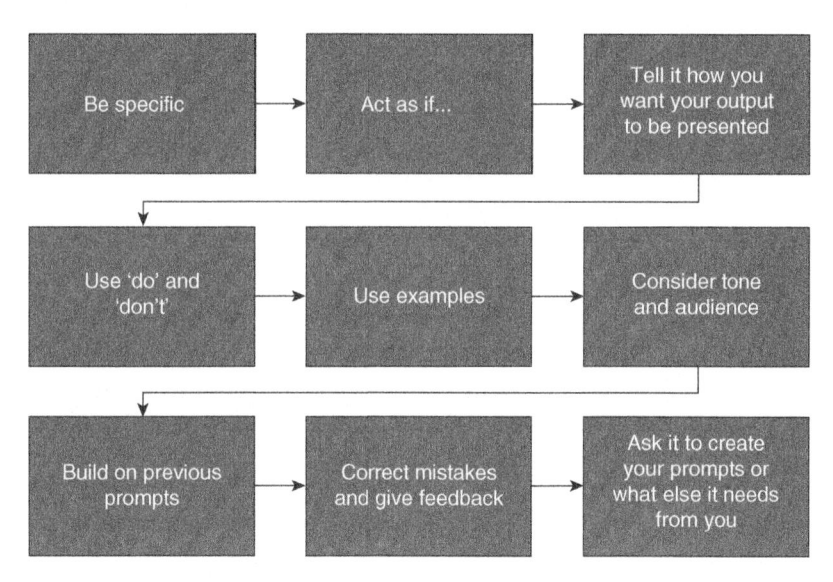

Figure 4.1 Getting started with prompting.

Table 4.3 Prompt frameworks

RTF	RISEN	RODES
R: Role	R: Role	R: Role
T: Task	I: Instructions	O: Objective
F: Format	S: Steps	D: Details
	E: End Goal	E: Examples
	N: Narrowing	S: Sense Check

4.9 Unpacking the AI tool kit

4.9.1 Introduction to tool types

The following section categorises Generative AI into four types of tools and introduces their relevance and use. The first type relates to writing and the correction or generation of text: AI writing tools. The second type will introduce image creation tools which can be used to support study and both formative and summative assignments. The third type relates to the generation of presentations or slides which will contain both text and images in relation to the prompt it is given. The final type will introduce AI video-based tools and explore how a medium such as text can then be transformed into video. It is worth stating here that the number and types of tools relating to Generative AI in all areas are both increasing and advancing. This means that all of the considerations in the first half of this chapter should be revisited each time you explore the use of a new AI tool: To sign-up or not to sign-up?; Free or Fee?; Officially Vetted vs the Wild West?; Novice or Pro? It also means that by the time this book is published, there will more than likely be several new contributions to each type of tool that are worth checking out but not covered here.

4.10 AI Writing tools

AI writing tools are programmes that utilise AI technology to analyse the text input and provide feedback on it or suggestions in terms of what to write next based on an algorithm. The use of AI to enhance writing-based products is not new. It was reported that Microsoft were using AI to enhance its spellcheck feature across Microsoft Office programmes in 2016 (Lopez, 2016). What has changed, however, is the increased capacity and ability of AI-based models to undertake a wider range of functions and at an increased level of accuracy. This has blurred the lines between what is or is not human output in terms of text generation. Real-time feedback has evolved further in relation to grammar, vocabulary, syntax, content and structure. Recommended improvements are often made via underlined text and an options tab that can be accessed by a click or hovering above it. This has been an accepted way of working within text-based programmes, such as Microsoft Word for a long time. More recently though, tools are expanding their functionality to do more than assist in reviewing written text and its style. AI tools are able to offer functions that generate writing or text for the user based on a prompt. This means that the boundaries between AI-assisted writing and AI-generated writing are increasingly blurred. The following tools present a brief overview of AI tools that can be used to aid students in developing their writing. If being used for formal purposes such as assignments, it is important that students are aware of two points:

1. If they can use such tools in the first place (see university/programme guidance on the use of AI tools).
2. How the use of such tools should be acknowledged or referenced, and any examples of this before getting started.

4.10.1 Grammarly

At the time of writing, this is probably one of the better-known grammar checkers available. As has already been detailed in this chapter, there is both a freemium and premium version. A version can be installed on your desktop meaning that with the correct permissions, it can be used across apps, word-processing programmes, emails and more. Something to be aware of, however, is that its use in conjunction with programmes that already have spelling/grammar checkers installed can mean that you get two lots of feedback relating to spelling and grammar. This can feel excessive at times, especially if one is set to US English and the other British English. The freemium version of Grammarly is a great place to start though!

4.10.2 Quill Bot (paraphraser)

Quill Bot seems to be offering an increasing number of AI-based tools to support the writing process including a grammar checker. The paraphraser tool is aimed at helping to reduce plagiarism as students can enter an original piece of text and Quill Bot will rephrase its sentences and paragraphs but retain the original meaning. Although you are limited in terms of the style of paraphrasing that you can access using the freemium version of Quill Bot, you can paraphrase up to 125 words at a time.

4.10.3 Hemingway editor

This is a free online version of the Hemingway App, which also has a premium version available for a monthly subscription. The online version has two modes: write and edit. The write mode presents a distraction-free interface where you can focus on writing your text. The 'Edit' mode introduces five coloured highlights that identify potential areas of improvement throughout your text as part of its analysis. It will feedback on your text's readability score, use of passive voice, word count, estimated read time and more. The freemium version can support you in reviewing your work to make it clearer, but you will have to take on board the feedback provided and make adjustments.

4.10.4 Paperpal

This tool is provided by Researcher.Life provides several other AI-based tools aimed at research and academic writing. The freemium version allows you limited access and usage to its online site. Once you have created an account you can begin writing or copy and paste a text you have already started for feedback. It has numerous features that can suggest edits and rewrite your text for you.

Paperpal has recently launched a 'Copilot' that specifically aids in the rewriting of the text, generating outlines, titles, abstracts etc. It will also offer guidance if prompted and generate further ideas and direction for the text. Paperpal is particularly useful for students who are learning English as a foreign or additional language and need to improve their grammar and writing skills.

4.10.5 Jenni.ai

This is an AI writing tool that specialises in generating academic and research-related content. It will build content outlines and extend initial input with an AI autocomplete function. It can rewrite or paraphrase the text, create in-text citations and check for plagiarism as well. Whilst it is marketed as supporting users to develop their critical thinking and skills, the temptation to automate all of the previous functions through AI-based technologies is real. A word of caution is needed around this, as it means that the content becomes AI-generated rather than AI-assisted, which is not an accurate representation of the student's level of understanding and, therefore, risks their academic integrity. However, this does potentially allow for the student to attempt mastery in terms of the proofreading, attribution of sources and final editing of the piece of work produced.

4.11 AI image creation tools

The ability to edit and manipulate images has become common practice since the launch and rise of Adobe Photoshop in 1990. Developments in cloud-based services have allowed such capabilities to become accessible beyond the mainstay of graphic designers and digital artists. With the development of AI-based image generators, not only is image manipulation possible, but image creation from a single prompt/input is a reality now. AI-generated image creators are trained on large datasets of images. The training process enables algorithms to learn different aspects and characteristics of the images contained within the dataset. Broadly speaking, the best quality AI image creators are currently subscription-based and include the likes of DALL-E 3, Midjourney, Dream Studios and Firefly (by Photoshop). However, if you are looking to create images to support tasks in or out of taught sessions, or for assignments, then there are a number of AI image creation tools that offer some free usage and are worth checking out. Some tools are discussed below in this section, but you can also use a search engine to explore 'free AI image creators' and explore the results presented, just remember not to sign-up for anything with a bank card or details! Please be aware that some of the free tools do have limited functionality and will not allow you to enter fully developed prompts to define the content/style of your image.

4.11.1 AI image prompting

Just as with any Generative AI tool, the quality and accuracy of the output largely depends on the input, aka 'the prompt'. Most Large Language Models (LLMs) are able to offer guidance on how to develop prompts, including those related to image generation. There are various components that you will want to consider when developing a prompt. The more components you include the more accurate your image will be to your command. Furthermore, you can use an LLM to create your image prompt, asking it to provide a prompt in relation to the components in Table 4.4.

Table 4.4 Image prompt components

Component	Description
Style of image	This should relate to the distinctive visual elements that you want to be incorporated into the image and can range from broad commands to very specific requests. For example, realism or abstract would be a general request, but requesting an image in the style of Andy Warhol's work would be very specific. Consideration should also be given to colour palette, texture and the use of light and shadow. There is also a wide range of considerations that can be made if requesting a life-like photograph. For example, portrait, landscape, macro, documentary, black and white, architectural etc.
Main subject	This relates to the main focus or the predominant theme that is to feature or be communicated in your image. This is typically what the viewer's eye is drawn to and what the image is aiming to represent. In a portrait, this would be the individual being portrayed, in a landscape the dominant feature such as trees or mountains. The main subject may be the sum of its parts, consider how an image or scene may be developed to represent a central theme or point in time. For example, the Dutch and Flemish Renaissance Painter, Pieter Bruegel the Elder's painting 'Children's Games' in 1,560 shows a town scene of many people but when you look closely you realise that many are children and playing distinct games
Detail of image	Details should serve to support the main subject and contextualise the image developing an image's layers of meaning and relevance. Using the example of Bruegel's Children's Games' above, it would be developing the main subject and types of games that are being portrayed to the contextual elements of the scene at the time such as clothing, buildings etc.
Form of image	The form should develop the visual architecture of the image and guide the viewer's focus and influence the interpretation. For example, will the image be two or three-dimensional, should the image be framed or not and consideration be given to how the image should be layered?
Aspect ratio	These are expressed as two numbers and separated by a colon, with the first representing width and the second height. The type of aspect ratio is usually informed by the medium that it will be presented in. For example, 4:3 (Traditional TV shape), 16:9 (widescreen), 1:1 (square and often used for social media), 3:2 (standard for 35 mm film) and 18:5 (is an example of a panoramic aspect ratio). Aspect ratio is an essential consideration in both the creation and display of images, as it affects framing, composition, and how the image is eventually viewed

> **Prompt 4.1 Example of an AI image prompt developed in ChatGPT and then entered into DALL-E (9/11/23)**
>
> **INPUT:**
>
> Generate a wide aspect ratio (1792 × 1,024) image that conveys warmth and empathy, featuring a diverse group of children and an adult facilitator in a circle during a support group session. The children should have engaged and attentive expressions, with one narrating a story. The adult's presence should be comforting and supportive. The room should have soft lighting and comfortable furnishings like cushions and bean bags, and elements such as plants or soft rugs, to enhance the atmosphere of a safe and nurturing space.
>
> **OUTPUT:**
>
> **Image 4.1** AI-generated images

4.11.2 Bing's image creator

Microsoft entered into an agreement with OpenAI, the creator of ChatGPT and DALL-E, when it brought AI to Bing. Bing's Image Creator is free and allows you to generate images by entering a prompt and clicking 'Create'. The results are good, and you can create more specific pieces of art by describing your images as comprehensively as possible.

4.11.3 Deep AI

This text-to-image generator is easy to use and produces viable results with the right prompts. There are many image styles available but only some are free. The freestyles include basic text-to-image, cute creatures, fantasy worlds, cyberpunk, old, renaissance painting and abstract, among others. All of these styles produce images according to their respective themes. Although the tool worked fine at the time of writing, there were an excessive number of adverts and pop-ups when using the site.

4.11.4 Magic Media App (image and video creation) in Canva (online graphic design tool)

The Magic Media App in Canva provides text to image based on the prompt you enter. There are several styles you can select that adhere to a theme, or you can include the style in your prompt. At the time of writing, the Magic Media App also had a BETA text-to-video function that can generate short 3- to 4-second video clips based on the prompt that is entered. However, credits to do so are limited for freemium users.

4.12 AI presentation/slides tools

This section is going to begin by covering the AI features that have been added to Microsoft PowerPoint that align with an AI-assisted approach to creating presentations. Next, AI tools that create both text and images to make up complete presentations will be considered. These latter tools fall into the category of AI-generated approaches and therefore need to be introduced with a word of caution. If you are going to use AI-generated approaches to create a presentation, you need to consider the reason you are doing so and explore your university's guidance on this. Remember that if you are using an AI assistant to inform or develop a presentation for an assessment, then this must be done so ethically and maintain academic integrity.

4.12.1 Microsoft PowerPoint

Microsoft PowerPoint's embedded AI features at the time of writing offer assistance in both the design and rehearsal of your presentation. The *AI design function* can be accessed via 'Home Designer', and it uses algorithms for machine learning to review the information on a slide and make design suggestions that align with it. The 'Designer' function also activates when you are inserting an image, as it will open a right-hand pane in the window and present the image in several different styles and arrangements from which you can select your preferred one. The Designer AI function professionalises the aesthetics of your presentation at the click of a button. This will save you time and effort, allowing for this time to be spent elsewhere and supporting your creative journey.

The second AI feature to be discussed here can be accessed via 'Slide show *Rehearse with Coach*'. Rehearse with Coach offers real-time feedback and analysis of your presentation as you present it. Selecting the feature starts your presentation and activates the microphone function on your device. The real-time feedback will offer encouragement as well as pick up on your use of 'fillers' in speech. When you finish the rehearsal, a report will be generated that covers the time spent presenting, the number of slides covered, the pace (words per minute), the use of fillers, repetitive language, inclusiveness and originality. This feature is excellent to develop your confidence and experience of presenting which are especially important when practising for a presentation-based assessment. Increasing your confidence will enhance the content and key messages of your presentation and help to maximise your grade in presentation-based assessments. Microsoft is also rolling out the AI-based Copilot assistant across its Office/Microsoft 365 programmes which is likely to mean that PowerPoint and other associated programmes will feature an increasing array of AI-powered features in the coming months. This means that Microsoft Copilot will be able to create (generate both text and images), edit and offer feedback in relation to questions that you ask about the content or concepts in a presentation. Furthermore, as most university sign-up for Microsoft's products and packages, this could be a key place to get started with AI-assisted learning and creation.

4.12.2 Gamma.app

This tool offers freemium access once you have created an account. At the time of writing, Gamma offers some of the best freemium functionality within the limitations of its 400 starter credits. Further credits can be earned for free by inviting others to use Gamma or to our workspace. Gamma allows you to create new documents from blank, including presentations. You can import Word and presentation-based documents into Gamma and work on these within Gamma's user interface. You can share or export your finished documents in a number of ways via a copied link, PDF file or PowerPoint file. This is a function that is typically only available with a subscription to similar tools.

By selecting the '+ Create new AI' option on Gamma's homepage, you are given two options. The first is to 'Generate' and the second is 'Text Transform'. This second option is great if you already have notes or ideas to input. The first option 'Generate', however, will generate a first draft outline based on the topic or title that you enter in the format that you select (word, presentation or webpage). This section will focus on creating a presentation. After selecting the presentation format, you are asked to add the 'Topic'. The AI is then able to generate a draft outline for the presentation based on your input. This outline is editable and allows you to make changes based on ideas that you may have but are not initially captured. This is a really useful part of the edit function. Once you are happy with the draft outline, you proceed to pick a theme for your presentation and create it. Presentations are typically about six to eight slides in the freemium version and offer a great starting place for a first draft. Each slide will be stylised, based on your chosen theme, and include text and relevant images. All of these aspects are editable with Gamma's AI design partner function, which can also assist you further in adding slides, text or images.

Returning to Gamma's homepage, an 'Import' option is also available. This allows you to import Google docs, Google slides (text only), Word documents or PowerPoint files (text only). This feature imports all of the text from the selected document and creates slides based on this. You can then select a theme for all slides, edit each slide with text and images, add additional slides and share/export the slides when complete. Gamma's AI design partner is also available in this option to support the creation of new slides, text and images. It can reinterpret text on slides and present it in a different style. For example, it can turn a bullet point list into a timeline, format text as a table and offer edits to make the text sound more professional. When you have finished editing, the file can be exported as a PDF or PowerPoint file, or a shareable link created.

4.12.3 Tome.app

Although Tome is being discussed here in relation to creating presentations, Tome states that it is used to 'tell stories, change minds, share information, pitch ideas, fund startups, educate patients, entertain friends and so much more'. Once you have created a free account, you will be taken to your workspace which is the base for your activities in Tome. In the bottom left-hand corner, you will see how many AI credits you have left. This is one of the main limitations of the free account. From the central workspace, select the 'Create' tab in the top-right-hand corner to create a 'Tome'. This will open up a new page and provide access to the command bar. There are numerous options that include:

- Create pages, presentations, narratives, landing pages, stories and outlines with AI
- Transform documents into presentations
- Create images with AI or search from photography libraries
- Add any kind of tile, including text, image, table or one of our integrations
- Change themes, record narration, export to PDF and rename your Tome

For the purpose of this section, we will explore generating a presentation with AI. This can be done by selecting the 'Create presentation about…'. Option in the command bar. Enter what you would like the presentation to be about, so its title or topic, and select 'Generate outline'. An outline will then be developed which you can edit and change in terms of order. Each page is then presented, with several options in terms of content and images. You select the preferred choice and then move on to the next page. This process allows you to edit each page as it is created and makes you feel slightly more involved in the process than Gamma's fully generated first draft of a presentation (although you can still edit every aspect just as in Tome, it is just a difference in order of doing this). Once you have completed your Tome and edits, you can then share by emailing a link to people and choosing their level of access (full access/can edit/can comment/can play) which is a useful feature. The share menu also offers a feature that automatically creates a QR code through which to access it and the QR code can be page specific, i.e., it can take the person using it directly to a specific page in the Tome instead of having to start at the beginning of the Tome. Unfortunately, in terms of exporting the Tome, this is only available to Pro users.

4.13 AI video creation tools

AI video creation is inherently more complex than the previously discussed writing, image and presentation-based tools. This is because videos or animations are sequences of images over time that are accompanied by audio. This area of AI creation is in the early stages of development than the previous areas discussed (text and image creation) as it draws on a greater resource of computational ability and algorithms through deep learning techniques in order to create or enhance videos. Tools have been developed that allow for automated video editing and AI-driven animations as well as deepfakes. Deepfakes represent a huge moral and ethical issue if the technology is misused, undermining the truth and reality. Concerns have already been raised about the impact such fakes may have on misinformation and democratic processes.

As this area is still developing rapidly at the time of writing, a list of functions that the evolving AI tools can undertake is provided in Table 4.4. Selecting the functionality in relation to the task you are undertaking should aid you in searching for an appropriate tool. Please remember to seek out freemium versions of any tool first. Initially, it was intended to only provide this list instead of actual tool examples as has been given in the previous sections. However, during the final edit of this chapter, OpenAI – the organisation responsible for the ChatGPT series – announced its first AI text-to-video model 'Sora' (OpenAI, 2024). Although Sora has not yet been publicly released, and when released will be subscription-based, it does highlight the evolving and impressive direction of travel for text-to-video AI assistants and platforms (Table 4.5).

Table 4.5 AI tool functionality for video creation and editing

Function	Description
Automated video editing tools	This will be one of the most common functions used as AI will enable the automation of editing that was previously manual
Text-to-video tools	This type of function is valuable if you want to convert a text input into a video output. For example, it could be a blog entry that is then turned into video clips, images and animations as relevant
AI video generators	Current uses relate to short illustrative clips or animations based on the input of a prompt. These can be used to aid in presenting an idea or scenario
Voice synthesis and lip syncing tools	Such tools can be used to generate voiceovers from text and be synchronised with lip movements of characters in a video to match, aiding in video presentations

4.14 Summary

This chapter has focused on the 'how' to get started with AI. It has discussed some of the practical considerations that you should make before engaging with AI tools and has aimed to allow for both reflection and direction. This chapter has also provided an introduction to 'Unpacking the AI Tool Kit' presenting the AI tools within four categories: AI writing tools, AI image creation tools, AI presentation/slides tools and AI video creation tools. All tools and functions should be approached with an understanding of 'why' you are using them and in relation to AI usage and guidance from your university. When using AI tools and their various functionalities your own intellect and insights should guide the prompts and therefore the outputs. Check that outputs are ethically sound and factually correct. You will remain responsible for any content that is generated and should be able to articulate the processes behind such generation as well as the attribution of ideas and relevant sources that you have drawn on. AI tools should be used as enhancements to your learning and study experiences to allow for more dialogue and critique around their application and development.

4.15 Chapter hacks

1. **Security in AI Tool Registrations:** Prior to signing-up for AI tools, consider setting up a secondary email account to maintain privacy and security. This safeguards your personal details, especially as many AI tools necessitate an account for access.

(Continued)

2. **Navigating Freemium Models:** Take advantage of 'freemium' models of AI tools to explore their functionalities without financial cost. When usage limits are reached, look for alternative tools offering similar free features instead of subscribing to premium services.
3. **Utilising University Resources:** Consult your university for officially supported AI tools integrated into your studies. This ensures you are utilising vetted tools with available institutional support and guidance.
4. **Developing Digital Navigation Skills:** When utilising AI tools from startups or less familiar platforms, be ready to adapt to new user interfaces and controls, thereby enhancing your digital fluency and adaptability.
5. **Progressing from Novice to Pro:** Begin with simple prompts to gauge an AI tool's response. Progressively tackle more complex prompts and stay abreast of the tool's new features to transition from a novice to a pro user.
6. **AI Tool Categories:** Familiarise yourself with the different categories of Generative AI tools, such as writing assistants, image creators, presentation generators and video tools, and understand their specific applications to your academic requirements
7. **Refining Prompts for Image Tools:** For AI image creation tools, the specificity and intricacy of your prompts directly influence the precision and quality of the generated images. Harness this insight to craft detailed prompts for improved results.
8. **Presentation Tool Features:** Investigate embedded AI features in applications like PowerPoint for design and presentation practice to refine the aesthetics and delivery of your presentations, conserving time and enhancing presentation proficiency.
9. **Exploring Freemium Tools for Presentations:** Use tools like Gamma.app to create presentations under a freemium model, which permits editing and customisation of AI-generated content to meet your specific academic needs.
10. **AI Video Creation Considerations:** As AI video creation is intricate and rapidly advancing, concentrate on the functionalities that align with your academic tasks and seek out freemium tools to dabble in automated editing and text-to-video transformations.

4.16 Chapter MCQs

1. What is a wise initial step prior to registering for AI tools to ensure privacy is maintained?
   A) Utilise your primary email address
   B) Establish a new, secondary email account
   C) Share your current passwords for security verifications
   D) Engage in anonymous web browsing solely

2. What benefit does utilising 'freemium' models of AI tools offer?
   A) They grant unlimited access to all functionalities
   B) They necessitate a long-term financial commitment
   C) They provide immediate accessibility without financial outlay
   D) They are accompanied by comprehensive customer support
3. Where should students primarily seek guidance for utilising AI tools within their studies?
   A) Forums on the web not associated with their university
   B) Social media collectives
   C) Their university's support services
   D) Helplines for commercial AI utilities
4. What strategy should be adopted when initiating the use of a new AI utility?
   A) Embark on complex tasks to assess the utility's capabilities
   B) Commence with uncomplicated prompts to gauge the utility's reactions
   C) Solely utilise tools recommended by acquaintances
   D) Bypass 'freemium' versions and proceed directly to paid subscriptions
5. What should students be aware of if using an AI assistant for a writing task?
   A) Merely the premium iterations are deemed acceptable for utilisation
   B) They must ascertain if such uses are permissible and how to acknowledge them if so
   C) The use of AI assistants for a writing task does not necessitate any form of recognition
   D) AI writing assistants are not appropriate for scholarly purposes

Correct answers:

1. Correct answer B
2. Correct answer C
3. Correct answer C
4. Correct answer B
5. Correct answer B

5

Using Generative AI Tools to Support Your Study

5.1 Chapter objectives

1. To explore the role of Generative AI in transforming traditional study methods
2. To demonstrate how AI-assisted approaches can enhance students' learning experiences
3. To examine the shift from lecture-based learning to more interactive approaches and the contribution of AI in this transition
4. To discuss the capabilities of AI tools in creating, organising and accessing study materials

5.2 Having read this chapter, you will...

- Explore the potential for AI to support and improve study habits and academic work.
- Begin to reflect on how Generative AI may be used to help you study.
- Gain insights into how AI can personalise and optimise the learning process for all educational needs.
- Consider how to effectively integrate Generative AI into your study routines and comprehend its potential impact on your studies.

5.3 Introduction

The purpose of this chapter is to detail how advances in Generative AI can inform and support students in their studies and assignments. It considers traditional approaches to study before connecting them with potential AI-assisted ways of studying moving forward. The intention here is to explore how AI-assisted approaches to study can become a core part of a student's learning journey in aiding them to study smarter and more efficiently. Previously, lecture halls were the mainstay of student learning, with note-taking a key part of this. Today, smaller, more interactive settings like seminars and tutorials are increasingly common. These allow for greater opportunities to engage and ask questions about the taught content as well as digital content covered in taught sessions being readily available via a University's Virtual Learning Environment. The role of Generative AI in this shift is crucial – it offers a more dynamic and flexible approach to studying and moves beyond traditional limitations. AI-based tools have the potential to redefine how students create, organise and access their study materials, making it possible to customise learning experiences to fit individual needs within the outcomes of the degree programme. This chapter will provide insights into the effective use of Generative AI for studying. By the end, students should have a clearer understanding of how to integrate Generative AI into their study routines and the impact these tools will have on their studies.

5.4 Traditional approaches to studying

5.4.1 Creating study notes: Handwritten or digital?

The stereotypical (and partly historical) image of note-taking during lectures lends itself to a lecture theatre, where many students are sat in rows with each eagerly making notes by means of paper and pen. Whilst subjects such as Law and Medicine may still have large cohort lectures in a traditional sense, for many social science-based subjects, there has been a conscious move towards seminars and tutorials. These typically involve smaller student numbers, include greater interaction and are of higher quality in terms of student experience. Lecture note-taking a decade plus ago relied on handouts of presentation slides and notes scrawled around them.

More recently, good practice dictates that access to session content is available for students to access electronically before sessions. This is usually via an institution's Learning Management System such as Canvas, Blackboard, Moodle etc., and means that a student does not have to wait for a taught session to receive input. This is particularly useful for neurodiverse students and students who have English as an additional language as session content can be reviewed beforehand. This will allow students to attend the taught session already having an insight into what will be covered and prepare any questions relating to the content.

Whilst some students may prefer to print out lecture content and make notes on them directly, purely from an economical perspective, students should consider doing so electronically to avoid the financial cost of printing. Most software tools now offer some form of 'comments' or 'notes function' when it comes to Word documents, presentations or PDFs. Taking such an approach will also contribute to students becoming increasingly digitally literate as they navigate the range of file types that contain information of relevance to their studies. Furthermore, study notes should make connections between what is being taught and relevant experiences of the student. This connection is key as students' progress in their studies and develop their analysis and critique. Ultimately, creating study notes in a digital sense will feed forwards into how these can then be accessed and utilised by AI-based tools.

5.4.2 Organise, store and access study notes

Note-taking may appear to be a simple process but the reality, once explored is far more complex when you consider what to do with your notes and how to organise them. Note-taking in real-time often takes the form of linear notes; this typically involves lists, bullet points, numbers, highlighting and underlining to identify key or important information, theory and concepts. The complexities occur when you revisit such linear notes and then consider how to go about organising them in a logical manner that will aid you in your studies. Burns and Sinfield (2022) offer a whole chapter on 'How to Make the Best Notes' with the core of each approach involving how you choose to organise your notes and the processes behind this. Their chapter covers this in detail:

Cornell Notes: This involves dividing a piece of paper into three sections: a left-hand margin for keywords, a wider right-hand section for main notes, and a smaller section at the bottom for summarising the main ideas discussed in the notes above.
Concept Maps: This involves visually representing and organising knowledge so that concepts and ideas are connected. This provides an overview of the relationships and hierarchical structure of the content covered.
Mindmaps: These start with a central theme or topic at its core. Related words, theory and concepts radiate outwards in a branching structure. This provides a holistic representation of the core theme and promotes a creative approach to understanding it.
Pattern Notes: This involves arranging notes in a non-linear pattern, typically a spider diagram or grid. This provides an overview of the relationships between concepts and is easily accessible.

Whilst the above methods were developed with non-digital tools, they can also be created with digital tools. Furthermore, digital notes and approaches to note-taking can be organised with relative ease. At a basic file management level, folders and file names can be created that give insight into the subject, concept, theory or date of study. However, Platforms like Microsoft One Note or Evernote also support digital categorisation, tagging and storing of notes. This means that notes in such systems become easily searchable by keywords or terms, portable across devices if stored in the cloud and can integrate multiple modes of media including image, audio and video.

5.4.3 Creating revision materials

The purpose of creating and then organising notes from your studies is to aid future retrieval. Such retrieval should go beyond rote memorisation of facts and allow for the application of the concepts to real-world situations relevant to your subject. This type of retrieval will be of benefit in preparation for an assignment, an upcoming exam or in aiding your decision-making on a placement. Creating revision materials from your notes traditionally meant revising your notes in full whilst making more digestible notes that are in an accessible format. Manual summarisation requires further engagement and analysis of the content further aiding your ability to make connections between content and its application. Typically, flashcards can be created, self-quizzes set and mind maps developed. These approaches often constitute the 'holy trinity' of revision methods as they aid memory retention and understanding through engagement and rearrangement of the information. It is, however, a timely process when creating all these resources from scratch; this shall be addressed later on in this chapter.

5.5 AI-assisted approaches to studying

5.5.1 Flipping the pyramid – Bloom's Taxonomy

Traditional approaches to teaching, learning and studying in Higher Education have been firmly framed within Bloom's Taxonomy (Figure 3) for decades. An exploration of lower to higher-order thinking skills are developed as students progress in their studies. Creating lecture notes, organising them and revising as discussed in the previous section links with the lower-order thinking skills: remember, understand and apply. Rivers and Holland (2023), however, explain how Generative AI means a reinterpretation of Bloom's Taxonomy. They argue that Generative AI essentially flips the pyramid model of Bloom's Taxonomy on its head. They liken Generative AI's ability to draw on vast amounts of information and ability to create content of many types instantly as the equivalent of jumping five levels in a video game. This may also explain why some students first feel that using Generative AI is like 'cheating' as the cognitive load needed to produce information is much less than if retrieving it from oneself. Using an initial prompt is a vast reduction in effort when compared to traditional approaches to study. It should also be emphasised here that the ethical use of Generative AI should mean that its role is seen as a tool for learning rather than a replacement for learning.

Students can use Generative AI to create text and output that will support them to remember, understand and apply their knowledge. Furthermore, Generative AI can address information overload and aid both neurotypical and neurodiverse

BLOOM'S TAXONOMY

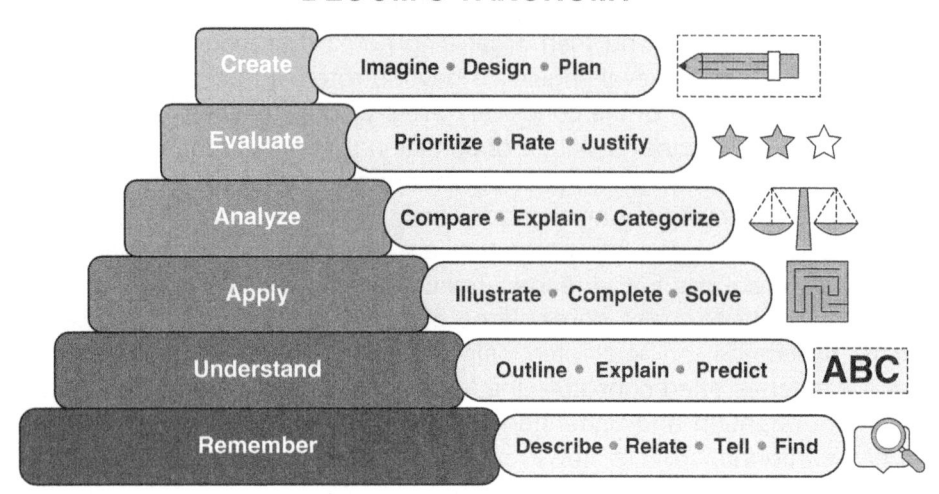

Figure 5.1 Bloom's Taxonomy.

students in how they interact with information. There are current limitations regarding Generative AI as it can be incorrect, overly formulaic, and lack detail and context. There is an assumption that failure to develop the traditional lower-order thinking skills will mean difficulty in developing the higher-order thinking skills. Flipping the pyramid of Bloom's Taxonomy, however, means engaging with generative AI to create, evaluate and analyse content as a starting point. This will promote the development of 'AI literacy' and allow students to develop their understanding, application and experience of this process (remember). Generative AI depends on the prompts that are put in, and this is where it is key to consider the content that you enter and make connections with the traditional approaches to study that have already been discussed (Figure 5.1).

5.6 AI-assisted study notes

Study notes will generally be created from attendance at lectures, seminars and workshops as well as by reviewing the digital content supplied. The main consideration to begin with is what you intend to use as your source material. A good place to start is the session materials. These should be accessible in advance via your University's Virtual Learning Environment (VLE; this could be Canvas, Moodle, Blackboard etc.). Review the session title and learning outcomes and consider how these align with the module and assignment outcomes. This will help you begin to connect what information is, and is not, important for your study notes. You could even prompt an AI assistant to help you in exploring potential connections (see Prompt 5.1).

Prompt 5.1   Connecting session learning outcomes to assignment learning outcomes

INPUT:

I am a university student studying for [enter course and study level here]. I am currently undertaking a module titled [enter module title here]. These are the Learning Outcomes for the assignment [list assignment learning outcomes here]. The upcoming session will focus on [enter session title]. Please analyse these and suggest connections between the assignment learning outcomes and the session learning outcomes to help develop my understanding.

5.6.1 Creating study notes from digital content before a session

Digitally available content refers to the files and links that are deposited within the module or programme folders on your university's VLE. This will often include presentation slides, PDF documents and links to recommended reading or video clips. You need to check what content can and cannot be analysed using third-party AI-based tools. This can be done by contacting your programme team and asking them. You should review/skim-read the digital content to get a feel for what is, and is not, relevant to you and your study. Next, you will need to ensure that the relevant electronic content is in a single format as this will make it easier to process via an AI tool without needing premium access. This will often mean converting the source files into a text-based document so that it can be entered into a Large Language Model for analysis. Where links are provided to videos or audio clips, a transcription tool is a good place to start as this will provide you with a script, which can then be combined into your other text notes. In order to explore transcription tools, search for 'Free AI transcription tools' with your preferred search engine and explore the results. Remember that you should prioritise open-source and free tools in the results. Once you have a complete document for that session combined of the slides, PDF files, suggested reading and transcripts of any audio or video linked to can be uploaded or copied and pasted into a Large Language Model for a summary, analysis and feedforward (see Figure 5.2).

Once Figure 9 has been followed, the Generative AI tool that you have selected should have produced a summary of the key aspects of the content in relation to your assignment, the learning outcomes and any initial ideas that you have inputted. It is important that you review any content produced by the

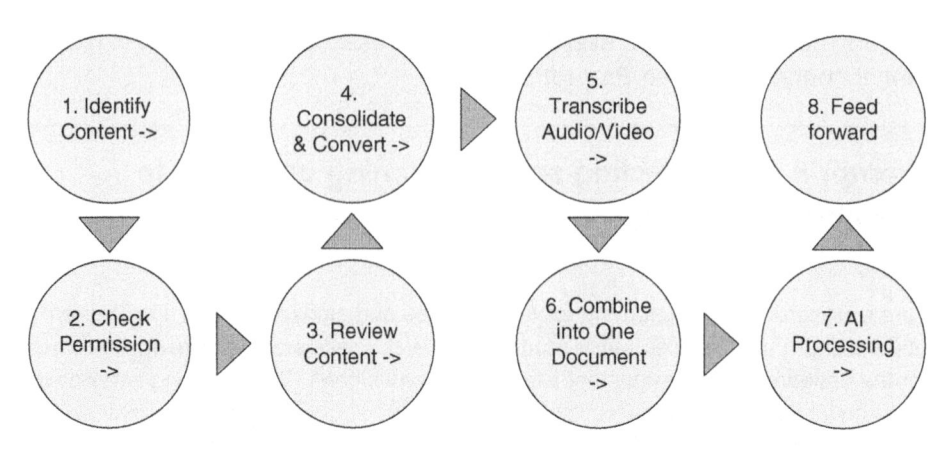

```
1. Identify Content ->  →  4. Consolidate & Convert ->  →  5. Transcribe Audio/Video ->  →  8. Feed forward

          ↓                           ↑                           ↓                           ↑

2. Check Permission ->  →  3. Review Content ->  →  6. Combine into One Document ->  →  7. AI Processing ->
```

Figure 5.2 Creating study notes from digital content.

Generative AI to ensure it is accurate and that you understand it. When you prompt the Generative AI based on the information you have entered, capture and save this information as it should aid in developing more focused and succinct study notes for later use. You can also ask for further clarification on any aspects that you are not sure of. The feedforward also provides you with information to take to that session in order to ask questions of the programme team and expand on the knowledge generated via the Generative AI tool, connecting it to your lecturer's experience of teaching and learning in the session.

This approach can also be followed after a session has been delivered, but you will not benefit from the opportunity afforded by the feedforward. The feedforward will allow you to expand on and make connections between the digital content for the session, your interests and experiences and the lectures' experience of teaching, learning and assessment on the module. The questioning in the feedforward will assist you in making further sense of and connection between the session content and your studies.

5.6.2 Creating study notes during a session – Is it being recorded?

It is a commonly expected practice for students to take notes in lectures and seminars. Sometimes digital content is available prior to the session (as has just been discussed), sometimes hard copies are handed out in session (but this is becoming increasingly less common) and sometimes handouts are distributed after the session (usually electronically). Hamano-Bunce (2017) states that four steps have to be considered when note-taking. These are:

1. What is being said
2. What it means
3. Whether it is important and whether to write it down
4. How to write it in note form

The four considerations of note-taking remain and will be picked up again in the next subsection. Many universities, however, have now developed policies in relation to the recording of taught sessions. This means that much of the input from the lecturer (all of the examples, experiences and anecdotes that are not captured in the originally supplied digital content) can potentially be accessible both during and after the taught session – as long as they are captured in the recording. If you are at a university where all taught sessions are expected to be recorded and shared with students, this is a great resource that can be utilised to enhance your understanding after the session, as discussed in the next section. However, recording each taught session may not be a blanket policy at your university and you must make further enquiries about this. For those universities that do not record taught sessions as standard, it may be possible for you to record the lecture yourself; however, permission to do so will need to be sought and the rationale behind it shared, as well as what your intentions are relating to the use of the recording. Fundamentally though, knowing that a session is being recorded should lessen the pressures and cognitive load needed in relation to note-taking. This should allow you to focus on Steps 1 and 2 above as well as the first half of Step 3: What is being said? What it means? Is it important? If a recording is possible, listen and ask questions more, and use your notes so that you know where to revisit the recording. A word of caution though, recordings do not always go to plan, so attendance of taught sessions is paramount, regardless.

5.6.3 Creating study notes from digital content after a session – What to do with a recording

In an ideal situation, you would have prepped your study notes before the session based on the previous section discussed and then attended the session in person. In session, you would have listened and interacted with the taught dialogue and activities asking your related questions to the content. Afterwards, you will then have access to a recording of the session. However, if you were not able to attend the session for whatever reason, you could still review the digital content and create study notes as has been discussed above. If there is a recording, then you could also review that. However, if you have been able to prepare, attend and access a recording, the recording can be utilised further. Figure 5.3 expands on how an AI-based transcription tool could assist in turning a video or audio file into a text file, and how this file could be used to extend your notes further.

Step	Consideration to be given	Type of AI tool	How it can aid
1	What is being said	Transcription tools that record audio and produce text or can take an audio recording and produce a script.	This will provide you with a full transcript that you can then use to assist you in creating further notes.
2	What it means (how it relates to what has been said)	Upload the transcription or parts of it to a Generative AI Tool/LLM and ask it to explain it to you.	Both explanations and summaries can be provided. If you do not understand what is generated, ask it to explain it to you like you are a 5-year-old—this approach often works well and can be used for the most complicated content.
3	Whether it is important and whether to note it down	Generative AI/ LLM	Using the LLM, upload the Learning Outcomes, ask for further explanation in relation to these. Extend your question and relate it to your assignment.
4	How to write it in note form	Generative AI/LLM	Using the LLM, ask it to summarise the key take aways, produce flash cards or a quiz etc.

Figure 5.3 How to analyse a recording of a lecture or taught session.

5.6.4 Organising study notes

By following the above guidance on AI-assisted study notes, you will create comprehensive notes for each session of a module and therefore each module of a programme. The next key consideration is how do you organise them. The key to organising something is making it accessible. This should mean that the initial thought of finding it is not totally defeatist as you have a rough idea of where to look. Organisation is also a skill expected in most professions and will stand you in good stead for future employment. There are two key considerations to begin with when organising your notes:

1. How do you want to organise them?
2. What tools or software do you have access to that will assist you with your answer to number 1?

It is important to reflect on your prior experiences of learning and consider which ways you were able to study best. This should be a key starting point. Typically, notes can be organised in relation to the topic or focus of them, the chronological order of when they were taught or their importance. This last option, importance, will often relate to the relevance the notes have for you and how you intend to use them in relation to assessments. Whilst assignments at Levels 4 and 5 may be fairly explicit and focused, you may see less guidance and more freedom in how you approach an assignment at Level 6 and beyond. This will mean that you instinctively attribute greater importance to certain content and draw on this to inform your assignments.

Deciding how you organise your notes initially is an important step as this will then inform how you curate or collect them as your studies progress. This is similar to traditional ways of organisation, but as already discussed, notes are often in a digital format. This is where AI tools can be used further to support your filing, organisation and retrieval of relevant information from your notes. If you have created study notes based on the previous guidance, you will essentially have a text-based document for each session. If your module has ten taught sessions you will have ten documents, arranged in chronological order because of the dates they were created. When studying, revisiting and writing assignments, the chronological order is of little importance to you, what is important are the key themes that have been covered and which key theme(s) are most relevant to your study now. You could turn each text document into a PDF file or you could combine all of the text documents into one, before converting it into a PDF file. Key points for consideration here are: is all session content important for the focus of your study? Or are there specific sessions that you know are not important and can be excluded? Therefore, you would only need to turn the relevant text files into PDF documents or combine the relevant text files into one PDF document. The next step is where the magic happens and the retrieval of information can be supported by an AI tool. There are several tools that will support you with this, but it depends initially on whether or not you have created a single PDF document or multiple PDF documents.

5.6.4.1 Single PDF document reader, e.g., Chat PDF (novice approach)

Some tools will only allow you to upload and interact with a single PDF document at a time. If you have created one master PDF then this is the initial type of tool you should use. Please be aware that there is a limit on how many pages such a file can contain with the freemium version of Chat PDF. Once you have successfully uploaded the master PDF of your notes, you will then be able to interact with it like a chatbot. As well as responding to the questions you ask about the uploaded file, Chat PDF is also able to draw on information from wider sources. This is a great opportunity if you want to ask for further explanations about a theory or a concept that is not in your uploaded notes. But it will be able to draw information from across the document in relation to topics, themes or the importance that you place on it.

5.6.4.2 Multiple PDF document reader – e.g., Humata (intermediate approach)

If you have created multiple PDFs of your notes, you will need to use a tool that allows for multiple PDFs to be uploaded and searched simultaneously. The advantage of using a multiple PDF reader is that you can also upload additional content in PDF format that is of relevance to your studies. An example of this could be further documentation or research that you have found in relation to your studies but was not covered in session. This is a key part of achieving higher grades, as it is important to complete independent research and expand on the core content and theories covered in taught sessions.

5.6.4.3 Tools that allow for analysis and concept creation (advanced approach)

PDF readers are a good starting place for you to explore retrieving information from your notes; however, there are also more advanced tools with freemium and premium access. These tools are aimed at optimising research and are generally aimed at the postgraduate level or beyond study. These tools, however, can be equally used and applied at the undergraduate level, as all study and assignment preparation is essentially secondary research. Here are two tools that may be of interest to those wanting to develop their digital and AI literacy skill set further:

Lateral.io: First you upload your notes in PDF form, before creating concept headings (think themes or focus), the AI tool will then search across all of the PDF files and suggest sections of text relevant to the stated concept. You can review each suggestion and choose to keep it or not. Essentially, the tool is skim reading your content and presenting the key points to you. You can upload any PDF, so this is another good way to extend your reading and research beyond the core content and theory.

Quivr.app: This tool presents an AI Cloud-based second brain. You can upload multiple file formats, including URLs (web addresses). Essentially, you create the 'brain' that is specialised in the information that you have given it. There are numerous ways that you can then interact with the tool, with one mode being an academic researcher and providing insight into the gaps in your information and its limitations.

5.6.5 Creating revision materials

With the creation of AI-assisted study notes and their organisation, it is important to consider how these can be utilised to create revision materials. One advantage of the developments in AI tools is their ability to take information in one format, for example, extended notes in text format, and promptly turn it into another format such as a multiple-choice quiz. As you have already created and organised your study notes using AI tools, you are just a prompt away from creating tailor-made revision materials for your needs. If you do not already have a preferred style of revising, then this is a key opportunity to experiment with different formats. This will allow you to tailor the resources that are created in relation to your preferences. If you are stuck for ideas, just ask an AI assistant to give you some suggestions on how to get started creating revision materials. Generative AI can cater for a diverse range of educational needs and preferences in this way. Furthermore, AI can be used to highlight additional but relevant information that may help you extend your thinking beyond your study notes. Drawing on wider literature and presenting original ideas will enable you to achieve the highest grades in your assignments.

5.6.5.1 Be clear on what it is you are creating revision materials for

Begin with reflecting and defining why you are creating revision materials in the first place. These could be to aid with a formative task, to recap on taught content so far or to prepare for a summative assessment. Establishing this clarity should help to inform the prompt or search term that you use, but this will be dependent on how you have organised your study notes as discussed in the previous section.

Revising for a Formative Task: These will often be specific and focused. They may involve quizzes, reading, discussion boards, reflections etc. Before starting the formative task, engage with your study notes to date. Any of the previous approaches to organisation (single or multiple PDF document reader or analysis and concept tools) should allow you to search for key terms from your formative task and ask questions in relation to them. This will help you to connect with the wider content and learn across the materials that have already been taught. You can also take the information that these tools give you and enter it into Large Language Models (LLMs) for further explanations. This should provide an informative and timely start to any formative task that is set. The key here is to make links with your prior learning and then to consider how this informs the formative task moving forward.

Recapping on Taught Content: This approach is more general. If you have uploaded your study notes to a single or multiple PDF document reader, it can ask you questions about the content if prompted to test you on it. This will enable you to revise questions and answers, seeing where this is situated within your study notes. If you want to revise with peers, you can ask such readers to create question-and-answer cards in relation to your content and turn them into flashcards. This approach can also be used to create Multiple-Choice Quizzes in the same way. You can then copy and paste the MCQ questions into instant messenger etc. and share them with peers.

Revising for a Summative Assessment: These will usually have guidance or a brief attached to them as well as learning outcomes appropriate to the content and level of study. This is important, as key information from here can be taken to inform your approach to revision. For example, develop a prompt that includes the type of summative assignment you are revising for, the limitations (word count or time limit etc.) and the learning outcomes aligned to the assessment. Use this prompt to ask the AI tool to assist you based on your study notes and your initial thoughts on the assignment. This should help you get started on preparing for your summative assessment. Furthermore, you can continue to prompt and ask the AI tool to make connections with your study notes, explain or clarify aspects you do not understand and inform your approach to your summative assessment.

5.7 Summary

This chapter has explored how AI-based tools can support academic study. The integration of these tools enhances the efficiency and effectiveness of learning by assisting in the curation and creation of study notes. This will aid in producing relevant revision materials and facilitating a deeper engagement with the course material. The capacity of AI to customise materials in relation to individual prompts has been explored and addresses both the personalisation of the study experience as well as the AI tool's capacity to meet diverse educational preferences and needs. By illustrating how AI can sift through vast amounts of data to provide targeted information, its role in creating a more efficient and focused study process is highlighted. Remember that aligning your prompts to the programme and module learning outcomes will help refine the AI assistants' responses further.

The use of AI tools to curate and review study notes will generate more succinct and accessible content, leading to further questions and exploration. This aids in expanding critical thinking and creativity. The ability of AI to simulate various scenarios can expose students to a wider range of learning experiences, preparing them for the multifaceted nature of real-world problem-solving. The enhancement of traditional study practices is addressed as the chapter details ways that AI tools can assist in note-taking and revision. Using AI tools to create and refine study notes should lead to a more succinct curation of them which will aid the organisation. The use of AI tools in the revision process also allows the student to save time in creating resources aligned with their preferred method of study or a combination of several. Engaging with AI-based tools in this way will develop them as learning tools that aid in deepening your understanding. Furthermore, the use of AI tools in such a way is one of the latest developments in ensuring that learning remains dynamic, interactive and personal. With Generative

AI assistants, a study experience is no longer a one-size-fits-all approach but an iterative journey that responds to the student's input.

5.8 Chapter hacks

1. **Pyramid Flip Technique:** Reverse the traditional Bloom's Taxonomy approach by employing Generative AI to start with creating and analysing content, thereby fostering higher-order thinking from the outset of your study.
2. **Prompt Precision Strategy:** Hone the art of crafting precise prompts for Generative AI tools, enhancing the utility and effectiveness of the AI's response for more targeted study sessions.
3. **Session Summary Approach:** Use Generative AI to summarise session materials beforehand, gaining an overview that can guide your focus and inform the questions you raise during live sessions.
4. **Recording Rundown Method:** Leverage Generative AI for transcribing recorded sessions, supplementing notes and offering additional clarity on complex discussions.
5. **PDF Power Utilisation:** Consolidate notes into a single PDF and interact with them through AI conversational interfaces, facilitating an engaging and dynamic review of topics and themes.
6. **Multimedia Merge Strategy:** Integrate various forms of media into your study notes, using Generative AI to create a rich, multimedia learning experience catering to diverse learning styles.
7. **Flashcard Fast-Track Method:** Transform detailed notes into flashcards or quizzes with Generative AI, injecting an interactive and time-efficient element into your revision process.
8. **Concept Crystallisation Technique:** Generate concept maps from study materials with Generative AI to aid in visualising and understanding the intricate connections between theories and concepts.
9. **Revision Reboot Method:** Re-engage with AI-generated notes to generate practice questions or simplify explanations, ensuring a more profound mastery of the subject matter.
10. **Personalisation Process:** Continuously refine your AI tool prompts to align the output with your advancing understanding and academic requirements.
11. **Independent Inquiry Initiative:** Expand your research horizons beyond session content using AI suggestions for further reading, thus promoting independent study and critical analysis.
12. **Study Sync Solution:** Maintain continuity in your study habits by synchronising notes across devices with cloud-based AI tools, allowing flexible study times and environments.

5.9 Chapter MCQs

1. How may Generative AI be of assistance to students?
   A) It completely supersedes traditional study methods
   B) It aids solely in memorisation, not comprehension or application
   C) It supports the creation of content to bolster memory, understanding and application of knowledge
   D) It heightens cognitive load during study periods
2. Which of the following is NOT identified as a current limitation of Generative AI?
   A) Tendency to be overly formulaic
   B) Lack of intricate detail
   C) Unfailing accuracy of results
   D) Occasional inaccuracies
3. The ethical employment of Generative AI ought to be regarded as:
   A) A substitute for conventional learning
   B) A means to eschew studying
   C) An instrument for learning
   D) A technique to hasten assignment completion
4. What should you do before reviewing the available digital content prior to a session?
   A) Submit content to a Large Language Model for analysis
   B) Participate in the session physically
   C) Transmute all files into a text-based document
   D) Review the session learning outcomes and available digital content
5. In what manner can AI tools be beneficial in structuring study notes?
   A) By autonomously attending sessions on behalf of the pupil
   B) By transfiguring notes into varied formats for revision resources
   C) By summarising notes based solely on their chronological sequence
   D) By fabricating a physical compilation of notes for each session

Correct answers:

1. Correct answer C
2. Correct answer C
3. Correct answer C
4. Correct answer D
5. Correct answer B

PART THREE

HOW TO APPROACH YOUR ASSESSMENTS WITH GENERATIVE AI

6

Essays

6.1 Chapter objectives

1. To understand the different types and purposes of essays
2. To develop skills in analysing essay titles and formulating responses
3. To explore the role of Generative AI in essay writing
4. To master the planning and structuring of essays
5. To enhance research and critical analysis skills
6. To reflect on ethical considerations and maintain academic integrity

6.2 Having read this chapter, you will...

1. Be able to distinguish between various types of essays such as argumentative, descriptive, narrative and compare and contrast. Understand the unique purpose, structure and content requirements of each essay type.
2. Learn how to deconstruct essay titles, identify key components and understand the expectations embedded within the prompts. Gain skills in formulating a title and structuring responses that directly address the essay's requirements.
3. Gain insight into how Generative AI can be utilised in various stages of essay writing, from brainstorming and planning to drafting and revising. Understand the benefits, limitations and ethical considerations of using AI in academic writing.
4. Learn how to effectively plan and structure their essays, ensuring a coherent and logical flow of ideas. This includes the creation of outlines, the development of arguments and the organisation of supporting evidence.
5. Consider ways to improve the ability to conduct thorough research, critically analyse sources and integrate findings into the essay in a meaningful way. Evaluate the credibility of sources and synthesise information to support the essay's thesis.
6. Consider academic integrity, including how to avoid plagiarism and ensure originality in writing, especially in the context of using AI tools. Learn about citing sources correctly, paraphrasing effectively, and maintaining their unique voice and critical perspective.

6.3 Introduction

Essays serve as a crucial bridge between knowledge acquisition and knowledge demonstration across many university assessments. Essays offer students a platform to demonstrate their understanding, critical thinking and communication skills. The various forms of an essay – from argumentative to reflective, from comparative to problem-solution essays – are designed to encourage a particular type of engagement with relevant literature and experience. Higher-level essays compel students to not only recall facts but also to make connections, evaluate evidence and express thoughts in a structured and coherent manner. This has made the essay a staple in Higher Education assessments, challenging students to demonstrate their knowledge within logical narratives that can be evaluated and appreciated.

This chapter begins by considering different types of essays, their purpose and what sort of approach each type involves. Understanding the rationale behind each type will allow students to align their writing with specific academic goals and expectations. Next, we will discuss the importance of essays in assessment, emphasising their role in promoting academic skills like research, analysis, organisation and time management. The chapter then considers how to interpret and respond to essay titles, utilising a blend of critical thinking and creativity. The role of Generative AI in essay writing is then explored, outlining strategies for leveraging technology to understand learning outcomes (LOs) and constructing an essay plan. Each section of this chapter includes practical advice, examples and insights to support students in approaching an essay.

AI assistants are not a substitute for the intellectual rigour and creativity that essays demand but a tool that offers new possibilities for assistance and enhancement. AI assistants can help students overcome writer's block, suggest diverse perspectives, and even ensure structural and stylistic coherence. It aids in brainstorming, structuring arguments and refining language, thus allowing students to focus more on the critical and creative aspects of their essays. However, it is imperative to strike a balance when using AI assistants, ensuring that the authenticity of the student's voices and the integrity of their critical thinking remain paramount. This chapter will also explore how to integrate AI into the essay-writing process, enhancing the quality and depth of the work without compromising on the personal engagement that lies at the heart of academic writing.

6.4 What is an essay?

The essay has been a stalwart of many university degree programmes for as long as any current academics and librarians can remember. However, its history

'Show what you know' type of essay	'Show what you think' type of essay
1. Argument/Discussion Essay	5. Definition or factual essay
2. Problem-Solution Essay	6. Review Essay
3. Cause and Effect Essay	
4. Reflective Essay	

Figure 6.1 Two types of Essays.
Source: Adapted from Hopkins and Reid (2018, pp. 9 and 10).

begins outside of the world of formal and Higher Education. The term essay was first coined by the French noble, Michel de Montaigne (1533–1592). Then, the British philosopher Francis Bacon used Montaigne's term and published his book 'Essays' in 1597. Both John Locke and David Hulme published titles that included the word 'essay' in them in 1689 and 1741, respectively. These early essays were quite different from the assessment-based, title-led and LO-focused approaches common today. The introduction of first unseen written examination in this style was introduced at the University of Cambridge in 1791 (Hyams, 2021). In its contemporary but simplest form, essays can be split into two types (see Figure 6.1): 'show what you know' and 'show what you think'. Furthermore, within each aspect, there are variations of the format that an essay may take. Whilst there is not a clear delineation between each subsidiary (nu.1-6 in Figure 6.1), there are core components of each which will be discussed now and examples are given.

1. **Argument/Discussion Essay:** These require you to investigate a topic, collect and evaluate evidence and present a reasoned and supported position. Such essays hold debate central to them and allow the student to construct and develop a well-supported position on the issue which has been identified. For example, an essay titled 'The impact of Social Media on Political Discourse and Democracy' should lead to a debate on both the positive and not-so-positive aspects of social media in relation to political discourse.
2. **Problem-Solution Essay:** This is a type of essay that identifies a problem and proposes one or more solutions. The solutions need to be supported by your investigation and research. Such essays are commonplace in courses or modules that are focused on addressing societal change and often encourage engagement with real-world issues. For example, an essay titled 'Addressing Homelessness in Urban Areas in the UK' should invoke more than an initial exploration of the causes of homelessness in the UK. It should also include an exploration of the work being done to combat homelessness and recommendations for policy and practice to address the issue of homelessness moving forward.
3. **Cause-and-Effect Essay:** This type focuses on reasons why something has or could happen (cause) and what happens or is likely to happen as a result (effect). In social

sciences, this can often involve an exploration of literature and data leading to a demonstration of how various social phenomena have been impacted or led to specific social outcomes. For example, 'The effects of Globalisation on Local Education Cultures' should include definitions of key terms, as well as consideration of dominant or global trends in education and how these influence educational practices at a local level.

4. **Reflective Essay:** This type of essay requires the writer to reflect and examine their own personal attitudes, experiences, thoughts and feelings about a specific topic or activity, and how this has impacted their learning and/or life. This type of essay is most common in courses where there is a practical component. For example, students undertaking teacher training may be asked to write a reflective essay on an example of practice: 'Reflecting on the use of adaptive teaching strategies to support numeracy skills in Key Stage 2'. Whilst such an essay should define key terms such as 'adaptive teaching strategies', the focus is on the student's reflection or experience of applying such an approach in relation to supporting pupils' numeracy skills in Key Stage 2. Whilst first-hand experience is important in a reflection, as it is still a piece of academic work, the connection must also be made to the purpose of the assignment (the LOs) and relevant literature.

5. **Definition or Factual Essay:** This allows for the exploration and explanation of what a specific term means. Terms can be concrete (e.g., greenhouse effect) or abstract (e.g., trust, caution and fear). Students might be asked to explore and define complex social phenomena or theoretical concepts, grounding their explanations in factual evidence and academic discourse. For example, 'Exploring the Concept of Social Capital'. Here, it is important to define social capital as a concept, before continuing to explore its various conceptions, i.e., the different explanations of what it is and how it works that can be found in literature and the student chooses to present in their essay.

6. **Review Essay:** These types of essays will ask you to summarise and critically evaluate one or more texts (e.g., a journal article, case study and chapter of a book). In doing this, students should demonstrate the ability to synthesise their findings and provide a comprehensive evaluation of the reviewed text(s). An example may relate to being given an essay title which includes an article's title to review: 'A critical evaluation and review of Paul et al.'s (2022) journal article: Perspectives of Children and Youth With Disabilities and Special Needs Regarding Their Experiences in Inclusive Education: A Meta-Aggregative'.

6.5 Why are essays used in the assessment process?

Essays are typically designed to be a heuristic process that enables a student an aspect of autonomy in relation to how they demonstrate understanding, engagement, analysis and critical thinking through the content in the essay. This allows the marker of the essay to pass judgement not only on the knowledge conveyed but also on how a student interprets and integrates different sources of information and viewpoints in their completed submission. The processes behind compiling an essay traditionally promote skills such as time management, organisation, research and idea generation. In turn, such skills foster independence and encourage students to take ownership of the process. Essays should allow for the exploration and development of nuanced arguments and the complexities of human experience and understanding.

The essay format also allows for students to receive feedback. Whilst many students prioritise the grade awarded for an essay submission, feedback and a feedforward should also be taken into account. Feedback may be in the form of on-script comments. These should highlight areas of strength in your essay and highlight areas for correction and development. On-script comments will also provide you with a window into the marker's views and attention. This should be reflected and built on to improve and strengthen future submissions. Feedback may also take the form of a narrative comment in the 'feedback' comments box. Feedback comments can also address the LOs for the assignment and how you have met them. This should provide feedback if you have not met the LOs and highlight what needs to be done to address.

It is increasingly common for feedback to also include a marking rubric. This will provide an overview of different areas (sometimes the LOs and sometimes specific knowledge or skills) and grade you on each aspect. This will also highlight your areas of strength and areas for development. Finally, you should also receive a feedforward. These are usually a few points that provide a focus on what you need to address to improve your next submission. It is important that you take these considerations forward as you prepare for the next essay or assignment. Overall, essays not only allow students to personalise how they respond to a given title or even create their own, but they also allow for a complex exploration that does not fit into a right or wrong check box. Chapter 10 explores further how a student can utilise the feedback and feedforward received from assignments with the help of an AI assistant.

6.6 Checklist to begin the assignment: Essay

6.6.1 A seven-step checklist to begin your essay

The checklist in Tables 6.1 and 6.2 is designed to help you reflect and contextualise your study environment and identify key information that will help you to begin and successfully complete your essay.

Table 6.1 Essay Checklist

	Essay Checklist
1.	Do you understand your module and key themes so far? Is there anything that you did not understand?
2.	Have you identified the level of study and depth and complexity expected in the essay? Are examples of previous essays or samples available?
3.	Have you reviewed the essay brief and any materials related to the assessment?
4.	Have you gathered and reviewed supporting materials such as lecture notes, presentations, slides, videos etc.
5.	Do you understand the purpose and format of the essay? What type of essay (refer back to Figure 6.6) is it?
6.	Do you have a title for the essay, do you need to choose one or can you create your own?
7.	When is it due? Work backwards from the due date to create a plan. What needs to be done when to keep on track?

Table 6.2 Essay Example: An example of applying the 7-step checklist

Step	Response
1	BA in Education Studies/Education and Technology
2	Level 5/Examples reviewed
3	Assignment brief reviewed
4	Keynotes on Education, learning, knowledge, change and development, personal development and achievement, Technology, Datafication, Human Data Interaction Theory, Universal Design for Learning, SAMR model
5	Assignment guidance: *Plan your 2000 words essay carefully before you start writing and give yourself time to do this. Begin by interrogating the title and identifying exactly what it is asking you to do (topic, focus and instruction). Your essay will need:* A clear introduction which signposts what is going to be covered and sets the scene for how you are going to answer the essay title. The main body of the essay is broken into paragraphs which introduce a clear point each. Logical progression through the paragraphs – each clearly linked to the essay title and your overall argument. A concise, relevant and useful case study included in a neat box (not more than 250 words) To demonstrate your engagement with academic reading to support your discussion. Ensure that your discussion is evidence-based and this evidence is clearly referenced using the Harvard system. To finish with a clear conclusion which summarises the key points made. A reference list at the end of your essay listing all the references used in alphabetical order, using the Harvard system.

(Continued)

Table 6.2 (Continued)

Step	Response
	Please note that your essay should include a case study based on your personal experience. Where the case study is included in your essay is up to you, it should be clearly boxed and will be included in your word count so should be concise. It will be important to expand on your case study during your essay, making relevant connections to your chosen essay title and academic literature.
6	Essay title options are: 1. Technology in 21st Century Education is a force for good. Discuss. 2. Children are passive in their engagement with technology. Discuss. 3. The current evolution of technology in the 21st Century will result in education becoming an 'individualised and non-social activity'. Discuss.
7	Five weeks to complete the essay

6.7 Understanding the assessment format

6.7.1 Fixed essay title – Deconstruction

Sometimes students are able to select an essay title from a range of options, or they may be given just one. Regardless, the essay will be marked in relation to the title, the LOs and relevant content. First, we will focus on understanding the title in general terms, before specifically focusing on the LOs to make further sense of it. We will deconstruct the following essay title as an example (Figure 6.2):

Children are passive in their engagement with technology. Discuss.

After deconstructing the essay title, ideas for the content need to align with and address the LOs that we will explore next. Stating the scope of the essay and

A	Key terms	Children, passive, engagement, technology-each needs defining in the context of the essay
B	Understand the Instruction Words	Discuss-the implication here is to develop an argument for and against the statement to provide a balanced overview.
C	Recognise the Scope	The scope of this title is set within the module it is situated. Therefore, the content that has been covered needs to be considered with the most relevant content selected.
D	Identify Implicit Assumptions	The assumption here is that children are passive in their engagement with technology. Does this assumption need challenging? Yes!
E	Connect to first-hand learning experiences	Having considered the scope of the module, make connections between the title, own interests/experiences and literature/theory.

Figure 6.2 Deconstructing an essay title.

defining the key terms in the essay title are important starting points for the essay. This will need to consider 'who' is meant by the term 'children' and how the adjective 'passive' and the noun 'engagement' relate to technology and education. The term 'discuss' means an exploration of key theoretical perspectives and practice experience of the student writing the essay. Exploring theory and practice will contribute towards achieving any LOs that require this. Further reflection and analysis in terms of the content may also be required by LOs as well. If we are to take the example of primary children accessing a maths-focused ed-tech programme both at school and at home, exploring issues of accessibility for all children would be a suitable consideration in relation to the passiveness of students with their engagement with technology. Furthermore, consideration can be given to categorising such a use of technology in relation to the SAMR model (Puentedura, 2013) as well as literature that consider the digital divide in such teaching practices (McDonald and Fotakopoulou, 2023), as this was covered in the module itself. Having established these initial ideas, a plan or structure can then be built from these in relation to the LOs of the Assessment (see Section 6.8 below). Of course, AI assistant can also be utilised to help you break down and understand an essay title (see Prompt 6.1).

Prompt 6.1 Deconstructing an essay title

INPUT:

I am a university student studying [enter programme and level of study]. I have been set an essay title and would like you to help me break it down further so that I can understand the key terms, the instruction words within it, the scope and any implicit assumptions before making connections to my own first-hand learning experiences. The essay title is [enter title here]. Can you help?

6.7.2 Developing an essay title – Construction

Deconstruction is often the precursor skill to construction. An infant can readily knock down a tower of blocks before becoming competent in the construction of one. At more advanced levels of study, it is likely that students will be asked to create their own essay titles to answer the assessment's LOs. Developing original essay titles should be a smoother transition if students have experienced answering set essay titles previously. Creating an essay title allows the student greater freedom, creativity and expression in addressing the LOs. This is especially relevant if a student is able to align their chosen title with a specific interest or specialist knowledge that they have. When developing an essay title, it is essential that the context of the module, the student's interests and the LOs for the assessment inform it. The below example LOs relate to the Education and Technology Module previously discussed and will be used to inform an example essay title.

Example of Learning Outcomes: Essay

A) Analyse the current and emerging role of technology in facilitating or inhibiting education.
B) Select and describe current debates related to the use of education technologies in the context of inclusivity and diversity within the learning environment.
C) Evaluate theoretical perspectives and their influence on practice.

Example of Essay Title

How can teachers use technology to support the development of student's reading skills in England?

The above essay title sets up a reflective essay that aims to draw on current uses of technology in supporting the development of student's reading skills by teachers. This will mean there is a focus on practice (relating to Learning Outcome C), with consideration given to the current and emerging technologies that teachers are using (Learning Outcome A). Learning Outcome B may be addressed in several ways, as the student may have general considerations in relation to inclusivity and diversity as we have already touched on, but the student may also want to explore specific tools and approaches. For example, Microsoft's Reading Coach (Tholfsen, 2022) and Reading Progress are innovative platforms that can be utilised to support reading. However, the debate aspect of Learning Outcome B here may be whether or not it is an assumption that everyone has access to and should be using Reading Coach at home as part of their homework. Furthermore, how inclusive is the programme for emergent and novice readers when compared to readers who are focusing on developing fluency? In this section so far, we have demonstrated how to develop an essay title based on LOs and in consideration of content. We have not yet considered how to plan or structure the essay or begin writing it. The rest of this chapter will now consider how the use of Generative AI can support students in this process, but first a reminder of the ethical and non-ethical use of Generative AI in relation to writing essays.

6.8 Understanding the learning outcomes

Every assignment should be comprised of several LOs. A LO is a specific statement that will detail exactly what the student will need to demonstrate in order to achieve it. LOs are the end product of taking a module. Taught sessions, related activities and independent study should therefore be aligned with and inform the process of learning on a module leading to the successful completion

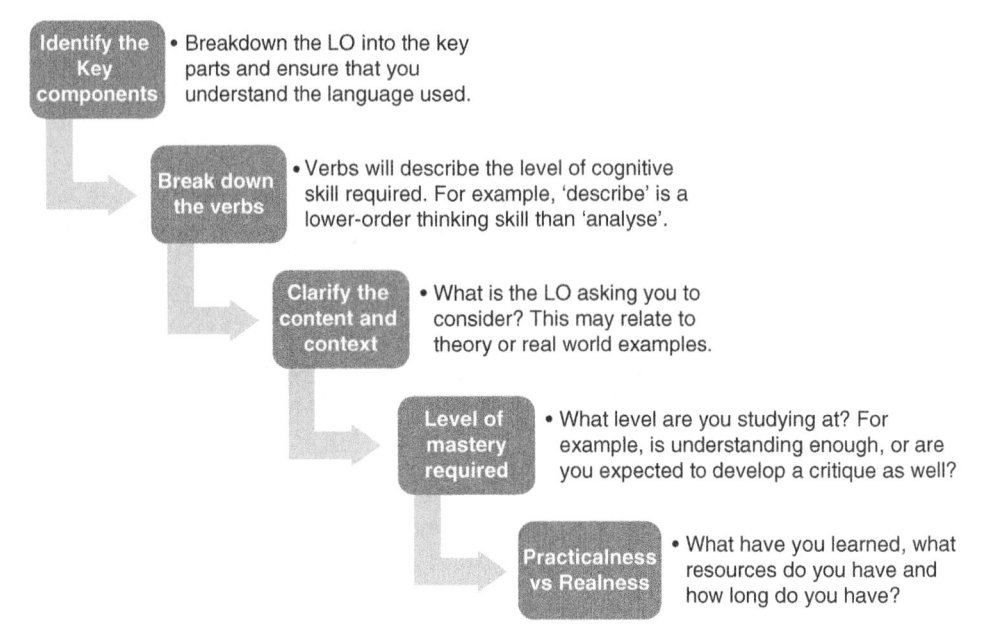

```
Identify the     • Breakdown the LO into the key
    Key            parts and ensure that you
components         understand the language used.

        Break down    • Verbs will describe the level of cognitive
         the verbs      skill required. For example, 'describe' is a
                        lower-order thinking skill than 'analyse'.

            Clarify the    • What is the LO asking you to
           content and       consider? This may relate to
              context        theory or real world examples.

                Level of      • What level are you studying at? For
                mastery         example, is understanding enough, or are
               required         you expected to develop a critique as well?

                    Practicalness    • What have you learned, what
                     vs Realness       resources do you have and
                                       how long do you have?
```

Figure 6.3 How to break down a learning outcome for an assignment.

of the assignment. LOs focus on what the student has learned and is able to demonstrate, not what the lecturer has taught. Often LOs will draw on the language of Bloom's Taxonomy such as understand, apply, analyse, evaluate and create. This enables the student to evidence such skills as well as the assessor to observe and pass judgement on them. The LOs should be easy to understand, related to the module and content, and easily achievable within the assessment design. For example, if a LO detailed 'work effectively in a group' but the assessment was an individual essay, then this would be a misalignment of assessment design with the LO. Just as we have discussed deconstructing an essay title, LOs should also be deconstructed to enable understanding as well (see Figure 6.3). Of course, Figure 6.8 can also be taken and adapted into a prompt (see Prompt 6.2).

Prompt 6.2   Understanding learning outcomes for an assignment

INPUT:

You are a world-renowned expert in [enter a subject that you are studying] and work at a world-leading university in [enter the country of study to provide context]. You are going to offer an explanation and breakdown of the following LOs. In this process, you need to:

1. Identify the key components of the LO.

> 2. Break down the verbs and provide examples of what this might involve in an essay.
> 3. Clarify the content and context of each LO.
> 4. Consider the key skills that need to be mastered in relation to each LO when studying at [enter your level of study here]. What is the appropriate level of mastery that you should be demonstrating at the level you are studying? For example, is understanding enough, or should you be expected to critique as well?
> 5. You are then going to finish by asking a number of questions that will help me to reflect on what has been taught so far and how this relates to each LO.
>
> The LOs for this assignment are [enter the list of LOs aligned to the assignment].

It is important to remember that the initial breakdown provided by an AI assistant is a starting place, not an end place, for understanding the LOs of an assignment. Prompt 6.2 was used and applied to the previous example LOs A, B and C. It can be seen from the AI assistant's response (AI Assistant Output 1) that each aspect of key component, verbs, content, context and key skills encourages reflection and connection to a student's prior learning and experience. This connection to the student's world (both experience and learning theory) is something that the AI assistant does not have access to. However, the AI assistant example does show that it is adept at identifying the differences in relation to the key skills that each LO are asking for the student to demonstrate. These are an understanding of 'educational technology' (LOA), 'inclusivity and diversity in education' (LOB) and 'theoretical perspectives and their practical implications' (LOC). Having developed an understanding of the LOs it is then important to consider these in relation to the title of your essay as previously covered in this chapter.

> AI Assistant (Bing.ai) Output:
>
> Sure, let's break down these LOs:
>
> A: Analyse the current and emerging role of technology in facilitating or inhibiting education.
>   Key components: Analysis, current and emerging role of technology, facilitation or inhibition of education.
>   Verbs: Analyse – This involves examining the topic in detail, and identifying key elements and their relationships.
>   Content and context: The focus is on how technology is used in education, both currently and in the future.
>   Key skills: Critical thinking, research, analysis, and understanding of educational technology.
>
> *(Continued)*

> B: Select and describe current debates related to the use of education technologies in the context of inclusivity and diversity within the learning environment.
> Key components: Selection, description, current debates, education technologies, inclusivity and diversity.
> Verbs: Select and describe – This involves choosing relevant debates and providing a detailed explanation of them.
> Content and context: The focus is on the intersection of education technologies with inclusivity and diversity.
> Key skills: Research, critical thinking, understanding of inclusivity and diversity in education.
> C: Evaluate theoretical perspectives and their influence on practice
> Key components: Evaluation, theoretical perspectives, influence on practice.
> Verbs: Evaluate – This involves making judgements based on criteria and standards.
> Content and context: The focus is on the impact of theoretical perspectives on practical applications.
> Key skills: Critical thinking, evaluation, understanding of theoretical perspectives and their practical implications.
>
> Now, let's reflect:
>
> 1. Can you identify a situation where technology facilitated your education? How about a situation where it inhibited your education?
> 2. What are some debates you've heard about regarding the use of technology in education, especially in terms of inclusivity and diversity?
>
> Can you think of a theoretical perspective that has influenced your practice or the practice of others around you? How did it do so?

AI Assistant Output 1

6.9 Connecting the Learning outcomes with assessment format and taught content

6.9.1 Developing an essay plan and structure

Before starting this part, students should have an essay title (fixed or self-created); be aware of the LOs for the essay and have some initial ideas about the theory and experiences they would like to bring to the essay (see Figure 6.4). If this is not the case, then please go back to the start of this chapter and review the preceding sub-sections to help you with this as it will help to ensure that your engagement with the AI tool is informed and connects with your prior learning. The components identified in Figure 6.4 will be needed in order to develop an essay plan that is relevant to what a student is to be assessed on and representative of their capabilities.

Essays

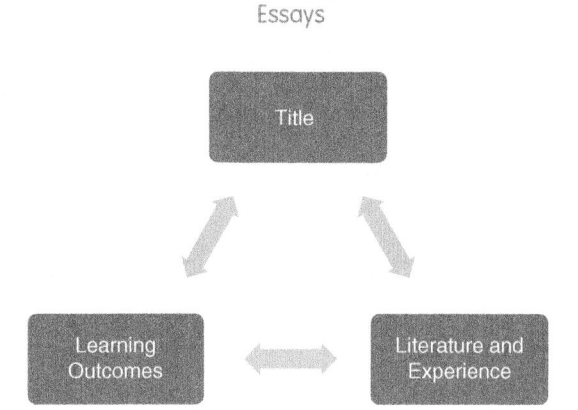

Figure 6.4 The main components needed to create an essay prompt with Generative Artificial Intelligence.

Prompt 6.3 Develop an essay plan and structure

INPUT:

Role: You are a world expert in [enter subject] who teaches at a university in [country]. You are going to provide support for a student.

Task: You are to provide a structured essay plan, broken down into sections totalling [enter number of words here] words. The essay plan must include an introduction and conclusion. The main body should consist of [enter the number of parts].

Format: When producing the plan you need to consider the essay title [enter essay title here], the LOs [enter LOs here] and this key information [enter relevant theory and experiences here]. Identify at each part of the plan which LO should be addressed. Please ask any questions needed for further clarification.

AI Assistant (Claude) Output:

Here is a proposed 2,000-word essay plan on "How can teachers use technology to support the development of student's reading skills in England?":

Introduction (200 words)

- Introduce the topic of using technology to support reading skill development
- Note the rising importance of technology in education
- Learning outcomes to be addressed: A, B

(Continued)

> Part 1: Current role and debates around educational technology (600 words)
>
> - Describe current major technologies used in developing reading skills (e.g., Microsoft Reading Coach)
> - Discuss the benefits and limitations of technology in reading skill-building
> - Address debates around the digital divide in access to technology
> - Consider inclusivity issues around the use of technology in diverse learner groups
> - Address learning outcomes: A, B
>
> Part 2: Theoretical perspectives on technology and reading (600 words)
>
> - Introduce the SAMR model of technology adoption
> - Explain how the SAMR model can be applied to the use of technology in developing reading skills
> - Give examples at each level of the SAMR model
> - Discuss theoretical implications of effective vs ineffective uses
> - Relate back to debates raised in Part 1
> - Address learning outcomes: A, C
>
> Part 3: Recommendations for best practice (500 words)
>
> - Building on analysis in Parts 1 and 2, provide recommendations for teachers
> - Give specific tips for using technology to improve reading skills
> - Emphasise the need to ensure inclusivity and access
> - Discuss setting up professional development for teachers on technology use
> - Address learning outcomes: B, C
>
> Conclusion (100 words)
>
> - Summarise key points raised in the essay
> - Note technologies as supplements for teachers, not replacements
> - Conclude that targeted, inclusive use of technology, informed by theory, can greatly support the development of students' reading skills
> - Learning outcomes: A, B, C
>
> Please let me know if you need any clarification or have additional questions as I develop this essay plan further. I'm happy to incorporate feedback.

AI Assistant Output 2

Prompt 6.3 outlines how to structure a prompt using the role, task and format framework to create a first attempt at an essay plan or structure. Prompt 6.3 has been used as an example, with the previous details covered in this chapter so far, in terms of an example title and LOs covered, being entered to complete the prompt. AI Assistant Output 2 is the output received from using this example prompt. This output clearly demarcates sections, word counts, content and which LO the section should link to. This provides a comprehensive plan to start from, which can then inform reading, research and eventually writing (see Section 6.11 in this chapter on 'Time Management').

The examples, Prompt 6.3 and AI Assistant Output 2, demonstrate how a coherent essay structure can be generated for the student to reflect on and begin writing. However, this is not always guaranteed and any content that has been generated by AI should be reviewed and critiqued by the student as standard. Utilising an AI assistant to help with understanding LOs and plan a structure for an essay can be deemed as an AI-assisted approach and complimentary when completing an essay. Up to this point, essentially, the AI assistant has taken the place of a more knowledgeable other, just as a fellow peer on your course may help you to develop your ideas. Such back and forth exchanges relating to the title, LOs and essay plan could also take place in a face-to-face taught session or within an online discussion board.

It is worth noting that the AI assistant is unable to replace the role of a lecturer in the module; although the AI assistant is efficient at processing and creating content, it is unable to master the context. Lecturers from your programme will have specific, insider and historical knowledge and experience of the assessment which the AI assistant does not have access to. It is also likely that the lecturer will be marking students' work. However, as can be seen from the response generated from AI Assistant Output 2, it does provide a valid start to planning and writing the essay if a lecturer is not available. Key to the continued development of AI literacy here is that the AI-generated plan is played around with, edited and tweaked as needed to capture the student's experiences, interests and voice. Such activity is essential to develop an authentic line of inquiry in the essay that proceeds it and will feed self-expression and human creativity (see Figure 6.5).

6.10 Is the use of GAI permitted in the final assignment?

The focus of using AI in this chapter so far has been on developing an AI-assisted approach to expand understanding and comprehension of the task/essay format at hand. The big question, however, as the sub-heading of this section suggests, is whether can Generative AI be used in the final creation or production of the essay. And if so, how? This will obviously differ across assessments, modules, universities and time essentially. So it is worth checking and double checking with the lecturer's who teach you. If examples of previous essays are available, then look out for how any use of Generative AI has been acknowledged or

Image created in Chat GPT 4: Create an image that represents this in images, no words:
• Check list- Your ideas, your writing, your voice. Don't lose it to AI. What are your lived experiences, what are your ambitions, what are your values and principles? Build out from them and come back to them.

Figure 6.5 The balance of AI input, self-expression and human creativity.

referenced. At the time of writing, this was also an evolving field as universities were considering their guidance on such matters.

6.10.1 The danger of using Generative AI to help with writing the essay for you

This chapter, and this book as a whole, present an AI-assisted approach to using GAI in supporting students with study and assessments, as opposed to creating them via an AI assistant, which would constitute an AI-generated approach. Whilst the next section will deal with how AI can be used to help get student's writing, it should not be used to generate a whole first draft of the essay. Admittedly though, AI assistants are very capable which was an initial source of panic in relation to students 'cheating'. Based on the author's experience of supporting students with using GAI, generating whole chunks of essay text leads to a debilitating effect in terms of the student then being able to write it better themselves. The elation at the speed of creation often subsides with a feeling of 'how can I do it better?'. This can lead to writing paralysis where the text generated by the AI assistant reads as best.

We can liken this to student's development in their use of direct quotations to effective paraphrasing. Embedding references and direct quotations in work is usually developed when students begin university. The concept of paraphrasing may also be introduced alongside or after direct quotations but is generally a more difficult skill for students to grasp. It is only after many attempts to put research and literature into a student's own words that it becomes a more familiar process. Although the use of direct quotes is still permissible, these complement arguments and paraphrased references. Whilst the journey from direct quotes to paraphrasing may be evolving, as long as referencing is accurate, academic integrity is intact. Submitting direct 'copy and paste' sections of an AI assistant's output lacks academic integrity as it risks misrepresenting a student's understanding and capabilities as discussed in Chapter 3. This is a major concern and why the prompting and generation of whole sections of essays should be avoided. Once an AI assistant's text response has been seen, it cannot be unseen; so it is advised against relying on it. Furthermore, the use of AI-generated content directly in student's work can be obvious and result in a referral for academic misconduct. Instead, there are other ways to use AI assistant in an assistive approach that will help with navigating any writer's block and continue to build on an ethical approach to using GAI. AI-assisted approach to using GAI. Albeit, you need to ensure that GAI can be used in the assignment as already stated.

6.11 Time management – When to research and write an essay with AI

Once you have a plan or structure for your essay in place, it is time to break it down into more manageable chunks. To do this, work backwards from the submission date to where you are now. Ideally, this will be a number of weeks, not days or hours! This will allow for flexibility in your approach and enable you to accommodate any unforeseen events that may crop up during this time. It should also allow for more time for final editing and proofreading. This is an area that students typically run out of time for. Two different examples of approaches to time management will be explored below. First, a general approach using an AI-generated ToDo list and secondly, a continued use of Claude.ai, which further breaks down AI Assistant Response 2 from earlier in this chapter.

6.11.1 General approach to action planning using 'Magic ToDo' by goblin.tools

Magic ToDo is a great place to start anything that you are not sure about and it is free to use. Whatever it is that you want to do (university or non-university related), just ask it, and it will create a step-by-step breakdown of how to approach it. Remember that the suggestions in the breakdown are just suggestions. For this example, however, the following prompt was used: 'I need to write an essay and have six weeks to do it'. The response in Figure 12 was provided (please note that an estimation of how much time should be spent on each step can also be generated for each step as below by using the drop down menu). This gives a good overview of the tasks that need to be completed and although the timings are not perfect (it is usually suggested that a third of the time is spent on researching/writing/editing), it answers the question of where you should start!

6.11.2 Detailed approach to action planning using an AI assistant

For a more tailored approach to time management and action planning, students can continue to use the AI assistant that has created the draft plan for them. Once a plan or structure has been suggested, then simply ask the AI assistant to provide an action plan within the timeframe that you have to complete the assignment (see Prompt 6.4). Please note, that for this example, a 'detailed action plan' was asked for and it continues to use the essay structure in AI Assistant Output 2. Once a response is generated to this prompt, more details can be asked for, or specific questions in relation to specific points, and the AI assistant will respond accordingly. Not only this though, but the action plan can also be turned into a table/checklist with a further prompt as shown in Figure 6.6 (please note it may need some slight formatting to get it looking exactly as it does).

Prompt 6.4   Action Plan for an Essay

INPUT:

This essay is due for submission in [enter how long in days/weeks etc]. Please write a detailed action plan of what to research and write based on the draft plan previously provided, please number each point based on Week 1, action a, b etc.

	I need to write an essay and have six weeks to do it.	
>	Brainstorm ideas for the essay.	1 hour
>	Research the topic and gather information.	7 days
>	Create an outline for the essay.	1 hour
>	Write the introduction.	1 hour
>	Write the body paragraphs.	2 days
>	Write the conclusion.	1 hour
>	Revise and edit the essay for clarity and coherence.	3 hours
>	Proofread for grammar and spelling errors.	2 hours
>	Submit the final essay.	2 days

Figure 6.6   Magic ToDo list for an essay.

AI Assistant (Claude) Output:

Here is a detailed 6-week action plan:

Week 1:

a. Read two-to-three journal articles and studies on current educational technologies used for reading skill development (e.g., Microsoft Reading Coach, other reading software/apps)
b. Read one-to-two reports/articles on debates around the digital divide and access to technology
c. Read one-to-two articles on inclusivity issues and using technology with diverse learner groups
d. Take two pages of typed notes summarising key points and citing sources
e. Write an introduction (200 words) introducing the topic and learning outcomes
f. Draft one page of Part 1 on current major technologies used for reading skills

Week 2:

a. Read two-to-three more articles on the benefits and limitations of technology for reading
b. Finish a one- to two-page draft of Part 1 summarising the debate around the digital divide and inclusivity (600 words total)
c. Search for two-to-three theoretical frameworks on technology adoption (e.g., SAMR and TPACK)
d. Take one-to-two pages of typed notes on theories relevant to the topic

Week 3:

a. Read in-depth on the SAMR model and implications for technology use
b. Make an outline for Part 2 relating SAMR levels to developing reading skills
c. Write a two- to three-page draft of Part 2 explaining the SAMR model (600 words)
d. Provide examples of effective vs ineffective use at each SAMR level

Week 4:

a. Finish a three- to four-page draft of Part 2 connecting SAMR to debates from Part 1
b. Search for three-to-five studies/articles with tips for best practices on using technology for reading
c. Take one-to-two pages of notes on recommendations

Week 5:

a. Make an outline for Part 3 on recommendations for teachers

(Continued)

> b. Write a three- to four-page draft of Part 3 on best practices and recommendations (500 words)
> c. Ensure discussing inclusivity, access and professional development
>
> Week 6:
>
> a. Finish one page conclusion summarising key points (100 words)
> b. Thoroughly proofread and edit a full six- to eight-page essay (2000 words)
> c. Double-check in-text citations and reference lists with at least eight sources
> d. Submit the final polished essay by deadline
>
> Let me know if you need any clarification or have additional questions! (Figure 6.7)

Week	Tasks	Checklist
Week 1	- Read 2-3 articles on educational technologies for reading - Read 1 article on digital divide - Take notes - Write-200-word introduction draft	[ ] Read articles [ ] Take notes [ ] Write introduction draft
Week 2	- Read 2 more articles on benefits/limitations of technology for reading - Finish 300-word part 1 draft on debates - Search for theoretical frameworks like SAMR, TPACK - Take notes	[ ] Read articles [ ] Finish part 1 draft [ ] Search for frameworks [ ] Take notes
Week 3	- Read in-depth about SAMR model - Make outline for part 2 explaining SAMR - Write 300-word part 2 draft on SAMR	[ ] Read about SAMR [ ] Make outline [ ] Write part 2 draft
Week 4	- Finish 600-word part 2 draft - Find 3 articles with best practices tips - Take notes	[ ] Finish part 2 draft [ ] Find articles on best practices [ ] Take notes
Week 5	- Make outline for part 3 on recommendations - Write 500-word part 3 draft on recommendations	[ ] Make part 3 outline [ ] Write part 3 draft
Week 6	- Write 100-word conclusion - Proofread 2000-word essay - Double check citations/references - Submit essay	[ ] Write conclusion [ ] Proofread essay [ ] Check citations [ ] Submit essay

Figure 6.7 Action Plan Checklist.

AI Assistant Output 3

6.12 Walk-through example: AI-assisted approach to creating an essay

6.12.1 Beginning your research

Once you have an initial structure to develop your essay, researching is made easier. There are two basic approaches to researching an essay from here that you can use interchangeably. The first is that you build out from the initial structure you have, researching each section's theme or key points. The second approach is that you research for more general themes (this is especially useful if you are finding it difficult to find specific literature relating to what you want to write about) and then relate what you find to your key sections. With this latter approach, you may need to revisit and tweak the sections further to accommodate the literature you discover. Although two approaches have been mentioned here, the reality is often somewhere in the middle! This involves a combination of searching based on your key themes but also adapting your structure to allow for unexpected but relevant content to be included. Most importantly, however, is that you research and develop content that relates to and expands on your essay title as well as meeting the LOs.

Whilst it does depend on what level you are studying at, both undergraduate and postgraduate level assignments expect students to draw on academic sources. Academic sources do not mean Googling your essay title and referencing the first few websites that are presented. It also does not mean prompting an AI assistant to generate your references for you. At the time of writing, AI assistants were still susceptible to hallucinations in such cases. What this means is that AI assistants will create both original and fake references for you if asked. If a student is discovered to be using fake references, then this may result in academic misconduct and a stern warning (the first time) or worse.

All courses will have a reading list. This should be any student's first place to begin when researching for the essay. For higher grades and more advanced levels of study, students should demonstrate further independent research. This means going beyond the suggested reading list. The online library portal that you have access to through your university should be utilised to ensure you are accessing academic literature. There are, however, AI tools that can also assist with this. Such AI tools are especially effective in identifying the sources that an article draws on (i.e. the sources in the reference list), as well as the proceeding sources, that draw on that article (i.e., literature published afterwards which has referenced the article you are reading).

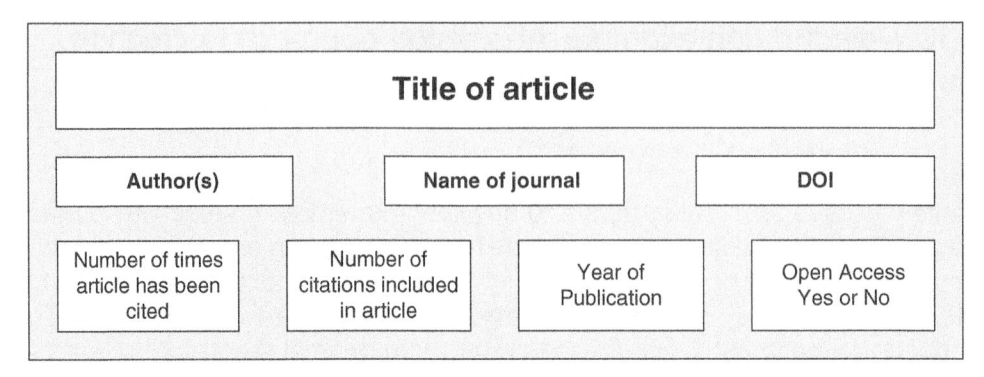

Title of article				
Author(s)		Name of journal		DOI
Number of times article has been cited	Number of citations included in article	Year of Publication		Open Access Yes or No

Figure 6.8 Inciteful overview.

An example of this will be demonstrated using the free Inciteful.xyz tool to explore an article by Stole et al. (2021) titled: 'Assessing children's reading comprehension on paper and screen: A mode-effect study. As can be seen in Figure 14, Inciteful.xyz will provide an overview of the seed article that is important for assessing the initial validity of the article. The example article by Stole et al. (2022) has been cited by 53 other articles and includes 31 citations. Furthermore, a map of these citations is then presented, which not only reveals the year of publication but also allows you to select each paper and link to visit its location online and read the abstract. It is worth noting that some papers may be open access, whilst others may require a further sign-in using your university credentials and some may be behind a paywall. Using tools such as Inciteful.xyz allows for a much more succinct and focused search in relation to your chosen essay title and aids in developing analysis, synthesis and critique. One of the dangers here, however, is that it can feel like a rabbit hole of endless reading. That is why it is important that you have planned your research time for the essay accordingly and stay disciplined within these limits (Figure 6.8).

6.12.2 Combatting writer's block with AI

By now, you know what you want the essay to be about (based on the title and LOs), you know what you want the essay to contain (based on your learning and research) and you know what sources you need to include (in-text citations and reference list). You just need to put it all together. This can at times feel much easier said than done and lead to procrastination in terms of writing the actual essay. Using an AI assistant to help create some sentence starters for each section is a great way to overcome this.

6.12.3 Sentence starters

This is a quick way to get writing by using the AI assistant to support you instead of the AI assistant doing the writing for you, which could be considered academic misconduct and unethical. Following on from Claude.ai's earlier output in relation to the essay plan (AI Assistant Output 2), the AI assistant was further prompted (see Prompt 6.5) and responded with AI Assistant Output 4. As can be seen in the output, the AI assistant takes relevant content and embeds this in the opening part of the sentences which then allows the student to complete them and continue writing.

Prompt 6.5 Sentence starters for an essay

INPUT:

Based on the essay structure that you have provided. Can you suggest a few sentence starters to get started for each section?

AI Assistant (Claude.ai) Output:

Here are some suggested sentence starters for each section of the essay plan:

Introduction.

- Recent years have seen a steady increase in the use of technology for developing reading skills as…
- With the advancement of education technologies, teachers now have an expanding set of tools such as…

Part 1.

- Major technologies currently utilised in building reading skills include programmes like…
- However, the integration of technology in reading instruction has sparked debates around…

Part 2.

- The SAMR (Substitution, Augmentation, Modification, Redefinition) model outlines four tiers of technology adoption, which can provide a useful framework for…
- Applying this model to the use of technology in reading, the substitution would involve instances where…

(Continued)

> Part 3.
>
> - Bearing in mind the potentials and limitations identified, best practice recommendations for teachers include...
> - A priority area should be ensuring inclusivity and access to reading skill technologies for all groups by...
>
> Conclusion.
>
> - In conclusion, while technologies hold much promise, they ultimately serve to supplement rather than replace...
> - Targeted and thoughtful integration of tools like...equipped with professional guidance, can significantly enrich the development of reading skills.
>
> Please let me know if you need any other suggestions for getting started on sections of the essay. I'm happy to provide additional ideas or examples.

AI Assistant Output 4

6.12.4 Searching for literature or references with AI Assistants or Specific AI Tools?

AI assistants: Using Large Language-based models such as Bing, Gemini or ChatGPT to recommend references is not currently recommended. This is because, at the time of writing, such AI assistants can hallucinate (as already mentioned) and create references which will at first seem real, but if searched for, will not be real. You could start with such an approach, however, and then check each reference that is recommended to see if it is real. But, the time spent doing this, may be better spent beginning with the recommended reading list and expanding your search from there. Remember, that you will need to draw on academic sources for your essay as well.

Using a specific AI tool for literature searches: There's an ever-increasing number of tools that do this. Some offer freemium access, such as Litmaps and Connected Papers, but there are also free tools such as Inciteful.xyz and Research Rabbit that do a similar job. These are all AI-based tools that will identify further literature based on the initial search term or reference that you enter. This is a great way to research and keep your reading succinct and specific to the focus of your research.

Essays

	Editing	**Formatting**	**Proofreading:**
Focus	Editing is an in-depth process which involves making changes and improvements to various elements of the text, including structure, clarity, style, and coherence.	Formatting pertains to the arrangement and style of the document. This includes the layout, font choices, headings, spacing, alignment, page numbering, and adherence to specific formatting guidelines (such as APA, MLA, or specific university guidelines).	This process primarily concerns itself with the identification and correction of surface errors in writing, such as typos, spelling mistakes, grammar, punctuation, and consistency in language use.
Objective	When editing the student should seek to enhance the quality of the content, ensuring that arguments are clear and well-presented, the narrative flow is logical, and the overall message is effectively communicated.	The goal is to ensure that the document is visually organised and meets any required standards or guidelines. Good formatting makes a document more readable and professionally presented.	The aim is to ensure that the text is error-free and reads smoothly. Proofreading does not typically involve making changes to the content or structure of the text.
When it Happens	Editing is done during the drafting of the document and can occur multiple times as the text develops.	Formatting can be done both during and at the end of the writing process. It is essential to ensure the document's final version adheres to the required formatting standards.	This is usually the final step in the writing process, conducted after all editing revisions have been made.
Can AI be used?	Although the student, or human should always remain the final editor and accountable for any work submitted as an assignment in their name, AI assistants can offer editing assistance.	AI assistants can be utilised to provide feedback on particular styles, especially in relation to referencing accurately and appropriately.	Yes- this can be utilised in the same way that you may ask a peer to read over your work and is especially useful for students with English as an additional language or students with SEND.

Figure 6.9 Editing, formatting and proofreading.

6.12.5 Editing, formatting and proofreading

The tasks of editing, formatting and proofreading an essay before its submission are distinct yet complementary processes. Figure 6.9 breaks down the different aspects of each concept and considers if Generative AI can assist with it. As with all other aspects of Generative AI usage, it is important to first identify whether or not this complies with the guidance on how AI can be utilised in your essay from your university/faculty/programme.

In summary, editing, formatting and proofreading are key stages in the preparation of an essay, each with its specific focus and objective. Editing enhances the content and clarity, formatting ensures the document is well-organised and adheres to the required guidelines, and proofreading ensures an error-free and polished text. AI assistants can be utilised to assist with all of these processes which will contribute to the overall quality and effectiveness of the final essay, provided this is in line with your assignment's guidance on the use of AI.

6.12.6 Introductions, summaries and conclusions

Every essay will need an introduction and a conclusion. For longer pieces of writing, it is wise to include mini summaries at the end of the main body of content and connect to wider aspects of the essay. However, doing all of these things can at times, feel like repetition, which it is in many ways, but it is demonstrating your understanding of numerous topics across and within the essay format. Once a student has focused on writing the main aspects of their essay, an AI assistant could be used to create an introduction and conclusion to this work.

Before considering this, however, double-check what the requirements are from your institution regarding the use of an AI assistant in such a way so that you are transparent about it and acknowledge it accordingly. Secondly, to generate a response (either introduction, summary or conclusion), you would need to upload your working draft or copy and paste it into an AI assistant. If you are happy to do so, please ensure that you are not sharing any sensitive information and it is best to anonymise or omit key details (e.g., student name/name of university etc.) in your draft before uploading. Once you are happy that you can use an AI assistant for this purpose and that the information you are uploading is appropriate, then it is simply a matter of doing so and asking the AI assistant to create a draft introduction/summary/conclusion based on this text (see Prompts 6.6 and 6.7). Please be aware, that this is a first draft and will need editing and personalising.

Prompt 6.6 Generate a draft introduction

INPUT:

[Enter text by copy and paste or document upload]

Review this text and create a detailed introduction for it. Ensure that you identify and define the key terms first, before discussing the focus and context of the essay. Next, signpost to the core parts covered in the essay and any key arguments that are made.

> **Prompt 6.7 Generate a draft conclusion**
>
> INPUT:
>
> [Enter text by copy and paste or document upload]
>
> Review this text and create a detailed conclusion of it. Ensure that you provide a summary of the core parts and any key arguments made.

6.13 Summary of chapter

This chapter has considered the different types of essays utilised in Higher Education and their key role in assessment. It has considered the steps necessary to start an essay and presents a detailed checklist and illustrative examples for clarity. Ethical considerations and applications of AI in academic writing are considered throughout the chapter, providing insights into AI-assisted research and editing. In doing so, students are encouraged to use AI tools in line with guidance from their university to ensure outputs are ethically sound and academic integrity maintained. The chapter aims to enhance students' understanding and skills in essay writing, advocating for the thoughtful integration of AI as a tool to enrich their learning experience. The use of AI assistants and tools is presented to assist students in essay writing as opposed to writing the essay for them.

6.14 Chapter hacks

> 1. AI-Assisted Brainstorming: Before starting your essay, use AI tools to generate ideas or themes related to your topic. This can help overcome initial writer's block and provide new perspectives.
> 2. Structuring Essays with AI: Utilise AI tools to help structure your essay. Input your main ideas and let the AI suggest a coherent flow, ensuring a well-organised essay.
> 3. Ethical AI Usage Awareness: Always be aware of the ethical implications of using AI in your writing. Understand your institution's guidelines on AI usage to ensure your work remains academically honest.
> 4. AI for Research Efficiency: Leverage AI tools to quickly gather and summarise relevant research materials. This can drastically reduce the time spent on preliminary research.
>
> *(Continued)*

5. Enhancing Writing Style: Use AI-based writing assistants to refine your writing style, grammar and syntax, ensuring your essay is clear, concise and professionally presented.
6. Regular AI Tool Updates: Stay updated with the latest features and updates of your chosen AI tools. Regular updates can bring new functionalities that might be beneficial for your essay-writing process.
7. Critical Review with AI: After completing your draft, use AI tools for an initial review. AI can provide insights on readability and structure, and even suggest areas for improvement before the final submission.

These hacks are designed to enhance the essay writing process in Higher Education, making it more efficient and effective by integrating AI tools thoughtfully.

6.15 Chapter MCQs

1. What is the key benefit of using AI tools for brainstorming essay topics?
    A) They guarantee a top grade
    B) They offer a variety of perspectives
    C) They write the entire essay for you
    D) They replace traditional research methods
2. How does AI assist in structuring essays?
    A) By automatically writing the introduction and conclusion
    B) By providing a coherent flow of ideas
    C) By choosing the essay topic for the student
    D) By guaranteeing plagiarism-free content
3. What should students be mindful of when using AI in academic writing?
    A) AI completely eliminates the need for proofreading
    B) AI use is always encouraged by all educational institutions
    C) The ethical implications and institutional guidelines for AI use
    D) AI tools can replace tutors or lecturers
4. What advantage does AI offer in the research phase of essay writing?
    A) It ensures all sources are academically credible
    B) It can provide a quick summary of relevant materials
    C) It automatically writes the literature review section
    D) It chooses the best research methodology
5. What is the importance of AI in editing and proofreading essays?
    A) It replaces the need for human review
    B) It can help identify grammatical and stylistic errors
    C) It changes the essay's original ideas
    D) It automatically increases the word count

Correct answers:

1. Correct answer B
2. Correct answer B
3. Correct answer C
4. Correct answer B
5. Correct answer B

7
Presentations

7.1 Chapter objectives

1. Understand the importance of presentations and the different formats they may take
2. Consider learning outcomes (LOs) for presentation-based assessments and enhance your own presentation skills
3. Use Generative AI ethically and transparently in the research and creation of presentations
4. Respond constructively to feedback on presentations as part of the development process

7.2 Having read this chapter, you will...

1. Differentiate between individual and group presentations, appreciating the unique opportunities and challenges each format presents.
2. Navigate the various presentation formats available within academic settings and understand how each can be tailored to meet specific LOs and assessment requirements.
3. Grasp the rationale behind the use of presentations in assessments, recognising their role and how these contribute to both academic success and employability.
4. Employ a structured approach to preparing for a presentation and effective time management.
5. Leverage Generative AI tools ethically and effectively in the preparation and creation of presentations, ensuring transparency in their use and alignment with academic standards and ethical guidelines.
6. Conduct thorough research to support your presentation and practice your presentation skills to ensure a polished and professional delivery.
7. Receive and apply feedback constructively to better engage your audience.
8. Critically evaluate the use of Generative AI in presentations.

7.3 Introduction

Presentations hold a unique space in the spectrum of university assessment. It is not uncommon for students to feel dread at their sheer mention, or avoid modules that have presentation-based assessments altogether. Presentations can now involve the in-person delivery or audio and visual recording of a student delivering the assignment. By combining knowledge and the need for verbal communication presentations challenge students to engage actively with their audience. Active engagement often involves the synthesis and presentation of complex ideas in a coherent and impactful manner. This interactive form of assessment supports the holistic development of students and needs planning, practice and confidence to be delivered effectively – skills that will benefit most graduates in the workplace.

This chapter begins by recognising the evolution of oral presentations from their historical roots to contemporary assessment practice. The chapter distinguishes between individual and group formats and considers the current and diverse approaches to presentation-based assessments, enabled by developing technology. The strategic design of presentations, emphasising alignment with LOs and the incorporation of ethical considerations, particularly in the use of Generative AI tools, is covered. The chapter provides a walk-through for students on a journey from the inception of a presentation idea to its delivery. The importance of thorough preparation, research and rehearsal is highlighted. Opportunities and limitations of using AI assistants to support presentation development while adhering to academic integrity are presented. This chapter stands as a vital resource for students wishing to move beyond the first blank slide of a presentation and not knowing where to start.

7.4 What is a presentation?

In a traditional sense, oral assessment has a long history and many forms as it predates written assessment. For example, in 16th-century England, university examinations were conducted in public, orally and in Latin, before a shift towards more written examinations in the 18th and 19th centuries (Stray, 2001). Oral or verbal-based assessments have continued as a mainstay of many disciplines and are linked to developing employability skills today. Traditional face-to-face presentations are still the mainstay for many programmes at university. Universities also have a wide range of experiences in facilitating online approaches to presentations due to the online nature of work during the coronavirus disease 2019 (COVID-19) pandemic in 2020. This has partly been of benefit for students who are anxious about presentations and online programmes. There are now feasible and equitable interpretations of traditional face-to-face presentations that foster inclusivity across the diverse student body, albeit the same LOs will still need to be met.

7.5 Individual or group presentations

Individual presentations tend to be more common than group presentations but can often be the most daunting as you prepare and present alone. Group presentations, however, can sometimes lead to complications because of the expectations students have of each other, rightly or wrongly. Regardless of initial experiences or preferences, both approaches can offer a range of opportunities and challenges (see Table 7.1).

Table 7.1 Individual and group presentations

Aspect	Individual presentations	Group presentations
Skill development	Develops individual skills in researching, creating and presenting	Develops beyond individual skills relating to teamwork, collaboration and communications
Accountability	Clear individual responsibility and a direct reflection of effort in grading	Shared responsibility, but individual contributions can vary. Grading can be on an individual or group basis
Learning experience	Allows for tailored learning in relation to personal interests	Offers peer learning opportunities and exposure to diverse viewpoints to develop analysis and scope
Confidence building	Builds self-confidence and individual presentation and speaking skills	For less confident students, there may be a temptation to shy away from presenting and allow more confident members of the group to lead. This will mean confidence is not developed
Pressure	All of the pressure is on the individual	Shared pressure among group members reduces individual stress. However, stress can increase if individual members are not contributing
Collaboration	Misses out on developing collaborative and teamwork skills	Enhances collaborative abilities but depends on group dynamics
Workload	The sole responsibility for all aspects of the presentation	The workload is distributed but requires effective coordination and action
Group dynamics		Can be challenging due to different work styles and commitment levels

7.6 Different types of presentation

The term 'presentation' involves a number of formats which are continuing to be reviewed in light of developing approaches to authentic assessment within Higher Education. All approaches to the presentation can be tailored to both individual and group-based tasks. There may be a learning outcome for the presentation that specifically refers to group working, or there may not. Whilst the below list is not exhaustive, it aims to capture the breadth and depth of various approaches to presentation-based approaches of assessment at university:

1. **Face-to-face presentation:** This is the most traditional in essence and involves the presenter, presenting relevant content to the audience within the same physical space. Typically, the presenter will position themselves where everyone can see them and should face the audience ensuring that they can be heard. A presentation is then given including the use of text and visuals to support their verbal delivery. Such presentations are often followed up with questions or feedback from the audience.
2. **Online presentation:** This format involves presenting online using audio-visual communication-based software. This could include tools such as Microsoft Teams or Zoom, or it could be held within a virtual classroom hosted by the university's Virtual Learning Environment such as Moodle or Canvas. Again, it will typically involve the sharing of text and visuals to support the verbal delivery. It is important to ensure that students have a suitable internet connection and speed for online deliveries, as a poor connection can result in many challenges for those listening to and marking the presentation.
3. **Pre-recorded presentation:** This format potentially mitigates situations where internet connection or speed is problematic for live presenting. It allows students to create, record and upload their presentation prior to a submission deadline. This is especially useful for students who are learning online from regions or countries with slower internet speeds and connections. The added benefit here is also that the recording itself can be paused, stopped and restarted as the student sees fit. Depending on the assignment brief and instructions, there is a range of tools that can be used to create and record presentations, before uploading them for submission.
4. **Poster presentation:** Posters are usually created to summarise a project or research on a particular theme. These are then typically displayed by the presenter, allowing the audience to ask questions. Sometimes, the student may be asked to 'present' the poster first, before questions are asked. Traditionally, this took place in a face-to-face environment, but it can also take place online or even as a pre-recorded walk-through of the poster.
5. **Interactive presentation:** This involves the interaction of the audience in the presentation itself and not just at the end of the presentation to ask questions. In a traditional sense, the interaction could have been encouraged through asking questions and audiences responding via a show of their hands, as well as think-pair-share approaches etc. However, presenters will need to be mindful of time restrictions, as interactions take up more time than a traditional presentation.

There is also a range of digital tools that can capture and share the input of the audience relating to polls, word clouds, interactive whiteboards etc. Examples of such tools include Kahoot, Mentimeter and Poll Everywhere.

6. **Workshop presentation:** These are often educational in the sense that they invite more active participation from the audience with the intention to teach about or explore a topic in depth. This usually involves teamwork and may be based on a role-play activity or case study exploration. This can often be a formative assessment task (not graded) but will help to develop an understanding of how people learn and what they engage with.

7. **Portfolio presentation:** This involves presenting a collection of work which may be made up of a range of artefacts but deemed relevant to the assignment. It is commonly used in creative subjects but is becoming increasingly popular in other subjects for students to demonstrate thought processes and development across a certain scope or time period.

7.7 Why are presentations used in the assessment process and why is feedback from them important?

Presentations in academic settings are designed to be a dynamic and active process. They grant students a degree of autonomy in how they convey understanding, engage with the audience, and demonstrate analytical and critical thinking skills. This format allows those marking it to assess a student's ability to synthesise and articulate diverse sources of information in a coherent manner as well as the depth of a student's knowledge. The process of preparing and delivering a presentation promotes skills such as effective communication, time management, organisation and the generation of ideas. These skills foster independence and should encourage students to take ownership of their learning journey. Such ownership and independence are an essential employability skill. While the grade awarded is a key output of any assignment, the feedback received during or after a presentation is important. Feedback should highlight strengths and areas for improvement in content delivery and public speaking. Constructive criticism can provide students with insights into the audience's reception and understanding of their work. This should aid in student's learning and help them to refine and tailor future presentations. Being able to receive feedback is also another key employability skill in the modern workplace.

Post-presentation feedback for presentations may also include written comments. These comments are essential for addressing how well the LOs of the assignment have been met, including specific pointers on areas of success and aspects needing further development. A comprehensive review might include feedback on the use of visual aids, the structure of the presentation and the effectiveness of the engagement strategies employed. Increasingly, feedback on presentations integrates marking rubrics which offer a detailed breakdown of various components, such as content accuracy, delivery, engagement techniques and use of technology. These rubrics can pinpoint specific strengths and development areas, providing a clear roadmap for improvement. Additionally, presenters often receive a 'feedforward' – constructive guidance focusing on aspects to consider or enhance for subsequent presentations. This forward-looking advice is crucial for continuous improvement and skill refinement in future endeavours and is discussed further in Chapter 10.

7.8 Checklist to begin the assignment: Presentation

7.8.1 A seven-step checklist to beginning your presentation

Complete this seven-step checklist before starting your presentation. It is designed to promote your AI literacy as it will enable you to:

- Avoid misunderstanding what is needed
- Think about the key details
- Know what relevant learning and ideas you already have (Table 7.2)

Table 7.2 Seven-step checklist

	Question
1.	Do you understand your module and key themes so far? Is there anything that you didn't understand?
2.	Have you identified the level of study and depth and complexity expected in the presentation?
3.	Have you reviewed the presentation brief and any materials related to the assessment?
4.	Have you gathered and reviewed supporting materials such as lecture notes, presentations, slides, videos etc.
5.	Do you understand the purpose and format of the presentation? Consider the key aspects it should contain in relation to communication and interaction.
6.	Choose or create a presentation topic and consider how you will engage the audience.
7.	When is it due? Work backwards from the due date with a plan. What needs to be done when to keep on track?

7.9 Understanding the assessment format

7.9.1 Understanding a presentation assignment brief

Assignment briefs may be presented in a range of formats, but they should be standardised across the modules you are studying. This ensures familiarity for the student, that quality processes have been followed in the design of the brief, and that the LOs are appropriate for that level of study. The following sub-sections offer generalised guidance on common aspects that should be included in a presentation-based assignment brief.

7.9.2 Assignment overview

Most presentation-based assignments will be composed of at least two parts: the speaking part and the content part. The speaking part is what the student says to accompany the content that they have developed. It is important that the content and what is said are linked. Content should be effective in conveying key messages. This may be done through text, photos, images, graphs, etc. Each part of the content should be covered in the verbal delivery of the presentation. If it is not, it may be assumed that the presentation was poorly planned or that it was forgotten as an oversight of the presenter.

7.9.3 Submission details

Be aware of what is due when, and in what format it is due for submission. If an assignment consists of two parts, one part may be due for submission before the other. For example, the content of the presentation may be due for submission the week before it is due to be verbally presented. This allows time for the lecturers to familiarise themselves with the content, prepare questions and check any indicators relating to academic misconduct.

7.9.4 Submission process

It is also worth noting how the submission should take place and where. For example, are you required to submit your presentation slides and a script? If so, can they be submitted separately or do they need to be submitted as one file? If one file, what type of file? For example, do you know how to convert files to a PDF and merge them if needed? Are they to be submitted through the university's Virtual Learning Environment system or is it an external portal using a third-party tool such as Turnitin? If so, how can such portals be accessed? If you are unsure about this, or how to do it, it is imperative that you seek further guidance from a lecturer or module leader in advance of the date the presentation is due. The worst thing that can happen is that a student puts time and effort into a presentation and then fails to submit it according to the guidelines, resulting in a penalty. Finally, ensure that you complete a final check and that you are submitting everything that has been asked for, including a reference list!

7.9.5 Assignment focus/selection

Is the focus of the presentation clearly stated in the brief or does it allow for further exploration? What does the core 'ask' of the assignment, and how does this relate to what has been taught and what your interests are? There will usually be more guidance around the focus for students who are new to university study. Such guidance, however, should gradually reduce as you develop your knowledge and skill set, progressing through the different levels of study. This means that the higher the level of study, the more freedom and encouragement you have to develop a focus. Ensure that the focus relates to the LOs for the assignment and that it is relevant.

7.9.6 Content requirements

As mentioned previously, presentations will often consist of two parts: the content and the verbal delivery. There may be guidelines for how the content should be developed, for example, it may ask for a clear introduction of the student and their student number, before moving on to begin the presentation. The presentation will likely need to consider a main body or discussion section, between a clear introduction of what will be said and a clear conclusion of what has been said. Ensure that the organisation of the presentation correlates with the requirements in terms of using visuals, being organised and any specific formatting. If using slides, ensure clear headings and subheadings are used. In terms of verbal delivery, as already mentioned, this needs to be clearly correlated to the content so that it provides the analysis required at your level of study. Presenters should also be mindful of the allocated timeframe, as well as the potential for questions or feedback afterwards. If it is a pre-recorded presentation, then there will not be live questions at the end, but you may have been given a few questions as part of the guidance that you need to answer in the recording.

7.9.7 Learning outcomes

Focus on achieving the LOs specified in the brief, which may include subject knowledge, analytical skills and effective communication. These should guide your understanding of how you need to present the content in relation to the key theme or title of the presentation. The LOs are what you will be marked on so a key point of guidance for what comes next: beginning your presentation.

7.10 Understanding the learning outcomes

Every assignment should be aligned to a set of well-defined LOs. A LO is an explicit statement that details the specific competencies a student is expected to demonstrate upon successful completion of the module. For instance, in a module with a presentation-based assessment, a LO might 'effectively employ verbal and non-verbal communication techniques in a presentation'. The LOs represent the ideal mastery achieved after completing a module's learning journey. Such a journey encompasses taught sessions, guided activities and independent study. All of these contribute to the learning process and ultimately, the successful attainment of the LOs.

A key point to remember about LOs, however, is that they focus on knowledge and skills acquired by the student, rather than the content that has been taught by the lecturer. Both will be connected though, as the taught content should provide the basis for further exploration and understanding in relation to the presentation which will be assessed. Again, the language in LOs often relates to Bloom's Taxonomy, covering words such as 'understand', 'apply', 'analyse', 'evaluate' and 'create'. As well as providing the students the opportunity to demonstrate their cognitive capabilities, it also provides a clear framework for lecturers to evaluate the students' competencies in these. For example, a presentation-specific LO relating to Bloom's Taxonomy may state, 'Analyse and synthesise diverse sources of information to construct a cohesive argument in presentation format'. Communication and articulation are the key skills needed here. This is done twofold through the visual aids/slides you create and your use of voice and language. Just as an AI assistant can be utilised to help understand essay-related LOs (see Section 6.8 and Figure 6.3 p. 102), it can also be used with presentation-based LOs (see Prompt 7.1 and AI Assistant Output 5).

Example Learning Outcome: Presentation

a. Demonstrate advanced presentation skills by effectively communicating complex concepts related to Early Childhood Education and Care to a variety of audiences.

Prompt 7.1 Understanding learning outcomes for a presentation

INPUT:

You are a world-renowned expert in [enter a subject that you are studying] and work at a world-leading university in [enter country of study to provide context]. You are going to offer an explanation and breakdown of the following LO which is part of a presentation-based assessment. In this process, you need to:

1. Identify the key components of the LO.
2. Break down the verbs and provide examples of what this might involve in an essay.

3. Clarify the content and context of each LO.
4. Consider the key skills that need to be mastered in relation to each LO when studying at [enter your level of study here]. What is the appropriate level of mastery that you should be demonstrating at the level you are studying? For example, is understanding enough, or should you be expected to critique as well?
5. You are then going to finish by asking a number of questions that will help me to reflect on what has been taught so far and how this relates to each LO.

The LOs for this assignment are: [enter a list of Learning Outcomes aligned to the assignment].

AI Assistant (Gemini.ai/Google) Output:

Breakdown of the LO: Advanced Presentation Skills in Early Childhood Education

This LO focuses on your ability to effectively communicate complex ideas in Early Childhood Education and Care. Let's break it down into its key components:

Key components

Demonstrate advanced presentation skills: This implies going beyond basic presentation techniques and showcasing a strong command of delivery and audience engagement.

Effectively communicate complex concepts: You'll need to break down intricate ideas related to early childhood education into clear and understandable terms.

Related to Early Childhood Education and Care: The content of your presentation should delve into specific topics within this field.

To a variety of audiences: This highlights the need to adapt your presentation style and language to suit different listeners, whether they are professionals, parents or policymakers.

Verbs and examples

Demonstrate: You might present a live talk, create a multimedia presentation or even design a captivating infographic (depending on the course format).

Effectively communicate: This involves using clear language, strong visuals and engaging activities to ensure your audience understands and retains the information.

Complex concepts: Examples could include brain development in early childhood, the impact of play-based learning or the importance of social-emotional development.

(Continued)

Content and context

The content of your presentation will depend on your specific course and chosen topic. However, the context is always related to Early Childhood Education and Care. This means grounding your points in research, best practices, and the overall impact on young children's development.

Skills at level 5

At Level 5, you're expected to go beyond basic understanding. You should be able to:

- **Analyse:** Break down complex concepts into their component parts and explain their relationships.
- **Evaluate:** Assess the strengths and weaknesses of different approaches in early childhood education.
- **Synthesise:** Combine information from various sources to create a new and insightful understanding.

Level of mastery

While a foundational understanding is important, Level 5 presentations require deeper analysis and critical thinking. Aim to not only explain concepts but also discuss their implications, potential challenges and research-backed solutions. You can demonstrate this by:

- **Presenting opposing viewpoints:** Briefly outlining and addressing alternative perspectives on the topic.
- **Evaluating research:** Examining the methodology and credibility of research studies you cite.
- **Proposing solutions:** Suggesting evidence-based strategies to address challenges faced in early childhood education.

Reflection questions

1. What are some of the most complex concepts you've encountered in your early childhood education studies so far?
2. How can you break down these concepts into clear and concise language for a non-specialist audience (e.g., parents)?
3. Have you identified any areas where research in early childhood education is ongoing or inconclusive? How can you present these areas in a way that highlights the need for further exploration?
4. Think about a specific challenge in early childhood education care. Can you brainstorm and propose some potential solutions based on your current understanding?

> By considering these questions and actively practising your presentation skills, you'll be well on your way to demonstrating advanced communication abilities in the field of Early Childhood Education and Care.

AI Assistant Output 5

7.11 Is the use of Generative AI permitted in the final assignment?

It is essential that before considering the use of GAI in assignments students have checked and double-checked, if and how they are allowed to use it:

1. Are students permitted to use Generative AI in the presentation? (this should provisionally be a yes/no answer)
2. Are there any limitations on how GAI should be used in the presentation? (this is slightly more complex and may evolve as time progresses but, for example, may permit GAI for structuring a presentation but not writing the script?)
3. Are examples provided of how GAI can be used in a presentation? (if no, ask for some!)

7.12 What could the ethical use of Generative AI in a presentation involve?

The key aspect of the ethical use of AI in beginning a presentation is to be transparent about what AI tools you have drawn on and how in line with your university's guidance. This may mean that each interaction with an AI tool needs to be recorded and documented or it could mean that an acknowledgement is provided of the sorts of interactions undertaken. AI assistants may be used to generate ideas in relation to the given title or theme of the presentation. AI assistants can also be utilised to generate a structure or plan of what the presentation could include. AI assistants may be used as sounding boards and asked to provide feedback on initial ideas for a presentation and how to develop them further. Ensure that you comply with and record your use of AI tools at every stage that is deemed necessary by the guidance provided by your department/faculty/university.

7.13 Time management – When to create and practice a presentation

Research: The vast majority of academic-related assignments will require you to undertake some form of research. This is no different for presentations, as they will need to include links to literature and a reference list. Once you know the title of your presentation, and what the LOs are, you will have an idea of what to research. You can take two approaches. You could do some general research from which to develop a structure before completing some final research to complement and expand on the initial literature/structure. Or, you could generate a structure for the presentation based on the main concept that you have to present, and then complete the research. See the previous chapter (Section 6.12) on 'Searching for literature or references with AI Assistants or Specific AI Tools?' to help get started with finding literature.

Creating and curating the presentation: Once you have a structure and have completed the relevant research, you need to create the presentation. This is where you need to hone your communication and presentation skills as you need to ensure that the key messages are captured in your presentation. This may involve the use of text, images, graphs, videos etc. As you will see in the next section (7.14), AI assistants can be utilised to create the first drafts of a presentation.

Practising the presentation: This is the one area that students often run out of time for. However, if you have planned accordingly, and used AI ethically in the creation of a first draft and so on, this will allow for more time to edit and practice. If it is a timed presentation, then it is essential to time yourself and work on this. If you are to receive questions at the end of your presentation, consider what answers may be asked. An AI assistant may be a good way of exploring potential questions and answers, tell the AI assistant what your presentation is about and ask it to ask you some questions about it.

Get feedback: Whilst there are presentation tools that will record you and provide feedback on your speech, for example, Microsoft PowerPoint's Speaker Coach, it is also a good idea to get feedback from a friend, family member or colleague. Practice presenting to them and ask for their input.

Timeline: How long have you got to do what you need to do? Are there any significant events outside of your control that you know of, and you will have to mitigate? For example, birthdays. Beginning with the date the presentation is due, work backwards so that you know how many weeks or days you have. This will be the first stage of creating your timeline. Now consider breaking down what needs to be done in order for you to successfully complete your presentation into smaller tasks. Align these tasks with your timeline. Allow extra time for slippage, in case you fall behind, or allow for extra editing and practising at the end of the timeline if on task. Of course, an AI assistant can support you in developing a timeline for your presentation.

> **Prompt 7.2   Action plan for a presentation**
>
> INPUT:
>
> I am a university student studying for [enter subject and level of study]. I am currently preparing for a presentation which is due in [enter days/weeks/months]. I want you to help me consider what I need to do and when I need to do it, in order to research, create and practice the presentation before the due date. The presentation title is [enter the title of presentation]. Please ask any further questions that will help you in providing a draft timetable for me to work on.

7.14 Walk-through example: AI-assisted approach to creating a presentation

7.14.1 Developing a plan and structure with Generative AI

The approach to 'Developing a plan and structure with Generative AI' discussed in Chapter 6 (Section 6.9) can easily be adapted to inform the development of a presentation. The key thing to be mindful of here is that it is not an essay but a presentation. Prompt 7.3 is an adaptation of Prompt 6.3 used to create the essay plan and structure.

> **Prompt 7.3   Develop a presentation plan and structure**
>
> INPUT:
>
> **Role:** You are a world expert in [enter subject] who teaches at a university in [country]. You are going to provide an example for your students.
>
> **Task:** You are to provide a structured presentation plan, broken down into sections totalling [enter a number of minutes here] minutes. The presentation must include an introduction and conclusion. The main body should consist of [enter a number of parts].
>
> **Format:** When producing the presentation plan you need to consider the title [enter presentation title here] and the LOs [enter learning outcomes here]. Identify at each part of the plan which LO should be addressed. This presentation is aimed at [enter the audience and purpose of the presentation here]. Please ask any questions needed for further clarification.

7.14.1.1 Presentation example: Child poverty in England

Prompt 7.3 has been used to develop a presentation plan focusing on 'Child poverty in England' and to address the following LOs:

a. Discuss the concept of childhood in the 21st century through various perspectives on a contemporary issue.
b. Explain key aspects of legislation and policy and how these affect services for children, families and communities.
c. Analyse the issues related to the meaningful inclusion of all children.
d. Identify and explain the inclusion of diverse families and communities in professional practice in Early Childhood Education and Care.

AI assistant (Bing.ai) Output:

As a world expert in childhood studies, I would like to present a structured plan for a 10-minute presentation on 'Child poverty in England'. The presentation will include an introduction, four main parts and a conclusion. The main body of the presentation will be broken down into four parts, each addressing one of the LOs. Here is the outline of the presentation:

I. Introduction
   Introduce the topic of child poverty in England.
   Provide a brief overview of the presentation structure.
   Explain the LOs that will be addressed in the presentation.
II. Concept of Childhood in the 21st Century
   Discuss the concept of childhood in the 21st century through various perspectives on a contemporary issue.
   Explain how child poverty is a contemporary issue that affects children's lives.
   Address LO (a).
III. Key Aspects of Legislation and Policy
   Explain key aspects of legislation and policy and how these affect services for children, families and communities.
   Discuss how legislation and policy can help alleviate child poverty.
   Address LO (b).
IV. Issues Related to the Meaningful Inclusion of All Children
   Analyse the issues related to the meaningful inclusion of all children.
   Discuss how child poverty can affect the inclusion of children from diverse backgrounds.
   Address LO (c).
V. Inclusion of Diverse Families and Communities in Professional Practice
   Identify and explain the inclusion of diverse families and communities in professional practice in Early Childhood Education and Care.

> Discuss how professionals can work towards reducing child poverty and promoting inclusion.
> Address LO (d).
> VI. Conclusion
> Summarise the main points of the presentation.
> Reiterate the importance of addressing child poverty in England.
>
> Encourage further discussion and research on the topic.
>
> I hope this presentation plan provides a useful framework for your fellow students to understand the complexities of child poverty in England. Please let me know if you have any further questions or need clarification on any of the points.

AI Assistant Output 6

The above structure provides a great starting point for reflection on the suggested outline of the presentation. Furthermore, it needs reviewing to ensure that it is appropriate and for the student to expand on it as needed in relation to the taught content and the student's interests. This will help to develop the student's voice within the presentation and ensure that the use of Generative AI is in an assisted way.

7.14.2 Generative AI-based presentation tools

This section will discuss how to take an outline or structure of a presentation and generate a first draft using AI assistants. Having shown and used this approach with students, it has often been commented that it feels like cheating. This step, as well as all other steps regarding the use of Generative AI, does have the potential to be treated as academic misconduct. Students need to remain clear on what the guidance is from their university and subject area on using such AI tools. Furthermore, students should also be clear on how they are expected to reference and evidence the use of Generative AI in a transparent way. At the time of writing, how to record and reference the use of Generative AI was and will continue to be an evolving area as new tools, processes and applications are developed. The key thing is to be aware of the guidance and seek further help or support from your university subject or library team as needed.

7.14.3 Creating a presentation with a key phrase or term

This approach does not take into account pre-planning or developing a structure beforehand, as has just been discussed. The following presentation-related AI assistants will take you through several steps to generate content. It is worth noting from the beginning that their focus on content is far more general in nature than what would be expected for university-level work.

7.14.3.1 Example: app.decktopus.com

This tool will take you through a step-by-step process, asking a range of questions (type of answer indicated in bracket afterwards), before creating your presentation:

1. What's your presentation about? (open response)
2. Who is your audience? (it will make a logical suggestion based on your content, which you can edit)
3. What's your aim for this deck? (open response, or select from the number of suggestions that have been generated based on your prior input)
4. How long do you have for your presentation? (select 10, 25 or 40 min)
5. Which template would you like to use? (a range of templates are provided which can all be edited at a later date.)

The above steps are logical and relevant to developing a presentation; however, they remain general. This means that the AI assistant generating your content will be guided on the few lines that you have inputted and then draw on information from the dataset that it has been trained on to create the presentation. This lacks recognition of the assignment brief and the LOs, and limits the input of your personal learning and ideas.

7.14.4 Creating a presentation with a structure

For the reasons that have just been discussed, students will achieve a higher quality first draft from a presentation AI assistant, if they have followed the seven-step checklist in this chapter first. This can then be entered into a Large Language Model, such as Bing.ai or Gemini etc. Once these steps have been followed and the structure created, this can be copied and pasted into a presentation tool. Two examples are explored below. The same six-part structure and text that was generated by Bing.ai in AI Assistant Output 6 was used to inform the following presentations (Figure 7.1).

7.14.4.1 Example: gamma.app

Once you have created a freemium account with Gamma you will be able to start creating. The home screen will present any existing 'Gammas' that you have as well as the option to import, create new from blank or create new with AI. It is this last option that will be discussed here. Once selected, it asks how you would like to get started and offers three options:

Understanding Child Poverty in England

In this presentation, we will delve into the complex issue of child poverty in England. We will explore the impact of legislation, policy, and societal perspectives on the lives of children and families, and discuss strategies for meaningful inclusion in professional practice.

Figure 7.1 Title slide generated by AI in Gamma.app.

1. Paste in text
2. Generate (this is similar to the decktopus.com option above and will generate a presentation in the same way)
3. Import a file (this is a useful option for transforming PPTs/Word docs/Google slides/Google docs into presentations)

With this example, the first option was selected, and the full structure created from Bing.ai was copied and pasted in. Gamma then allows you to select the output as either a presentation, document or web page. It then presents you with a prompt editor. This allows you to edit the settings such as the text content, amount of text per card, audience and tone) and the content (which can be presented in freeform or card-by-card). The continue button will also indicate how many credits (you get a number of free credits when you sign up) it will cost you. Once you continue you then select a theme (style) for the presentation and 'generate' it. Within a few seconds, a full first draft is created with text and images that expand on the structure that was inputted.

7.14.4.2 Content analysis of the first draft using Gamma.app

Although a first draft has been generated on the structure that was created, it needs to be critiqued further to develop student's AI literacy and criticality skills. An initial analysis is presented below using a traffic light system to indicate how successfully content has been created. As can be seen, the

Gamma.app has developed a structure with slide titles and sub-titles appropriately based on the prompt. The majority of slides also include images, which is a good start. However, the level of written text is below the standard expected for university-level presentations as it reads overly descriptive. Finally, there are no references or citations included. This final point is a key indicator that more work needs to be done on the content of this draft if it is to meet basic academic standards (Table 7.3).

Table 7.3 Gamma presentation content analysis

				Content included		
AI tool	Slide number	Title	Sub-title	Level of text	Images	References
Gamma	1	Yes	n/a	Appropriate	One	None
Gamma	2	Yes	Yes	Very general, no analysis	None	None
Gamma	3	Yes	Yes	Very general, no analysis	None	None
Gamma	4	Yes	Yes	Very general, no analysis	One	None
Gamma	5	Yes	Yes	Very general, no analysis	One	None
Gamma	6	Yes	Yes	Very basic conclusion.	One	None

7.14.4.3 Example: tome.app

Once you have created a freemium account with Tome you will be able to start. On the top right-hand side of the home screen, there is a 'create' option. The create option will take you to a new window which is black and displays a chat bar at the bottom centre asking 'What would you like to do?' When you select the chat bar, there is a wide range of options available (from prompt writing tips to contacting Tome support). For the purpose of this example, select 'create a presentation about...'. It will then ask you 'What is the presentation about?' and you will need to copy and paste in the structure that you have developed. This example continues to use the previous structure from AI Assistant Output 6. Once the structure has been copy and pasted in, choose 'generate layout'. This will then present you with a first draft layout of the slides by title. These can be regenerated or edited if needed. There is an option to choose the style of slides and this can be completed for each individual page, or the option to generate all pages can be selected (Figure 7.2).

Figure 7.2 Example slide generated by Tome.app.

7.14.4.4 Content analysis of the first draft using Tome.app

Whilst Tome.app does demonstrate some slight improvements on Gamma's attempt at a first draft in terms of slightly more images created and a better conclusion, the same trends that persist in terms of what makes this a first draft and not a final draft persist (Table 7.4).

Table 7.4 Tome presentation content analysis

				Content included		
AI tool	Slide number	Title	Sub-title	Level of text	Images	References
Tome	1	Yes	n/a	Appropriate	None	None
Tome	2	Yes	Yes	Too text heavy, with no analysis	Two	None
Tome	3	Yes	Yes	Very general, no analysis	None	None
Tome	4	Yes	Yes	Very general and descriptive	One	None
Tome	5	Yes	Yes	Very general, no analysis	Two	None
Tome	6	Yes	Yes	Some key points identified but lacking in analysis	One	None

7.14.5 Summary of creating presentation content with presentation AI assistants

It is important to highlight here that neither presentation tool in the examples above advertises itself as a university-level presentation tool. For this reason, any presentation that has been created by them, even with a detailed structure, should be viewed as a first draft. Credit should be given to both tools' abilities to create a visually appealing and clearly structured presentation with images. Using this sort of tool would be highly beneficial for those who have not yet gained experience in presentation design and construction. However, presentations are expected to mirror and demonstrate an appropriate level of analysis and critique just as an essay would. In the examples explored above, both tools fall short of this. Students would need to give clear consideration in relation to what needs to be done next in order to up-level the presentation.

7.15 Summary of chapter

This chapter provides an in-depth exploration of presentations in relation to university-based assessments. It started with the historical evolution of oral assessments to the present-day incorporation of presentation formats across a range of assessment styles. It addresses the distinction between individual and group presentations, highlighting the unique challenges and opportunities each format presents, such as skill development, accountability, collaboration and managing group dynamics. The chapter explores the different types of presentation styles including face-to-face, online, pre-recorded, poster, interactive, workshop and portfolio presentations, and discusses their alignment with LOs and assessment requirements. It underscores the significance of presentations in fostering critical thinking, effective communication and other employability skills, thereby enhancing students' academic and professional competencies.

The chapter offers guidance in terms of preparing for a presentation covering understanding the presentation brief, conducting appropriate research to create engaging content and practising for the final delivery. Emphasis is placed on the ethical use of Generative AI tools in aiding presentation preparation and creation, ensuring transparency and adherence to the academic standards and guidance at your university. In conclusion, this chapter has considered the skills necessary to effectively plan, develop and deliver presentations where Generative AI may be used to complement the process. Fundamentally, presentations are a vital component of academic assessment and contribute to developing a well-rounded skill set for success in both academic and professional contexts.

7.16 Chapter hacks

1. **Leverage Generative AI Responsibly:** Utilise Generative AI tools to assist in the initial drafting of your presentation but always ensure that the output is critiqued appropriately. Remember to use these tools as a support mechanism rather than a complete solution, maintaining transparency about their use in your work.
2. **Start with a Clear Structure:** Before delving into content creation, outline your presentation's structure, ensuring that it addresses LOs and the core message you intend to convey. This structured approach will provide a solid foundation and ensure that your presentation remains focused and coherent.
3. **Practice Makes Perfect:** Allocate ample time for practising your presentation. Rehearse not just for content delivery but also for managing time, engaging with your audience, and any potential questions that you may receive. Consider recording your practice sessions to identify areas for improvement.
4. **Visual Aids Are Your Allies:** Use visuals judiciously to complement your narrative. Ensure they add value and clarity to your presentation, avoiding overcrowding your slides with text or irrelevant images.
5. **Know Your Audience:** Tailor your presentation to your audience's knowledge level and interests. Engage them with relevant examples, analogies and interactive elements, if appropriate.
6. **Time Management:** Work backwards from your presentation date to create a timeline of tasks, including research, content creation, slide design and practice. Use simple checklists and reminders in your calendar to stay on track.
7. **Ethical Considerations:** Be mindful of the ethical use of content, including proper citation of sources and the respectful use of copyrighted material. Ensure your presentation adheres to academic integrity standards.

7.17 Chapter MCQs

1. Which of the following best describes the evolution of presentations in academic settings?
   A) Presentations have remained largely unchanged since the 16th century
   B) Presentations have evolved from public oral examinations to include diverse formats like online and pre-recorded presentations
   C) Presentations were only introduced in the 20th century with the advent of digital technology

(Continued)

D) Presentations have decreased in importance as written assessments have become more prevalent
2. What is the key difference between individual and group presentations?
   A) Individual presentations do not allow the use of visual aids
   B) Group presentations are less formal and do not require a structured format
   C) Individual presentations focus solely on personal skill development, while group presentations emphasise collaboration and teamwork
   D) There is no significant difference; both formats follow the same assessment criteria
3. Which of the following is NOT a recognised benefit of using presentations as an assessment tool in academia?
   A) Presentations limit students' ability to develop critical thinking skills
   B) They offer students autonomy in conveying understanding and engaging with the audience
   C) Presentations promote effective communication and time management skills
   D) They allow assessors to evaluate students' abilities to synthesise and articulate information coherently
4. In preparing for a presentation, what is the first step according to the chapter's guidelines?
   A) Creating the presentation slides
   B) Practising the presentation delivery
   C) Understanding the module themes and identifying the expected level of study
   D) Collecting feedback from peers
5. How does the chapter suggest students should approach the use of Generative AI in presentations?
   A) Use Generative AI for all aspects of the presentation, including content creation and delivery
   B) Avoid using Generative AI as it compromises academic integrity
   C) Employ Generative AI tools ethically, ensuring transparency and complementing them with critical personal input
   D) Only use Generative AI for visual design and not for content development

Correct answers:

1. Correct answer B
2. Correct answer C
3. Correct answer A
4. Correct answer C
5. Correct answer C

8
Exams

8.1 Chapter objectives

1. Understand the various types of exams and question types that are used at universities
2. Consider the significance and role of exams in assessments
3. Investigate the ethical use of AI in exams and what it might involve as well as its role in supporting exam preparation
4. Navigate the exam roadmap considering the stages along the way
5. Apply AI-assisted learning strategies
6. Critically engage with AI outputs in relation to exams

8.2 Having read this chapter, you will...

1. **Be Familiar with Different Exam Formats:** Understand the nuances and requirements of various exam types including closed, restricted, open-book and take-home exams, and how they are designed to evaluate different aspects of your knowledge and skills.
2. **Recognise Various Question Types:** Gain insight into the structure and purpose of different question formats such as essay-based, short-answer, and multiple-choice questions, and how to approach them effectively.
3. **Appreciate the Role of Exams in Educational Assessments:** Recognise the significance of exams within the broader framework of assessments and their contribution to measuring learning outcomes.
4. **Navigate the Ethical Considerations of AI in Exams:** Be aware of the ethical implications of using Generative AI and other technological aids in exams and understand the importance of maintaining academic integrity.
5. **Utilise AI for Enhanced Exam Preparation:** Learn how to leverage Generative AI tools for studying, revising and preparing for exams, making your study sessions more productive and tailored to your learning needs.
6. **Master the Exam Process:** Be equipped with strategies for effective exam preparation, from understanding the format and content to managing your time and resources efficiently during the study phase.

7. **Implement AI-Assisted Learning Techniques:** Apply AI-enhanced strategies in your study and revision routines to deepen your understanding of the subject matter and improve retention.
8. **Critique AI-Generated Content:** Develop the ability to critically assess AI-generated materials, ensuring that you can distinguish between valuable insights and potential inaccuracies, enhancing your critical thinking skills.

8.3 Introduction

Examinations, or exams, are a core component of many university courses. For some courses, they may serve as both a rite of passage and a critical assessment tool. Exams can act as significant milestones along the academic journey and present a challenge for students to demonstrate their subject mastery and the ability to apply knowledge in various contexts. Beyond mere assessment, exams also shape the learning process, guiding students in identifying key areas of focus and encouraging a deeper engagement with the curriculum. They are a reflection of the educational standards and expectations within Higher Education and aim to demonstrate rigour and discipline within and across programmes.

This chapter offers an exploration of the role of exams within the academic framework. It begins by categorising exams into various types, such as closed, restricted, open-book and take-home. The chapter unpacks the different question formats encountered by students, including essay-based, short-answer and multiple-choice questions, highlighting the distinct skills each format aims to assess. A significant focus is placed on the ethical considerations surrounding exams, particularly in light of the increasing integration of Generative AI tools in academic settings and how these may be utilised in the process. The impact of such technologies on the traditional exam format is considered alongside a discussion on the evolving strategies for effective exam preparation and performance.

8.4 What is an exam?

The concept of an 'examination' is a worldwide one, meaning that most countries will usually have some form of examination situated at key points within their education system. The conception of these examinations though, who they are for, what they include and what they can lead to, differs. One country where exams have been part of the social fabric for most of the last 2000 years is China. The Kjŭ exam served as a mechanism to select the empire's highest officials, beginning in 605 CE and continuing until its abandonment in 1905 CE. O'Sullivan and Cheng (2022) believe that the thousand-year-plus history of the Kjŭ offers us many insights into test development, measurement and communication. Western colonialism is also seen as a historical force for the spread of examinations in the 20th century by Furuta (2021), and this has led to an increasing frequency of high-stakes exams across countries. This leads us to the question of 'what does an exam look like today for university students?'. As with each type of assessment considered in this book, what an exam will involve for students will depend on the programme that they are undertaking. Many teaching and learning websites from universities also provide their interpretation and explanation of the type of exams they use. To begin, we will explore exam formats and potential question types.

8.5 Types of exam

8.5.1 Closed exams

These are the stereotypical pen and paper-based exams that prohibit the use of external resources. The restriction on resources distinguishes this type of exam from others although the same restrictions relating to timing and communication may exist. Because the use of external resources is restricted, students must rely on their own cognitive capabilities to recall information, understand concepts and apply knowledge to problem solve. Closed exams are usually administered within a controlled environment where invigilators ensure adherence to the rules.

8.5.2 Restricted exams

Students are allowed to bring in certain specified items into the exam room. These items are usually clearly predefined by the exam guidelines and can vary depending on the subject and level of study. Example items could be a one-page cheat-sheet created by the student, a textbook or a formula sheet. The key here is that only those items that have been defined prior to the exam are allowed in. Although this style of exam still relies on a student's cognitive capabilities, enabling a restricted item allows for further application of knowledge and skills beyond initial memory and recall. Restricted exams are also conducted in a controlled environment to ensure compliance with the rules regarding permitted materials.

8.5.3 Open-book exams

These are used in Higher Education and within particular professional fields. Students taking open-book exams are allowed to bring and refer to some materials and sometimes access online resources. The specific resources allowed will be stipulated by the exam's guidelines. These types of exams focus on a student's ability to use the resources they have in order to better understand concepts, solve problems and construct arguments. Questions are often designed to be more complex to provoke deeper thinking, analysis and critique.

8.5.4 Take-home exams

This type of exam offers a different experience for the student as they are typically undertaken over a longer period of time, unlike traditional exams. Time periods can range from several hours to several days. This extended time frame allows for more in-depth research and thoughtful responses. Students are generally allowed to use a wide range of resources, including textbooks, notes, online materials and possibly discussions with peers, depending on the exam rules. The extended time period allows for a greater focus on developing research and analysis in the student's submission. Such exams can simulate real-world tasks, such as writing reports, developing a project plan or conducting a detailed analysis within a time-constrained amount of time.

8.6 Typical question types in an exam

8.6.1 Essay-based questions

These are utilised across a range of academic disciplines, particularly in the humanities and social sciences and emphasise critical thinking and written communication. Essay-based responses require the students to formulate a response in their own words and demonstrate a depth of understanding, analysis and communication in long-form, something other style questions do not allow for. This style of question and response is usually designed to allow students to demonstrate their application of higher-order thinking skills. Furthermore, they also allow for the assessment of writing skills relating to a student's capacity to organise their response, draw on appropriate evidence and effectively communicate. Questions can range from broad, thematic discussions to specific, detailed analyses of particular concepts or texts.

8.6.2 Short answer-based questions

These style questions require a short-form response and are used to assess a student's ability to be concise and provide a relevant response to a question or problem. The answer will usually consist of a few sentences or a paragraph. This type of question will be aimed at ensuring students understand key terms, definitions, formulas or principles. A wide range of content can be covered, but this will be done in a much more focused manner. Questions may range from fill-in-the-blank or completing this sentence to more complex answers that require an explanation or analysis. Ultimately, this style of question tests a student's quick recall and understanding of specific key concepts.

8.6.3 Multiple-choice questions

This involves both questions and possible answers, hence the 'choice' aspect. Both correct and incorrect answers will be provided. Sometimes more than one correct answer will need to be chosen or it may be the case of a 'best fit' answer to the question. Multiple choice-style exams can be used across a broad range of subject areas. They are flexible enough to cover a range of content, test knowledge, comprehension and application. The format allows for straightforward and objective scoring as the answer is deemed to be either right or wrong, eliminating the potential bias on the part of the marker for longer-style question/answer formats. These exams are usually completed within a time limit and under typical exam conditions.

8.6.4 Case study-based questions

These style questions will be based on real-life scenarios or complex situations and require students to apply their knowledge to address the problem or respond appropriately to the issue presented. Case studies are usually drawn from realistic scenarios that the student would be likely to encounter beyond their studies and once in employment. The case study may be comprised of a narrative, specific data or both. Essentially, a case study tests a student's application of theory and processes to a practical situation. This usually involves the synthesis of information from multiple sources and the ability to make decisions or recommendations based on logic and evidence.

8.7 Why are exams used in the assessment process?

Exams are a steadfast part of assessment for many courses in Higher Education. They allow for the standardisation of what is being assessed as well as the breadth and depth of what needs to be assessed. This standardisation and objectivity can allow for large student numbers to receive the same questions within the same environment. This is seen as contributing to the fairness of the process. Summative-based exams also offer an endpoint of assessment for students to prepare for. This provides a measurement/score/grade of how effectively students have met the learning outcomes of that module. This format allows for a prompt turnaround in terms of marking is a key benefit in managing large volumes of assessments and ensures timely feedback for students.

Repeating the use of the exam format also allows for the creation of revision materials in terms of past exam questions and papers. Such an approach allows students to familiarise themselves with the style and format, as well as the sort of content that the exam is based on. With students knowing the structured application of an exam, as well as the importance of high-stakes nature of it if a final assessment piece, a student's motivation for revision can increase. When used as a summative assessment it is a key opportunity for students to demonstrate their level of knowledge and analytical skills in relation to that subject. Ensuring that all students pass an exam also means that a minimum level of knowledge has been gained. Finally, as with most assessment practices, students are usually allowed more than one attempt if they are not successful the first time, they take an exam.

8.8 Checklist to begin the assignment: Exam

	Question
1.	Do you understand the content and key themes of your module so far? Are there any aspects that are unclear to you?
2.	Have you grasped the expected level of study, including the depth and complexity required for the exam?
3.	Have you examined the exam brief and materials related to the assessment? Are there past exams that you can look at?
4.	Have you collected and reviewed supporting resources such as lecture notes, textbooks, slides and videos? Have you used an AI assistant to support you with this? See Part 2 Chapter 5
5.	Do you understand the structure of the exam? Reflect on the crucial elements it will encompass in relation to the knowledge you need, the skills to be demonstrated and likely areas of analysis.
6.	Determine or narrow down the topics that are likely to be examined and think about how you can effectively demonstrate your understanding and critical thinking.
7.	When is the exam scheduled? Develop a revision timetable by working backwards from the exam date. What tasks need to be completed and when to ensure you remain on track?

8.9 Understanding the assessment format

8.9.1 Understanding exam preparation and strategy

Exam preparation strategies and requirements will differ based on the type of exam you are preparing for. Overall, regardless of the exam type, each assessment should be presented in a standard format that is aligned with your programme, faculty or university guidelines. This ensures consistency across all assessments and means that students are clear about the expectations for that module. It also ensures that quality standards are maintained and the learning outcomes appropriate for the academic level of study. The instructions for the exam should also include essential information such as the exam format (closed-book, restricted-book, open-book or take-home), clear information that the student needs to know, indicative content and assessment criteria related to the assignment tasks.

8.9.2 Exam overview

As discussed in this chapter, exams can take various formats, so begin by identifying the nature of your upcoming exam. Each type of exam involves different preparation strategies. For a closed-book exam, you may have to focus on memorising key concepts and details of theory. For other types of exams, there is less pressure with regard to memorisation, as you will have access to resources, but you will still need to demonstrate understanding, analysis and critique. The content might require an understanding of theories, problem-solving skills, analytical abilities or the creation of essays. Once you are clear about the type of exam, you can tailor your revision to cover the necessary content areas and skills to prepare you. If possible, review past exam papers or sample questions and seek feedback on practice answers to understand what is expected for higher marks.

8.9.3 Submission details

For any exam, it is crucial to be aware of the date and time, as well as any specific instructions related to the exam setting or submission process. This will be especially important for take-home exams as you will not want to spend time trying to figure out how to submit a take-home exam when you could be completing or finalising it.

8.9.4 Exam process

Ensure that you are aware of what expectations surround the exam process. For example, closed-book exams will be under exam conditions. For online or take-home exams, understand the submission format and platform requirements. Check and double-check the submission details. If unsure, seek clarification from your lecturer well before the deadline to avoid any penalties for incorrect submission. Ensure that everything required, including references if applicable, is included in your final submission.

8.9.5 Content requirements

Make sure that you know what key areas of study the exam is due to cover and that you have considered how these relate to the course's learning outcomes and your own understanding and experience. Depending on the type of exam, the question style will vary. Be aware of this so that the content and format do not catch you off guard. Whilst you are preparing and revising, familiarise yourself with the type and style of both questions and answers by reviewing past examples.

8.10 Is the use of GAI permitted in the final exam?

It is still to be seen what impact Generative AI and such tools will have on exam formats, but the initial assumption for most exam-based assessments is that AI assistants are not allowed to be used in the assessment itself. It will depend on the guidance that accompanies the assignment, but it is unlikely that Generative AI will be allowed in an open-book exam, very unlikely that it will be allowed in a restricted exam, and almost certain that it will not be allowed in a closed exam. Indeed, if used when the guidance specifically forbids the use of Generative AI, then this would constitute academic misconduct and be taken very seriously. The one exam format that has not been mentioned yet is the 'take-home exam', this is the most likely to allow the use of GAI. Again, the assignment guidance should clearly state in what capacity AI assistants can be utilised and how this use should be recorded. Where Generative Artificial Intelligence (GAI) may be used the following questions should be considered:

1. In what capacity can GAI be utilised in the exam?
2. Are there restrictions on how AI should be used?
3. Are there examples from past exams that demonstrate the use of AI in accordance with the guidance?

8.11 What could the ethical use of AI for an exam involve?

The ethical use of Generative AI hinges on transparency, integrity and the augmentation of the student's own efforts. Students should, therefore:

- Acknowledge the assistance of AI assistants in the learning process where required.
- Ensure that reliance on AI assistants does not hinder the student from developing academic skills and therefore misrepresent their capabilities in an exam.
- Use AI assistants as a supplementary tool to enhance their learning experience, rather than as a means to shortcut the learning process.

8.11.1 Study phase

During this phase, students will engage with new material and concepts. This should form the foundation to build knowledge that will be needed for the exam. AI assistants can be utilised in this phase to clarify concepts, provide additional examples or simulate real-world applications of theoretical knowledge. For instance, AI-generated summaries of lengthy readings can help students grasp the main ideas before delving into a detailed study. However, to complement the learning process, students need to critically engage with the AI-generated outputs, cross-referencing them with course content and their own experiences. This will ensure accuracy and depth of understanding are developed and contribute to successful exam preparation.

8.11.2 Revision phase

In this phase, the focus shifts to reinforcing and consolidating knowledge gained during the study phase. Generative AI can play a role in creating customised quizzes or flashcards based on the course content. This will aid in active recall and spaced repetition, which are effective revision strategies. Students should use AI to identify areas that need greater focus and target their revision efforts. AI assistants can be utilised to personalise the revision process in response to a student's input. One of the most effective strategies for doing this is to employ the Socratic method of learning which will lead to a series of questions and answers between the AI assistant and the student (see Prompt 8.1).

Prompt 8.1   Socratic-based prompt for revision

INPUT:

Role: You are a Socratic tutor specialising in study and revision practices.

Task: Engage the student in a critical dialogue for [exam revision/study preparation/learning activities] in [subject or topic specialisation].

Format: Initiate a series of questions that prompt deep reflection in relation to the above subject.

8.11.3 Exam preparation phase

As exams approach, preparation involves using the knowledge gained through the previous two phases and applying it to the relevant exam format and question types that you will undertake. Seeking past exam papers or questions from your lecturers will introduce you to the format and style. Such questions could also be entered into an AI assistant and it prompted to generate further questions in the same style, but on other relevant topics that the exam could cover. This would help to generate a number of questions on a range of subjects and broaden student understanding through practice. If using an AI assistant, it is important to remember that generated exam-style questions should be critiqued by the student in terms of the expected standards and level of study that they are working at.

8.12 Time management: What needs to be done when preparing for an exam?

As with each type of assessment covered in this book so far, knowing the due date, or in the case of exams, the date they will take place, should be your starting point. From there, you can work backwards and calculate how many weeks you have to prepare. It may be that you are given exam dates for the whole year at the beginning of the year. It would be logical to prioritise the exams that come first, but ensure that you are not leaving yourself short of time to prepare for the later exams. It is also a good idea to factor in any significant events outside of your studies such as holiday periods, birthdays etc., so that you can accommodate these in your planning. When you have worked out a timeline in terms of the number of weeks that you have to prepare for an exam, review the previous section and the three phases: study, revision and exam preparation. Allocate sufficient time to each phase across your timeline so that you can identify what you should be focusing on and when. If you fall behind, you will also know what you need to do to catch up. Of course, an AI assistant can support you in developing a timeline for your exam preparation and revision.

Prompt 8.2   Action plan for an exam

INPUT:

I am a university student studying for [enter subject and level of study]. I am currently preparing for an exam which is due in [enter days/weeks/months]. I want you to help me consider what I need to do and when I need to do it in relation to studying, revising and preparing for the exam. The exam will be on [enter focus of examination]. Please ask any further questions that will help you in providing a draft timetable for me to work on.

8.13 Familiarisation with the learning outcomes that the exam is based on

Depending on how many assignments there are in a module or programme, all or a select amount of the learning outcomes may tested in the exam. This means that an exploration of the relevant learning outcomes, even before the exam has been set, will help prepare the student in advance. The general assumption is that relevant content or skills are covered in the taught sessions, this is called constructive alignment as it aligns taught sessions with the assessment and learning outcomes. However, depending on the level of study there may be a greater emphasis on self-directed or independent study outside of sessions. Regardless, the learning outcomes aligned to the exam assignment can help as guidance for both the study and revision phases.

8.13.1 PROMPT-assisted preparation for an exam

To create a prompt for an AI assistant to help you get started ensuring that you have all of the following information:

1. Title of course you are studying
2. The level you are studying at
3. The title of the module
4. The type of exam and the sort of questions it will involve

---

Prompt 8.3   Preparing for an exam

INPUT:

Role: you are coaching me on how to prepare for an upcoming exam which is a [enter the style of exam here] exam.

Task: The exam is part of a [enter level and title of programme] module called [enter the name of the module here]. It will involve [enter the type of questions that are expected in the exam]. It will be based on the following learning outcomes: [please list all relevant learning outcomes].

Format: please suggest a step-by-step process that will help me study for and revise for the upcoming exam.

8.14 Walk-through example: AI-assisted approach to a take-home exam assignment

8.14.1 Preparation

For the purpose of this example, we will explore a Level 4 assessment as part of a BA in Sociology. It is an introductory module designed to test students' knowledge of relevant sociological theories and methods. The module includes a take-home exam and gives students a 24-hour period to complete the assessment. The exam is based on a comparison of two journal articles (the exact articles are confirmed when the assessment is released) and involves the following learning outcomes:

> **Example Learning Outcomes: Exam**
>
> A) Identify the relationship between theory, methodology and methods
>
> Categorise the theories and methodologies discussed in this module in peer-reviewed journal articles.

Based on the example information above, the prompt was adjusted and entered into Claude.ai. Claude.ai's response to the prompt provided some key insights that would help start the preparation for the upcoming exam:

> **AI Assistant (Claude.ai) Output**
>
> 1. Review the learning outcomes and make sure you understand what they are asking for. It seems this exam will focus on applying sociological theories and methods, so refresh yourself on the key theories and methods you learned.
> 2. Re-read any notes or textbooks related to the theories and methods covered in class. Make flashcards or summaries to help memorise key points.
> 3. Find two-to-three peer-reviewed journal articles that apply sociological theories/methods. Read them closely and take notes on the theories, methods, results and comparisons made.
> 4. Practice comparing the articles – how do they apply theories similarly/differently? Do they use qualitative or quantitative methods? What are their findings? Get comfortable discussing the comparisons.
> 5. Plan to spend a significant portion of time on the exam analysing and comparing your selected articles. Be ready to identify theories and methods, relate them to concepts from class and draw conclusions.
> 6. On the day of the exam, carefully read through all instructions and questions. Create an outline of your response before writing. Stay focused on addressing the learning outcomes.

7. Budget your time wisely so you can thoughtfully respond to each part of the exam. Leave time to thoroughly proofread your work.
8. Check in with your professor if you need any clarifications on the exam requirements. And get plenty of rest ahead of time!

AI Assistant Output 7

Planning your time to answer the exam question once it has been released.

> This take-home exam allows for a 24-hour period within which students are to compare and evaluate the two articles in relation to the following aspects:
>
> - Methods
> - Methodology
> - Theoretical background
> - Inductive/deductive approach
> - Standpoint
> - Epistemology
> - Ontology
> - Axiology
>
> Article 1 can be found here*.
>
> Article 2 can be found here*.
>
> Remember:
>
> - Do not use bullet points – write out your answers in full sentences
> - Provide definitions for the terminology
> - Justify your points using the two articles as evidence
> - There is no word limit – but the guidance is 1,000–2,000 words
>
> Fill in and include the Sociology Assignment cover sheet with your submission.

*the exact articles have been omitted from this example

Once the exam questions and more details have been provided, an AI assistant can also be utilised to help draft and structure the time available to complete the exam. Furthermore, if you continue to use the same AI assistant that was used to help with the study phase, the revision phase and the exam preparation phase, then the AI assistant will be able to tailor its responses further based on this as well as the specific instructions of the exam. Make sure that the AI assistant is able to recap what has been discussed so far by asking it to provide a summary. If there is anything significant that is missed in the summary, correct the AI assistant and make sure this is acknowledged moving forward. From there, you can share the take-home exam instructions with the AI assistant and prompt it to provide a draft structure of the timings and actions that would be needed in order to successfully complete the exam within the time period. AI Assistant Output 7 is an example response from Claude.ai based on the example learning outcomes and instructions in this section. Please note that the initial response from Claude did not include time for breaks or sleep, so the AI assistant was asked to rework its guidance to incorporate this.

> **AI Assistant (Claude.ai) Output:**
>
> **5 pm: exam instructions and details released.**
>
> **5:30–7:30 pm: Read Articles and Take Notes (2 hours)**
>
> Thoroughly read both articles, taking detailed notes on key aspects like methods, theories, etc.
>
> **8 pm–9 pm: Dinner**
>
> **9 pm–12 am: Define Key Terms and Detailed Outline (3 hours)**
>
> Based on articles and class notes, write out definitions for all key terms you need to address. Create a thorough outline for your essay, noting how you'll compare the two articles for each key term.
>
> **12–1 am: Get ready for bed**
>
> **1 am–6 am: Sleep**
>
> **6 am–7 am: Wake up and Breakfast**
>
> **7 am–12 pm: Write First Draft (5 hours)**
>
> Spend significant time writing your full first draft, aiming for 1,500–2000 words. Refer frequently to the outline.
>
> **12–1 pm: Lunch break**
>
> **1 pm–3 pm: Review and Edit Draft (2 hours)**
>
> Carefully re-read the first draft, editing for clarity, concision, depth of analysis and meeting requirements.
>
> **3 pm–4 pm: Final Edits (1 hour)**
>
> Do final edit focusing on tightening analysis and proofreading.
>
> **4 pm–4:30 pm: Submit (30 min)**
>
> Complete the cover sheet and submit the final draft. Double-check you met all requirements.

AI Assistant Output 8

As can be seen from the above structure, the AI assistant has successfully split the time available into the logical tasks that would need to be undertaken in order to successfully complete this assignment. Whilst such a structure may need amending further to make it realistic on the student's part, it is a good attempt at covering the essential tasks such as reading, planning, writing, reviewing, finalising and most importantly – submitting. This last point is often an area that may get pushed out of consideration due to the immediacy of the other section's pressures. However, allowing a 30-minute window and then a 30-minute buffer afterwards should hopefully address any potential delays in submitting the essay successfully!

8.15 Summary of chapter

The chapter began by defining exams and situating them within the broader context of university assessment, highlighting their significance in evaluating student knowledge and skills. It has explored various types, such as closed, restricted, open-book and take-home exams, considering their unique characteristics. The chapter considers different question formats, including essay-based, short-answer, multiple-choice and case study questions, explaining how each type assesses different aspects of student learning and comprehension. The discussion then shifted to the role of exams in the assessment process, underscoring their utility in standardising the evaluation of student performance and facilitating the fair and objective measurement of academic achievement. The chapter then addressed the strategic aspect of exam preparation, offering insights into effective study techniques, time management and the use or creation of exam papers to familiarise oneself with the exam format and expectations.

A significant focus of this chapter is placed on the ethical considerations and potential implications of using Generative AI in exam settings. It examines the rules surrounding the use of AI tools in various exam formats and discusses the importance of transparency, integrity and the augmentation of student efforts when integrating AI into the learning process. The chapter provides practical advice on leveraging AI during the study and revision phases to enhance learning outcomes. It suggests ways in which AI can assist in creating customised revision materials, such as quizzes or flashcards, and emphasises the importance of a critical engagement with AI-generated content to ensure depth of understanding and knowledge retention. Finally, the chapter presents a detailed walk-through of an AI-assisted approach to preparing for a take-home exam, illustrating how AI can help structure study and revision schedules, clarify complex concepts and simulate exam conditions to improve exam performance.

8.16 Chapter hacks

1. **Leverage AI for Efficient Study**: Utilise Generative AI to create summaries, flashcards and practice questions tailored to your course material. This can significantly streamline your study process and ensure a more engaging and productive revision session.
2. **Master Exam Formats**: Familiarise yourself with the specific format of your upcoming exam (closed, restricted, open-book and take-home) and tailor your preparation accordingly. For instance, focus on memorisation and recall for closed exams, and on the application and analysis for open-book or take-home exams.
3. **Question Type Strategies**: Use AI assistants to develop specific strategies for different question types. For essay questions, practice structuring your thoughts and arguments coherently. For multiple-choice questions, hone your skills in identifying key information and eliminating incorrect options.
4. **Ethical AI Use**: Understand the boundaries of ethical AI use in exams. Use AI tools for preparation but ensure you can demonstrate your knowledge independently, respecting the guidelines set by your educational institution.
5. **Simulate Exam Conditions**: Create practice exams for yourself under the appropriate conditions. This will not only help with time management but also reduce exam day anxiety by familiarising you with the pressure of completing an exam.
6. **AI-Assisted Mock Exams**: Use AI to generate or provide access to a variety of practice questions and mock exams. Critically evaluate the AI-generated answers and feedback to deepen your understanding and application of the material.
7. **Feedback Loop**: Incorporate feedback from AI tools, peers, and educators to refine your knowledge and exam strategies continually. Use AI-generated quizzes and assessments to identify areas of weakness and focus your revision efforts accordingly.
8. **Time Management Blueprint**: Plan your exam day strategy, allocating specific times to reading, planning, writing and reviewing your answers. Use AI to help draft a realistic schedule, including breaks, to maintain focus and energy throughout the exam period.
9. **Learning Outcomes Alignment**: Ensure your preparation aligns with the learning outcomes of your course. Use these outcomes as a guide to focus your study and revision on the most relevant and critical areas.
10. **AI for Last-Minute Prep**: In the final run-up to the exam, use AI to quickly revisit key concepts, definitions and summaries. This can be especially useful for reinforcing your understanding and recall of crucial information.

8.17 Chapter MCQs

1. What is the primary purpose of closed exams?
   A) To allow the use of external resources during the exam
   B) To assess students' ability to recall and apply knowledge without external aids
   C) To evaluate students' research and analysis skills over an extended period
   D) To test students' ability to access and utilise online resources
2. Which type of exam typically allows students to bring specified items into the exam room?
   A) Open-book exams
   B) Take-home exams
   C) Closed exams
   D) Restricted exams
3. Open-book exams focus primarily on a student's ability to:
   A) Memorise and recall information
   B) Use resources to understand concepts and solve problems
   C) Write extensive essays on a wide range of topics
   D) Complete the exam within a very short time frame
4. Essay-based questions are particularly utilised in which fields?
   A) Natural Sciences and Mathematics
   B) Humanities and Social Sciences
   C) Engineering and Technology
   D) Business and Management
5. What is a key advantage of multiple-choice questions in exams?
   A) They allow for subjective grading
   B) They require long-form written responses
   C) They enable straightforward and objective scoring
   D) They are primarily used for in-depth case studies

Correct answers:

1. Correct answer B
2. Correct answer D
3. Correct answer B
4. Correct answer B
5. Correct answer C

9

E-portfolios

9.1 Chapter objectives

1. Understand the concept and purpose of different types of e-portfolios
2. Recognise the role of e-portfolios in assessment
3. Explore, select and utilise appropriate e-portfolio tools
4. Consider ethical issues such as privacy, consent and intellectual property, when planning and creating an e-portfolio
5. Reflect and personalise your e-portfolio but integrate multimedia aspects and a diverse range of content
6. Ensure that e-portfolios and their associated tasks contribute to continued professional development

9.2 Having read this chapter, you will...

1. **Identify Different Types of E-Portfolios**: Understand the distinct purposes and functionalities of various e-portfolio types, including assessment, developmental, showcase, reflective and professional e-portfolios.
2. **Align E-Portfolios with Learning Outcomes**: Learn how to effectively link your e-portfolio content to specific learning outcomes (LOs), ensuring that your portfolio demonstrates your competencies and understanding of the subject matter comprehensively.
3. **Select and Use E-Portfolio Tools**: Gain insights into the selection of appropriate digital platforms and tools for creating and maintaining your e-portfolio, along with an understanding of their features and how to leverage them to your advantage.
4. **Incorporate Reflective and Diverse Content**: Develop the skill to create a reflective narrative within your e-portfolio, integrating various forms of content, including multimedia, to showcase your academic achievements and personal growth effectively.
5. **Navigate Ethical Considerations**: Become aware of the ethical implications involved in creating e-portfolios, especially concerning content that includes or affects others, and

learn how to navigate these considerations responsibly in relation to the use of AI assistants.
6. **Apply Theoretical Knowledge Practically**: Learn to connect theoretical knowledge from your field to the practical experiences and achievements showcased in your e-portfolio, enhancing the depth and relevance of your content.
7. **Manage Your E-Portfolio Project**: Explore effective time management and planning strategies for developing your e-portfolio, ensuring a coherent and comprehensive presentation of your work within set deadlines.

9.3 Introduction

An electronic portfolio, commonly referred to as an e-portfolio, is a digital collection showcasing an individual's achievements, learning experiences, and future goals tailored for a specific audience or purpose. The 'electronic' aspect of an e-portfolio extends beyond the traditional, paper-based folders and scrapbooks, by encompassing the digital as a medium. Many university courses include e-portfolios as a type of assessment. For this reason, the range and variability of what an e-portfolio involves are difficult to capture in a single chapter, but they commonly act as spaces that allow students to capture their growth, skills and aspirations. E-portfolios can evidence the connection between learning experiences and personal development for students. This chapter will explore some of the most common features of an e-portfolio with specific examples.

The chapter is structured to guide you through the various dimensions of e-portfolios. It will explore the types of e-portfolios ranging from assessment-focused to developmental and showcase portfolios. Part of this will involve consideration of their specific applications within the context of a university. This discussion extends to the use of e-portfolios as assessments and their role in capturing the breadth and depth of students' competencies. Practical aspects are also considered, including the selection of appropriate tools and software, the formulation of impactful LOs and the ethical considerations relating to the use of Generative AI in relation to e-portfolio design and creation. This chapter will equip students with the knowledge and insights necessary to approach and complete e-portfolios ethically and appropriate way.

9.4 What is an e-portfolio?

E-portfolios often evidence the journey and processes that have informed student's learning. They are used across a broad range of subject areas in a diverse number of ways. For many subject areas, the development of e-portfolios demonstrates a range of skills that contribute to experience and employability beyond it. An e-portfolio is a digital collection showcasing an individual's achievements, learning processes and future aspirations. It involves more than a compilation of works as it should integrate various multimedia elements like text, images, videos and audio. This can allow for a dynamic and personalised presentation. E-portfolios are used for different purposes, including reflective learning, assessment and professional development. They embody a learner's progress over time and are tailored to specific audiences, often utilising online platforms for easy access and sharing. This approach is an essential contribution in terms of assessment types for modern and future-facing subject areas. E-portfolios can also relate to the professional field to demonstrate competencies, encourage self-reflection and support continuous professional growth.

There are a range of e-portfolio types:

1. **Assessment E-Portfolios:** These are used specifically for evaluating a learner's performance against predefined criteria. They often contain assignments, projects and other forms of assessment that are evaluated to meet educational or accreditation standards. Assessment e-portfolios are commonly used in universities for grading or competency evaluation and may incorporate aspects of the other types of portfolios mentioned below.
2. **Developmental (or Process) E-Portfolios:** These e-portfolios focus on the development and progress of the learner over time. They typically include reflections, feedback and evidence of learning growth. They can be used for self-assessment and to track the evolution of skills and knowledge. Or they may be an assessed item which aims to capture a student's development each year and across their programme of study. This will enable students to break down their experience into key areas of growth and consider future areas for development. For example, students on a teacher training programme may be required to create a portfolio to capture their growth and application of knowledge in understanding how pupils are taught and learn. This could include supporting documentation such as planning and reflections on lessons, as well as action points that were addressed in follow-up sessions.
3. **Showcase (or Product) E-Portfolios**: Unlike developmental portfolios, showcase e-portfolios are often used at the end of a learning period to present the best work of an individual. They are curated to demonstrate the highest level of achievement in specific areas, suitable for job applications, academic evaluations or professional credentialing. These can be based on final-year outputs such as a thesis or project. The idea here is to really demonstrate and celebrate the level of mastery that you have achieved. For example, a sociology student who chooses to investigate the impact of urban regeneration on the community could showcase their key findings and recommendations with local media outlets, councillors or MPs to advocate for the community.
4. **Reflective E-Portfolios:** Central to this type of portfolio is the element of reflection. Learners are encouraged to think critically about their learning experiences, skills acquired and knowledge gained. Reflective e-portfolios are valuable for personal development and reflexivity, aiding in the synthesis of learning experiences and the development of confidence. They are particularly useful for practical or real-world

experiences such as work placements. For example, psychology students may be asked to reflect on their personal growth and understanding of psychological theories through practical experiences, such as internships or research projects and record this.
5. **Professional E-Portfolios:** These are typically used by individuals entering or already in the workforce to demonstrate their achievements. This may cover work experience, skills and career goals. Professional e-portfolios are often shared with potential employers or professional networks and are particularly important in business and creative-related industries. Professional e-portfolios can be linked to professional standards to ensure that students evidence their competence at the required level for that sector. For example, social work students may be required to complete case studies regarding placement experience, reflections on policy and procedure and certificates from completed training courses in preparation for meeting professional standards.

9.5 Why are e-portfolios used in the assessment process?

A key reason for using e-portfolios is to enable the student to tailor the content and key messages so that they relate to and identify with the student's experience and ability. This offers a level of flexibility and personalisation within the process. Depending on the type of e-portfolio, individualised goals may be set, evidenced and achieved to demonstrate, personal, academic and professional growth. E-portfolios can also allow for the curation of a range of artefacts that showcase a student's achievements and work. This process is both reflective and reflexive in nature, aimed at creating a deeper level of understanding and connection between learning, assessments and a student's own growth. E-portfolios can provide a structure to make sense of and connect a range of achievements across a student's journey. They provide a platform for students to draw on as they progress through their studies and begin to think about employment opportunities beyond. Creating and maintaining e-portfolios also evidence digital literacy skills, organisation, critical thinking and communication.

A well-managed approach to e-portfolios offers students, staff and employers ways of:

- Evidencing employability skills and attributes
- Assessing learning in a more authentic way
- Making sense of learning and achievements across various parts of the curriculum
- Engaging with personal and continuing professional development
- Making coherent links between different stages of learning
- Achieving deeper learning through reflection and dialogue
- Developing lifelong learning skills

(JISC, 2021)

9.6 Checklist to begin the assignment: E-portfolio

A seven-step checklist to completing your e-portfolio.

Table 9.1 A seven-step checklist to completing your e-portfolio

	Questions
1	Do you understand your course's definition of an e-portfolio and its associated LOs? Reflect on how these outcomes should be represented in your e-portfolio's structure.
2	Have you identified where to source information for your e-portfolio? Are there specific requirements, or is it more open-ended? Consider the relevance of potential content in relation to the LOs.
3	Have you planned what content to include, mindful of timing and ethical considerations, such as permissions for using content involving others?
4	Are you ready to actively engage with the e-portfolio process, seeking assistance where necessary and starting to compile your content?
5	As you engage, have you thought about how to effectively integrate your experiences and create connections that underscore your learning journey?
6	Are you regularly reviewing your e-portfolio to ensure it aligns with your initial plan, addressing any discrepancies promptly?
7	Finally, consider how the entire e-portfolio creation process and learning that your evidence can help you beyond this assessment and your course of study.

9.7 E-portfolio tools and software

The tool, software or how you are expected to submit your e-portfolio will be determined by the course you are studying. Just as the format, shape and size of an e-portfolio varies, so too do the tools that can be used to create them. Sometimes, these tools will be within your university's Virtual Learning Environment – for example, you may be asked to submit it as a blog post within Blackboard or an e-portfolio within Canvas. You may be asked to use a sanctioned third-party tool such as Mahara or you may have the freedom to choose how you create and capture it yourself. If it is your decision what tool you use, then you should also consider the submission format. For example, can you share a link to your e-portfolio or does it have to be downloaded and submitted as a certain file? If you are given such freedom, great! But please do ensure that you have checked and double-checked that you will be able to submit your portfolio within the parameters of the required format.

9.8 Understanding the assessment format

9.8.1 Understanding an e-portfolio assignment brief

Assignment briefs will vary in format based on the type of e-portfolio you are being asked to complete, but they should still be presented within a standard brief format for your study programme/faculty/university. This ensures consistency across all assessments. Such standardisation means that students are familiar with the requirements, quality standards are met and LOs align with the academic level of study. The brief for the e-portfolio should also include what essential elements are needed, clear objectives which the student should be able to understand, content expectations, and assessment criteria related to the e-portfolio tasks.

9.8.2 Assignment overview

As previously mentioned in this chapter, assessed e-portfolios can take different formats, so begin identifying what type of e-portfolio your assignment is: process, showcase, reflective or professional? All types will in involve multiple components, including the creation of content and the relevant commentary or analysis expected for that format. The content may need to be composed of various forms of media such as text, images, videos and audio. What is important here is that once you are clear about the type of e-portfolio required, you begin to identify the types of media and what they will cover, to ensure the LOs of the assignment are met. If possible, ask to see previous examples, or part examples of previous portfolios. As well as example portfolios, ask to see examples of feedback that was given to higher scoring portfolios as this will help you understand what the highest scoring e-portfolios do well.

9.8.3 Submission details

As for any assignment, please check the submission dates for all aspects of the e-portfolio. Depending on your module, you may have the opportunity to submit drafts of the portfolio or discuss them with a lecturer for feedback. Sometimes e-portfolios can be submitted in stages/sections, meaning that different sections will have different due dates. Such a phased approach allows for lecturers to provide feedback as well as a feedforward in relation to future sections.

9.8.4 Submission process

For e-portfolio submissions, understand the format and platform requirements. Determine if components like reflective narratives and multimedia elements should be combined into a single file or submitted separately. Know the acceptable file types, how to convert and merge files, and whether to submit through the university's Virtual Learning Environment (VLE) or an external portal like Turnitin. If unsure, seek guidance from your lecturer well before the deadline to avoid penalties for incorrect submission. Ensure everything required, including references, is included in your final submission.

9.8.5 Content requirements

Make sure that you know what the key components of the e-portfolio need to cover and that you have considered how these will relate to your learning and experience. Guidance will vary depending on the type of e-portfolio as well as the level of study. Typically, more freedom may be given to higher-level portfolios or where an aspect of specialised subject knowledge is chosen by the student. Guidelines may require an introduction to the portfolio and each section, as well as summaries and a conclusion. This will more than likely include a title, contents, headings and subheadings (these can be written, spoken or visualised). Overall, a clear and coherent structure should enable the lecturer, when reviewing or marking your e-portfolio, to navigate it with ease.

9.8.6 Learning outcomes

E-portfolios should integrate LOs that align with the expectations of the style required. For example, a reflective e-portfolio will include an LO relating to reflection, whereas a process-based portfolio may include LOs relating to problem-solving and creativity. A key opportunity afforded by the use of e-portfolios is to allow for evidence of student development rather than content delivery. Using language from Bloom's Taxonomy, such as 'evaluate' or 'create', in LOs will aim to assess a students' ability to apply theory to practice. When done well this will demonstrate a deep and reflective approach to the portfolio. If there are any aspects of an LO that you do not understand – then make sure you ask your lecturer or peers in your group. An AI assistant may also be utilised to help you understand the LOs for your e-portfolio (see Prompt 9.1).

Prompt 9.1   Understanding learning outcomes for an e-portfolio

INPUT:

You are a world-renowned expert in [enter a subject that you are studying] and work at a world-leading university in [enter the country of study to provide context]. You are going to offer an explanation and breakdown of the following LO which are part of a [enter type of e-portfolio here]. In this process, you need to:

> 1. Identify the key components of the LO.
> 2. Break down the verbs and provide examples of what this might involve in the e-portfolio.
> 3. Clarify the content and context of each LO.
> 4. Consider the key skills that need to be mastered in relation to each LO when studying at [enter your level of study here]. What is the appropriate level of mastery that you should be demonstrating at the level you are studying? For example, is understanding enough, or should you be expected to critique as well?
> 5. You are then going to finish by asking a number of questions that will help me to reflect on what has been taught so far, how this relates to each LO and its potential use for the e-portfolio.
>
> The LOs for this assignment are: [enter a list of LOs aligned to the assignment].

9.9 Is the use of GAI permitted in the final assignment?

Before using Generative AI in e-portfolios, students must verify permission and usage guidelines with the module team:

1. Is Generative AI allowed in creating the e-portfolio?
2. What are the restrictions on using Generative AI (e.g., permitted for organising content and summarising reflections but not for generating reflections)?
3. Are there examples of acceptable Generative AI use in e-portfolios? If not, request guidance.

9.10 What could the ethical use of GAI in an e-portfolio involve?

Generative AI will be able to assist in your approach to creating an e-portfolio in a number of ways. Firstly, as will be discussed in the next section, AI assistants can support students with generating ideas for their e-portfolio based on the LOs and assignment brief, by entering them as a prompt and asking for further explanation and ideas. Generative AI can create frameworks in response to the LOs and provide students with initial ideas for the portfolio in advance of starting it. Some e-portfolio tools or platforms may have Generative AI features within them that can help with content creation and organisation; however, how this should be acknowledged or referenced will depend on the guidance from the teaching team. Generative AI can also enable students to diversify the range of content within their e-portfolio; for example, using text-to-image tools to visualise a text entry and enhance that section. Generative AI can assist students in organising and presenting ideas, thoughts and reflections. Further feedback on design, purpose and audience can also be gathered. In each of these suggested areas, the key is for students to use GAI as a tool to enhance their own work, not replace it. Ethical use involves clear acknowledgement of GAI's role in the process and ensuring the final e-portfolio authentically represents the student's own efforts and learning achievements.

9.11 Example learning outcomes from an E-portfolio

For the e-portfolio LOs below, a different approach will be taken to understanding them than used for the previous sections on essay and presentation. This is because these e-portfolio LOs can be viewed as more holistic in terms of their construction and evidence within the e-portfolio. Therefore, viewing the key components of each LO as parts of the whole e-portfolio will aid in developing your understanding of what the e-portfolio may cover. Prompt 9.2 was edited to accommodate the below example LOs and the response can be seen in AI Assistant Output 7.

9.11.1 Example Learning Outcomes: E-portfolio

a. Recognise and understand key reflective models and apply critical reflection for personal, academic and professional learning.
b. Identify key professional behaviours and perform these behaviours when engaging with children, young people and professionals.
c. Understand effective ways of working with others and plan, lead, reflect upon and evaluate interventions or activities, supporting other practitioners, with children and young people.
d. Work as part of a team, critically reflecting on your own contribution and leadership role.

Prompt 9.2   Connecting learning outcomes to placement/ work experience

INPUT:

Role: You are a senior academic who teaches on [enter your course here].

Task: to provide a breakdown of the following LOs capturing the sentiment of what each one is asking for, explaining how they could be connected and their relevance for an e-portfolio.

Format: to consider what sort of experiences or evidence may be captured towards each LO for an undergraduate student on a work placement [Enter the LOs].

AI assistant (Gemini.ai/Google) Output:

Breakdown of LOs for Undergraduate Work Placement:

a. Reflective Models and Critical Reflection:
    - Sentiment: This LO emphasises understanding and applying frameworks for examining your own experiences and learning from them.
    - Placement Experiences:
        - Observe and participate in reflective practices used by the organisation.
        - Engage in individual and group reflection on your placement experiences.
        - Present a reflective piece using a specific model (e.g., Gibbs).
    - Evidence:
        - Reflective journals or reports using chosen models.
        - Feedback from supervisors on participation in reflective activities.
        - Examples of applying insights from reflection to improve practice.
b. Professional Behaviours with Children, Young People and Professionals:
    - Sentiment: This LO focuses on identifying and exhibiting appropriate conduct and ethics in various workplace settings.
    - Placement Experiences:
        - Shadow different professionals to observe their interactions with children, young people and colleagues.
        - Participate in team meetings and observe communication dynamics.
        - Undertake tasks that require professional behaviour (e.g., leading activities and presenting).
    - Evidence:
        - Supervisor observations and feedback on professional conduct.
        - Self-reflection on adherence to professional codes and ethics.
        - Examples of successfully navigating professional interactions.
c. Collaboration, Intervention Planning and Supporting Practitioners:
    - Sentiment: This LO highlights teamwork, planning and supporting colleagues in working with children and young people.
    - Placement Experiences:
        - Collaborate with other professionals on planning and delivering interventions or activities.
        - Provide support to colleagues (e.g., co-leading activities, observing and providing feedback).
        - Reflect on teamwork dynamics and the effectiveness of interventions.

(Continued)

> - Evidence:
>   - Joint planning documents and evaluations of interventions.
>   - Peer feedback on collaboration and support provided.
>   - Reflection on personal contribution to teamwork and intervention outcomes.
> d. Teamwork, Self-Reflection on Contribution and Leadership:
>   - Sentiment: This LO emphasises working effectively in teams, critically evaluating your own role and demonstrating leadership potential.
>   - Placement Experiences:
>   - Take on various roles within teams (e.g., leader, follower and mediator).
>   - Observe and reflect on the leadership styles of others.
>   - Seek feedback on your own contributions and leadership potential.
>   - Evidence:
>   - Peer and supervisor feedback on team participation and leadership.
>   - Self-reflection on strengths and weaknesses in teamwork and leadership.
>   - Examples of taking initiative and contributing effectively to team goals.
>
> Additional Tips:
>
> - Connect these LOs to specific placement tasks and responsibilities.
> - Discuss with your placement supervisor how you can best achieve these outcomes through your placement activities.
> - Seek regular feedback from supervisors and peers to track your progress.
> - Use various methods to capture evidence of your learning, such as journals, reports, presentations and portfolios.
>
> Remember, a successful work placement involves actively seeking opportunities to learn and grow within a specific context. By actively engaging with these LOs, you can gain valuable skills and experiences that will benefit your personal, academic and professional development.
>
> I hope this breakdown is helpful! Please let me know if you have any other questions.

AI Assistant Output 7

As you can see from AI Assistant Output 7, each LO is summarised using key words and then broken down further in relation to sentiment, placement experience and evidence. Gemini.ai also provides some valid 'Additional Tips'. Although these are still generalised and not specific to the student, type of placement to be undertaken or the format of the e-portfolio, they are a valid bank of statements to get students thinking about what needs to be experienced in order to create the e-portfolio and key place to start when planning what to do!

9.12 Time management – What needs to be done by when for an e-portfolio?

The essentials of action planning for any assignment remain true: know your due date and work back from there. This will tell you how many weeks you have. Once you know how many weeks you have, you can then begin to assign relevant tasks to the number of weeks you have to complete the e-portfolio. If the e-portfolio is based on a placement experience as the example LOs are in the previous section, students will only be able to get ahead so far and need to wait for placement to start. This is because the actual experience of placement informs the e-portfolio. However, this does not mean that you should not aim to stay focused in terms of what you will need to do to complete the e-portfolio. For example, in response to the example LOs and Gemini.ai's response an example action plan could look like.

Table 9.2 E-portfolio Action Plan

E-portfolio due in...	On placement	Actions
6 weeks	No	1. Review all e-portfolio guidance. Mind map initial ideas
5 weeks	No	2. Review all placement guidance. Review mind map
4 weeks	Yes	3. *Learning Outcome B*: observe a member of staff in their professional role. Action plan key points that you will take forward in terms of practice
3 weeks	Yes	4. *Learning Outcome D*: Seek feedback from a senior member of staff on your contributions to placement so far. Action plan key points for development
2 weeks	Yes	5. *Learning Outcome C*: collaborate with members of staff and support in the delivery of tasks relating to their professional role. Seek feedback once completed
1 week	No	6. *Learning Outcome A*: Reflect on placement experience to date- how have each of the activities undertaken across the three weeks of placement informed your practice going forward? Use a reflective model
		7. Compile e-portfolio
E-portfolio due for submission!!!		

Table 9.2 is an example of how you can take LOs, break them down into tasks and plan accordingly in chronological order. It is important to note, that LOs A–D, were not simply transferred to weeks one to three of placement, but the order was changed based on a logical interpretation of what would be best to do first and consideration of which LOs build on the others. Ensuring that you are guided by both your experiences as well as the appropriate LO will help to make connections between them more easily, and this is a key step in both undergraduate and postgraduate enquiry.

9.13 Connecting theory and literature to an e-portfolio entry using an AI assistant

This chapter has so far focused on the details of the different types of e-portfolios, practical considerations in terms of the format and explored some example e-portfolio LOs. However, what has not been discussed so far is how to establish links between the content of an e-portfolio and relevant theory. Of course, this will fundamentally depend on your subject area, programme of study and requirements of the e-portfolio. You should already have some key insight regarding the type of theory that needs incorporating from the taught sessions and module reading lists etc. However, an AI assistant may also be able to help you make some connections beyond this theory and encourage original research on your part.

9.13.1 Text-based entry

The below example is based on a fictitious reflection that has been created for the purpose of this activity. Remember that when using real reflections or data, identities and identifiable information should not be shared with an AI assistant. Such information should be changed or deleted to protect your and others' privacy. Three parts will be presented below before they are discussed. The first is an example reflection, the second is the prompt (see Prompt 9.3), and the third is the output from the AI assistant (AI Assistant Output 9). The reflection is not a real reflection but based on a realistic scenario. Prompt 9.3 is constructed using the Role/Task/Format approach. AI Assistant Output 9 is what Bing.ai/Microsoft Copilot has returned. This AI assistant has been used because at the time of writing it was able to include links to websites and sources of information in its response (as indicated by the underlined text in its response). This is especially useful, as it means sources can be validated by following the links provided. Here is the example reflection.

E-portfolios

Reflection

Today's phonics session with the five-year-olds was far from what I had anticipated. My objective was to explore the letters, 's', 'a', 't', 'p', 'i' and 'n'. The reality was a stark contrast. The children found it difficult to remain focused and attentive meaning that the session did not result in the outcome I hoped. Several factors may have contributed to this session's outcome. Firstly, the energy level of five-year-olds is naturally high, and my session perhaps did not sufficiently accommodate their need for movement and interaction. The seating arrangement and the structure of the session might have been too restrictive as well, limiting their engagement with the material.

In the next session, I will incorporate more movement and interactive activities that will engage them and align more closely with their stage of development. For example, I will look for using phonics games that involve physical movement or smaller group activities that could capture their attention more effectively. I will also review my approach to behaviour management and maybe use visual cues or signals to signify 'listening time'. I will also seek further guidance from my mentor.

Prompt 9.3 Connecting theory to practice in a reflection

INPUT:

Role: You are going to act as an academic coach and support me in developing a reflection for an undergraduate e-portfolio.

Task: Review the reflective entry. Do not rewrite it. Make suggestions for suitable literature or theory that would support and extend the reflection in relation to [enter subject area, key theory etc., that has been covered in your course] child development, early literacy teaching, phonics instruction and reflective practice.

Format: Prioritise academic sources in your response.

AI Assistant (Bing.ai) Output:

Thank you for sharing your reflective entry. It's evident that you're thoughtfully considering ways to enhance your phonics sessions with five-year-olds. Let's explore relevant literature and theories that can enrich your reflection:

1. Constructivist Theories:
    - Jean Piaget's Constructivism: Piaget's theory emphasises that children actively construct knowledge through their experiences and interactions with the

(Continued)

environment. Consider how this theory aligns with your intention to incorporate movement and interactive activities in your sessions1.
    - Vygotsky's Sociocultural Theory: Vygotsky's theory highlights the role of social interactions and cultural context in cognitive development. Reflect on how collaborative learning and peer interactions can enhance phonics instruction1.
2. Ecological/Contextual Theories:
    - Bronfenbrenner's Ecological Systems Theory: This theory emphasises the impact of various environmental systems (microsystem, mesosystem, exosystem, macrosystem and chronosystem) on child development. Consider how the physical environment (seating arrangement and session structure) influences engagement and attention during phonics sessions1.
3. Reflective Practice:
    - Schön's Reflective Practitioner Model: Schön's work focuses on professional reflection. Explore how reflective practice can inform your teaching decisions and lead to improvements in your sessions2.
    - Brookfield's Critical Reflection: Brookfield's approach encourages critical examination of assumptions and beliefs. Reflect on your assumptions about teaching and learning, and consider alternative strategies2.
4. Phonics Instruction:
    - Systematic Synthetic Phonics (SSP): Research supports the effectiveness of SSP in teaching children to read. SSP starts with simple letter-sound correspondences and gradually builds to more complex code. Investigate studies on SSP and its impact on early literacy34.
    - Marie Clay's Reading Recovery: Clay's approach emphasises individualised instruction based on continuous assessment. Reflect on how personalised strategies can address diverse needs in your phonics sessions1.
5. Child Development:
    - Language Development Theories: Explore theories related to language acquisition, such as Chomsky's Universal Grammar and Skinner's Behaviourist Theory. Consider how these theories inform your understanding of language development in young learners1.

Remember to delve into recent academic sources to deepen your insights. Here are some relevant resources:

- Literature Review on Reflection: This comprehensive review explores the theoretical concept of reflection, associated challenges and empirical evidence behind its benefits5.
- Piaget, J. (1977). *The development of thought: Equilibration of cognitive structures.* Viking Press.
- Vygotsky, L. S. (1978). *Mind in society: The development of higher psychological processes.* Harvard University Press.
- Brookfield, S. D. (1995). *Becoming a critically reflective teacher.* Jossey-Bass.

> - Clay, M. M. (2005). *Literacy lessons designed for individuals: Part one: Why? When? and How?* Heinemann.
>
> Happy reading and continue refining your practice!📚✨

AI Assistant Output 9

AI Assistant Output 9 is pretty impressive. Having directed the AI assistant in the direction of the general theory that this reflection relates to, it is then able to interpret the reflection and in its response, not only direct to external sources, but also ask prompting questions that are relevant. For example, 'Consider how the physical environment (seating arrangement, session structure) influences engagement and attention during phonics sessions' is in direct response to the reflection. However, although hyperlinked sources are a great place to start as they highlight key and relevant theories, they tend to be websites and pages, as opposed to academic journals and books. This means that an additional literature search would be required to find appropriate academic sources.

9.13.2 Image-based entry

At the time of writing, image analysis was not as freely available as text-based analysis. It is hoped, however, that by the time of publication, image-based analysis will be more freely accessible within AI assistants. Essentially, when the AI assistant model allows, you can copy and paste any image into the prompt box of the AI assistant and ask it to perform an analysis. This is assuming that the image is yours and appropriate to be shared with an AI assistant. Once the image has been shared with the AI assistant, see what the initial analysis provides as it may need the analysis to be corrected. Once a relevant analysis has been arrived at, the AI assistant can be used to make recommendations for relevant theory and academic literature. Once a list of suggested theories has been returned, these will need researching and analysing further in relation to the portfolio. Remember, that whilst the use of an AI assistant in such a case may relinquish some degree of control and initial thinking on your part, you cannot relinquish your responsibility and accountability in terms of making sure that the output is researched, critiqued and applied ethically within your portfolio.

9.14 Summary of chapter

This chapter began by exploring the concept of e-portfolios by recognising their use and significance for universities. Several categories of e-portfolio are then considered detailing their distinct purposes and advantages. The integration of e-portfolios within assessments is then explored with an emphasis on the enhancement of learning and demonstration of competencies. Practical guidance on selecting appropriate e-portfolio platforms and tools is provided, alongside strategies for aligning e-portfolios with specific learning objectives. Ethical considerations, crucial in the construction and use of e-portfolios are also highlighted, ensuring students navigate the use of AI tools responsibly and in accordance with the guidance from the institution they are studying at. The chapter aims to introduce university students to the steps that would need to be taken to complete an e-portfolio using an AI assistant. Connections are made throughout the chapter in relation to how AI assistants can act in assistive roles and scaffold both student's learning and the development of e-portfolios, developing their skill base and application for future use.

9.15 Chapter hacks

1. Understand the Purpose of the e-Portfolio: Recognise the specific type and purpose of the e-portfolio you are tasked with creating, whether it is for assessment, showcasing your best work, development, reflection or professional use. This understanding will shape the content and structure of your portfolio.
2. Align with LOs: Ensure your e-portfolio content is directly aligned with the LOs of your course or module. This alignment demonstrates your competency and understanding of the subject matter.
3. Select the Right Tools: Familiarise yourself with the e-portfolio tools recommended or required by your course. Whether it is a platform provided by the university or an external tool, understanding its features and limitations is crucial.
4. Incorporate Varied Content: E-portfolios can be more than text. Include various multimedia elements like images, videos and audio to make your portfolio more engaging and demonstrate your skills.
5. Reflect and Personalise: Use the e-portfolio as a space for reflection, not just a collection of works. Personal insights and learning reflections add depth to your portfolio, showcasing your growth and learning journey.
6. Ethical Considerations: Be mindful of ethical considerations, especially when including content that involves others. Obtain necessary permissions and respect privacy and intellectual property rights.
7. Utilise Generative AI Ethically: If employing Generative AI to assist with your e-portfolio, ensure its use is permitted and ethical. AI can help generate ideas and organise content but should not replace your original contributions and sentiment.
8. Connect Theory to Practice: When possible, link the content of your e-portfolio to relevant theories and literature from your field. This not only demonstrates your understanding but also your ability to apply theoretical knowledge to practical scenarios.

9. Time Management and Planning: Develop a clear plan for completing your e-portfolio, considering all necessary components and deadlines. Breaking down the task into manageable steps can help ensure timely and effective completion.

9.16 Chapter MCQs

1. What is the primary purpose of an assessment e-portfolio?
   A) To display the best work at the end of a learning period
   B) To evaluate a learner's performance against predefined criteria
   C) To document the professional achievements for job applications
   D) To encourage self-reflection and personal growth
2. Which type of e-portfolio is specifically designed to track and demonstrate a learner's development over time?
   A) Showcase e-portfolio
   B) Reflective e-portfolio
   C) Professional e-portfolio
   D) Developmental e-portfolio
3. What is a key feature of reflective e-portfolios?
   A) Highlighting the highest level of achievement in specific areas
   B) Encouraging critical thinking about learning experiences and acquired skills
   C) Evaluating performance for academic grading
   D) Showcasing professional achievements to potential employers
4. Which of the following is an ethical consideration when creating an e-portfolio?
   A) Ensuring the portfolio is aesthetically pleasing
   B) Including as many multimedia elements as possible
   C) Obtaining permission for content involving others
   D) Using the most advanced e-portfolio platform available
5. How can Generative AI assist students in creating e-portfolios?
   A) By generating reflections and personal insights
   B) By replacing the need for student input and creativity
   C) By providing frameworks and initial ideas based on learning outcomes
   D) By evaluating and grading the e-portfolio content

Correct answers:

1. Correct answer B
2. Correct answer D
3. Correct answer B
4. Correct answer C
5. Correct answer C

PART FOUR

HOW TO EXPLORE FEEDBACK WITH GENERATIVE AI

10
Grades and Feedback

10.1 Chapter objectives

a. To understand the role of grades and feedback as indicators of academic performance and areas for improvement
b. To explore how AI assistants can be used to support, scaffold and assist in the process of understanding feedback, making it easier for students to interpret and develop actions to move forwards
c. To present strategies that will aid with the effective and personalised interpretation of student feedback, across single and multiple assessments
d. To consider the use of AI assistants as a tool to prepare for discussions with lecturers about feedback

10.2 Having read this chapter, you will...

1. **Understand the Importance of Feedback**: Recognise the critical role that both grades and feedback play in your academic journey, serving as indicators of your strengths and areas for improvement.
2. **Appreciate the Dual Role of Feedback**: Acknowledge how grades and feedback can be both motivating and demotivating but engage with it constructively to enhance your academic performance.
3. **Leverage AI for Feedback Interpretation**: Become familiar with how AI assistants can aid in the initial interpretation of feedback, making complex academic feedback more accessible and easier to understand.
4. **Identify Patterns in Feedback with AI Assistance**: Learn how to use AI tools to detect recurring themes and areas for improvement across different pieces of feedback, helping you to focus your efforts more effectively.
5. **Develop Actionable Insights from Feedback**: Transform feedback into concrete action plans for academic improvement based on insights gained from AI analysis.

6. **Enhance Readiness for Discussions with Educators**: Be better prepared for in-depth discussions with your lecturers about your feedback, armed with a clearer understanding of the feedback's content and context, facilitated by AI tools.
7. **Apply Feedback More Effectively in Future Work**: Understand how a deeper engagement with feedback, supported by AI tools, can lead to significant improvements in your approach to assignments and overall academic outcomes.
8. **Grasp the Complexity of University-Level Study**: Gain insights into the broader context and complexity of university-level study, beyond the specifics of the feedback content, enhancing your overall educational experience.

10.3 Introduction

Grades and feedback are a key part of the university experience. They have the potential to be equally motivating and demotivating. Whether your grades are alphabetical or numerical, they provide an indicator of the strength of your work at the level you are studying. These can, and often will, change for several reasons across a student's study experience. With an increased familiarity and understanding of university expectations, students improve as they progress with their studies. Furthermore, there may be certain topics or modules that students particularly enjoy and therefore have more interest or knowledge of to start from. Regardless of motivation, grades and feedback are a key indicator of what a student has done well and the areas for improvement in relation to their study. Understanding this feedback and being able to apply it to future assignments is one of the most logical ways that a student can make progress. However, many students who pass or achieve the grade they want may overlook the feedback they receive, and this is a missed opportunity.

This chapter explores some simple steps that use AI assistants to support, scaffold and assist with understanding feedback. It is assumed that an increased understanding of feedback will impact positively on the future application of it. This chapter explores the potential of AI assistants in explaining feedback so that it is easier to interpret and develop actionable insights. Such an approach will capitalise on the feedback provided and enable students to consider multiple approaches to refining their approach to assignments, develop their understanding and improve their outcomes, i.e. achieve higher grades. This chapter will provide strategies that support the effective interpretation of feedback, recognise patterns across feedback and suggest ways to action these points. This personalised insight into student feedback is one of the key advantages that an AI assistant can offer ; however, it does not replace discussing your feedback with a lecturer who marked your assignment. As you will see, using an AI assistant can better prepare you for such conversations, allowing you to explore the context and complexity of university-level study, as opposed to only the content.

10.4 What are university grades and feedback based on?

Level descriptors define the depth and complexity of each academic level and outline the academic skills, amount of prior knowledge and amount of learner autonomy required to pass a programme or module at that level. The descriptors are closely aligned to the Framework for Higher Education Qualifications (FHEQ) and often with the more discipline-specific Quality Assurance Agency (QAA) Subject Benchmark Statements. It is the level descriptors, FHEQ and Subject Benchmarks that ultimately inform a programme's Learning Outcomes, and therefore a module's Learning Outcomes, on which an assignment or assignments are based. It is the marking academic's role to identify where the student's work is meeting these outcomes and where there are opportunities for further development. As a general guide, it is important to be aware of the skills that you are required to demonstrate at the level you are working at as indicated in Table 10.1.

Table 10.1 Adapted from UCL's Guidance on Level Descriptors (UCL, 2023)

Level	Description
4 (Undergraduate)	Introduction of evaluation and interpretation of concepts within the field of study, with an emphasis on developing arguments and making judgements based on theories
5 (Undergraduate)	Expansion to critical understanding and application of principles outside the initial context, including employment contexts. Introduction of enquiry methods and critical evaluation of problem-solving approaches
6 (Undergraduate)	Enhanced focus on systematic understanding, detailed knowledge at the forefront of the field, and application of advanced analysis and enquiry techniques. Introduction of current research and scholarship commentary
7 (Postgraduate)	Increased emphasis on critical awareness of current problems and insights at the forefront of the field, originality in the application of knowledge, and a comprehensive understanding of research and scholarship techniques

10.5 Understanding what grades and feedback mean at your university

Before exploring how AI assistants and Generative AI tools may be utilised in helping to understand feedback, it is important to acknowledge and clarify the diverse range of approaches that inform the concepts of 'grades' and 'feedback' at university-level study. Familiarise yourself with your university's assessment and feedback policy. Such policy or guidance can usually be accessed via your university's website and will provide details of the approach taken to assessment and feedback. For now, however, some of the key approaches to grades and feedback will be mentioned below. Grade, in whatever form presented, is usually a key indicator of how successful a student is in completing their assessment and therefore contributes to successful completion of the programme of study. Grades are therefore important to understand and be aware of. However, they provide little more than an indication, so although important overall, for students who want to do better and improve, it is not only the grade that needs to be known but the feedback that should be understood.

10.6 Types of grades used at universities

Letter Grades: These range from A (excellent) to F (fail), with plus and minus variations to provide more specificity. An A typically signifies outstanding understanding and mastery of the material at that level, while a C may indicate satisfactory or average performance, and an F represents failure to meet the basic requirements.

Percentages: Some assignments are graded on a 100-point scale, with scores reflecting the percentage of the total possible points earned. The exact thresholds for letter grade equivalents vary between universities.

Pass/Fail: This binary system simply indicates whether the student has met the minimum requirements to pass the course or assignment, without providing a detailed measure of performance.

Grade Points: Often used in GPA (Grade Point Average) calculations, grade points are numerical values assigned to letter grades, such as 4.0 for an A, 3.0 for a B, and so on.

10.7 Types of summative related feedback used at universities

Each of the below types of summative feedback plays a role in conveying assessment expectations and outcomes to students. They offer varying levels of detail and specificity, as well as areas for performance and growth.

Narrative Comment: This provides a concise summary or comment that provides an overview of the student's performance on an assessment. It usually highlights key strengths and areas for improvement, offering qualitative insights into how the student has or has not met the learning objectives. This type of comment allows for a more personalised response as well as acknowledgement of the key themes or general points that can be addressed to improve future assignments.

Extended Narrative Comment: This builds on the previous type of feedback but offers a more detailed and comprehensive version, providing an in-depth analysis of the student's performance. It may cover various aspects of the work, such as conceptual understanding, analytical depth, application of knowledge and quality of application. This type of comment will also highlight specific areas for improvement.

On Script Feedback: This involves comments and annotations made directly on the student's submission (e.g., on an essay, exam script or project). This can include margin notes, underlining, and specific comments tied to sections in a student's work. This allows for targeted feedback, connecting directly to the work which helps students understand exactly where and how their responses met or did not meet the assessment criteria and how this can be improved.

Rubric-Checklist Focused: This will present a list of criteria or essential components that the student's work should contain, often in a yes/no or present/absent format. It is a straightforward method for assessing the inclusion of required elements. To quickly and clearly identify whether key components or criteria have been met in the student's work, offering a clear and concise method for both the marker to assess and the student to work to.

Rubric-Learning Outcome Focused: This is a rubric that is explicitly aligned with the learning outcomes of a course or module. It assesses student work based on how well the work demonstrates achievement of these outcomes with descriptors for varying levels of performance. This aims to provide clarity and transparency in relation to the student's performance across the assessment's learning outcomes.

Rubric-Analytic Focused: This style presents a detailed breakdown of the assessment into multiple criteria, each with its own scale for scoring. Each criterion addresses a different aspect of the work, such as clarity of argument, use of evidence, organisation, presentation, referencing etc. This type of rubric provides a range of indicators across multiple dimensions of the student's work, allowing for an understanding of strengths and areas for improvement in relation to that assessment.

10.8 Why is feedback important?

Feedback plays a crucial role in a student's ongoing academic journey by highlighting achievements and offering insights for continued growth and improvement. In relation to summative assessments, feedback helps clarify what was expected in terms of learning outcomes and performance standards. It can offer students a glimpse into the marker's perspective, especially where feedback

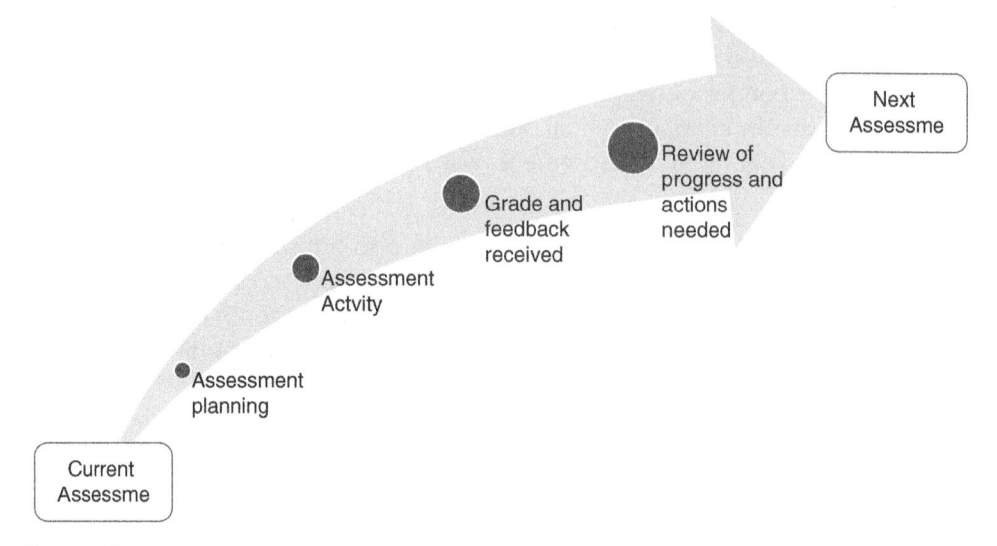

Figure 10.1 Assessment to assessment process.

highlights areas of strong and not-so-strong work. Such feedback will help students to understand what their strengths and areas for growth are in relation to academic development. Sometimes, this can confirm what students already know or it may highlight areas they were unaware of. Although summative feedback is sometimes received by the student after the teaching sessions for a module have concluded, it can inform approaches to future assessments and overall learning strategies. The feedback and feedforward should help inform the basis of what actions a student needs to consider in their next assessment (see Figure 10.1). Ultimately, feedback should contribute to a student's learning journey. Failure to read and understand feedback is a missed opportunity within the learning cycle. AI assistants can be utilised to support students in such a process.

10.9 Using AI assistants to help understand initial assignment feedback

This section needs to begin with a disclaimer. Once feedback and a grade have been received for an assessment, if the student has any initial questions, the first thing that they should do is reach out to the lecturers who have taught that module, the person who marked their assessment and potentially the module leader. These are the professionals who are best placed to support a student with understanding feedback in relation to the assessment and module that it is part of. Furthermore, a core part of any university lecturer's job role is supporting students to do well in their assessments, to which feedback is central. Should a student want to explore their feedback in a more general sense, potentially in preparation to meet with someone from the teaching or marking team to discuss it further, an AI assistant is a great start. An AI assistant may be able to provide a student with initial insights and help develop their understanding in relation to the feedback that then sets the student up for a well-informed discussion with the relevant lecturer about it. Remember to set the context before discussing assignment feedback with an AI assistant. This will involve sharing details of which country you are studying, the course or programme, the level you are studying at and details of the assignment. Please note that identifiable information (e.g. student name and name of university) does not need to be shared and should be anonymised.

10.9.1 Initial feedback – Narrative or extended Narrative

Once the context of your study and assignment have been shared, some of the phrases that may be useful to ask the AI assistant to consider before the actual feedback is provided may be too.

Ask for a summary of the feedback in relation to:

- Overall comment
- Strengths
- Areas for improvement
- Specific suggestions
- Additional feedback

Remember not to share anything that you would not want to be public, so delete any references to your name or private information. It is useful to include the grade you were given so that the AI assistant can acknowledge this in its response, and you can enquire directly about what may be needed to improve this. This approach has been trialled across a number of AI assistants with varying levels of success. This may be because the feedback given can vary in content, meaning that the AI assistants' algorithm-based response will also vary because of this. Overall, however, AI Assistants can reinterpret feedback and simplify it for a student to understand in an accessible manner. If the student still does not understand or has any further questions, then the student can ask for further clarification from the AI assistant or take such questions to the teaching team. If you will have the opportunity to discuss your feedback further with a lecturer from your course, you could also use an AI assistant to help you think of some questions to ask about your feedback (see Prompt 10.1).

> **Prompt 10.1   Understanding assignment feedback**
>
> **INPUT:**
>
> Role: You are a Learning Development Advisor supporting a student studying at [enter the level of study here] on [enter the programme of study here].
>
> Task: The student has received a grade and feedback for an assignment. They would like you to help them understand the feedback, think of further questions to ask about the feedback and make an action plan to address significant points of their feedback.
>
> Format: Explain the key points of the feedback first, with hypothetical examples to make it easier to understand. Develop three follow-up questions that can be asked about the feedback to a course lecturer. Suggest three areas of focus to improve on moving forward.
>
> Are you ready for the feedback?

10.9.2 Rubric-based feedback

At the time of writing, all freely available AI assistants could interpret text input but not all of them are capable of interpreting a table. This is important to note as the most common format that marking rubrics are presented in is a table. How you access the table will depend on how it is presented to you as part of your feedback. The quickest way that the author has found is to use the 'snipping tool' function that is common on both Microsoft and Apple platforms. Once an image of the rubric has been captured, check that it does not have any personal, identifying or sensitive information on it. When you are happy, you can then upload it to an AI assistant. Google's Gemini and Microsoft's Bing/copilot were able to analyse images at the time of writing (see Prompt 10.2).

> **Prompt 10.2   Analyse a marking rubric with an AI assistant**
>
> **INPUT:**
>
> [Upload Marking Rubric First]
>
> - What does this marking rubric show?
> - What grade has it given me? (to check that it is interpreting the upload correctly)
> - According to the rubric what do I need to do to improve my grade?
> - Can you suggest other ideas to help me improve?

The questions in Prompt 38 are designed to support the AI assistant to tailor its analysis of the rubric that you upload. Hopefully, this will help to develop your understanding as you will be able to ask further questions and for the AI assistant to suggest ideas of how to approach relevant aspects moving forward. What it cannot do though, is offer the insight and level of detail that your lecturer will be able to provide, but it can be a good starting place to develop your understanding.

10.10 Interpreting feedback across assignments

One of the revelations of Generative AI and its capabilities has been its ability to provide an efficient analysis in relation to inputs. Due to this capability, an AI assistant could be used to interpret your feedback and make you aware of commonly occurring aspects across the feedback. It may highlight patterns across your feedback that you did not realise were there. Table 10.1 shows a pre-AI example of what tracking and mapping feedback may look like. This would involve the student reading each piece of assignment feedback, interpreting what the core aspects of it are, and plotting it in a table for each assessment (Table 10.2):

Table 10.2 Tracking and Mapping Feedback

Aspect of feedback	1	2	3	4	5	6	Aspect Totals
Structure	X	X		X			3
Accurate Referencing	X	X	X	X			4
Clarity	X		X		X		3
Academic Tone	X	X	X	X			4
Analysis	X	X			X		3
Evidence Needed	X	X	X	X	X	X	5
Ass Totals	6	5	4	4	3	1	

With the use of an AI assistant, however, the above is not needed. Check that all of your feedback is ready (i.e. no private or sensitive information is contained) and enter all pieces of feedback into an AI assistant and ask it to provide an analysis. You can prompt for further information by asking it to identify key terms and themes throughout the feedback. Once it has identified these, it can inform further analysis. If there are aspects that you do not understand, ask the AI assistant to explain them further. Finally, ask the AI assistant to use the key findings from its analysis to inform an action plan going forward. You can also add in any extra aspects that you want to improve on but might not necessarily have been highlighted in your feedback.

10.11 Summary of chapter

This chapter began by situating grades and feedback as an important part of the university experience highlighting their dual role as motivators and potential sources of demotivation. It emphasises the importance of understanding and applying feedback if a student wants to improve their academic performance. It is recognised that many students can overlook feedback should they have achieved the grade they wanted but this is a missed opportunity. It presents simple steps for utilising AI assistants to support, scaffold and assist with the feedback interpretation process, enhancing students' ability to develop actionable insights from their feedback. AI assistants can help in making feedback easier to understand and more accessible. Students are then able to refine their approaches to assignments, deepen their understanding, and ultimately achieve better grades. It also suggests that a more nuanced understanding of feedback, facilitated by an AI assistant, will positively impact its future application. Strategies are then discussed that aid in the effective interpretation of feedback, recognition of patterns across feedback, and the formulation of action plans based on these. While the chapter advocates for the use of AI assistants as a valuable tool in understanding feedback, it also cautions that this does not replace the invaluable insights gained from discussing feedback directly with the academics who provided it. The use of AI assistants is positioned as a preparatory step that can enhance students' readiness for more in-depth conversations with their lecturers, allowing them to engage with the broader context and complexity of university-level study beyond the content of the feedback itself.

10.12 Chapter hacks

1. Use AI Assistants for Initial Feedback Interpretation: Leverage AI tools to get a preliminary understanding of your feedback. These tools can break down complex academic feedback into simpler, more digestible insights, helping you identify the key areas of strength and improvement in your work.
2. Identify Patterns in Feedback: Use AI to recognise recurring themes or areas for improvement across different pieces of feedback. This can help you understand broader trends in your academic performance and guide you in focusing your efforts on specific areas that need attention.

Grades and Feedback

3. Develop Actionable Insights: Once you understand the feedback, use AI assistants to create action plans based on the insights. This can involve setting specific goals, like enhancing your research skills or working on your writing style. What is important is that these are based directly on the feedback you have received.
4. Prepare for In-depth Discussions with Educators: Armed with the initial analysis provided by the AI assistant, engage in more meaningful conversations with your lecturers. You will be better prepared to discuss specific aspects of your feedback, ask relevant questions and understand the context and nuances of the feedback.
5. Reflect and Apply Feedback in Future Work: Reflect on the feedback and the insights provided by the AI assistant to improve your future assignments. Consistently applying what you have learned from previous feedback will lead to continuous improvement in your academic work and potentially, higher grades.

10.13 Chapter MCQs

1. What is the primary role of feedback in a student's academic journey?
   A) To assign grades only
   B) To highlight achievements and areas for growth
   C) To replace the need for exams
   D) To focus solely on weaknesses
2. How can AI assistants aid students in relation to feedback?
   A) By completely taking over the role of educators
   B) By providing initial insights and helping to develop understanding
   C) By ensuring students no longer need feedback from educators
   D) By making feedback unnecessary
3. What is the key benefit of understanding feedback for future assessments?
   A) It allows students to ignore feedback in the future
   B) It makes feedback less important over time
   C) It informs approaches to future assessments and overall learning strategies
   D) It guarantees higher grades without effort
4. What should students do first if they have questions about their feedback?
   A) Ignore the feedback
   B) Only rely on AI assistants for clarification
   C) Reach out to the educators who provided the feedback
   D) Assume the feedback is incorrect
5. What does the effective use of AI in understanding feedback require from students?
   A) To disregard educator input
   B) To share personal and sensitive information with AI

(Continued)

C) To set the context and share relevant details about the assessment with AI
D) To fully automate their learning process

Correct answers:

1. Correct answer B
2. Correct answer B
3. Correct answer C
4. Correct answer C
5. Correct answer C

References

Advance HE. *Degree attainment gaps*. Advance HE. https://www.advance-he.ac.uk/guidance/equality-diversity-and-inclusion/student-recruitment-retention-and-attainment/degree-attainment-gaps. Accessed on February 29, 2024.

Arora, A. (2023). Moravec's paradox and the fear of job automation in health care. *The Lancet, 402*(10397), 180–181.

Bloom, B. S., Engelhart, M. D., Furst, E. J., Hill, W. H., & Krathwohl, D. R. (1956). *Taxonomy of educational objectives: The classification of educational goals. Vol. Handbook I: Cognitive domain.* David McKay Company.

Burns, T., & Sinfield, S. (2022). *Essential Study Skills: The complete guide to success at university* (5th ed.). SAGE.

Department for Science, Innovation and Technology. (2023). *Cyber security breaches survey 2023: Education institutions annex*. GOV.UK. https://www.gov.uk/government/statistics/cyber-security-breaches-survey-2023/cyber-security-breaches-survey-2023-education-institutions-annex. Accessed on February 11, 2024.

Eaton, S. (2021). *Plagiarism in higher education*. Bloomsbury.

Eaton, S. (2023). *6 tenets of postplagiarism: Writing in the age of artificial intelligence*. Learning, Teaching and Leadership. https://drsaraheaton.wordpress.com/2023/02/25/6-tenets-of-postplagiarism-writing-in-the-age-of-artificial-intelligence/. Accessed on February 29, 2024.

Estienne, S. (2016). *Artificial intelligence creeps into daily life*. https://phys.org/news/2016-12-artificial-intelligence-daily-life.html. Accessed on January 27, 2024.

Euronews. (2024). *Google's CEO admits Gemini AI model's responses showed 'bias'*. euronews. https://www.euronews.com/next/2024/02/28/googles-ceo-admits-gemini-ai-models-responses-showed-bias-and-says-company-is-working-to-f. Accessed on February 29, 2024.

Fido, D., & Harper, C. (2023). *How to use ChatGPT to help close the awarding gap*. The Campus Learn, Share, Connect. https://www.timeshighereducation.com/campus/how-use-chatgpt-help-close-awarding-gap. Accessed on February 29, 2024.

Furuta, A. (2021). *Western colonialism and world society in national education systems: Global trends in the use of high-stakes exams at early ages, 1960 to 2010*. https://journals.sagepub.com/doi/epdf/10.1177/0038040720957368. Accessed on December 21, 2023.

Hamano-Bunce, D. (2017, September 28). *Lecture listening and note-taking: Developing an efficient approach*. English Language Education Centre for Open Learning. University of Edinburgh.

Harvard University. (2023). *Getting started with prompts for text-based Generative AI tools*. https://huit.harvard.edu/news/ai-prompts. Accessed on March 2, 2024.

Hopkins, d, & Reid, T. (2018). *The academic skills handbook*. SAGE.

Hutson, M. (2023). DeepMind AI creates algorithms that sort data faster than those built by people. *Nature, 618*(7965), 443–444.

Hyams, A. (2021). *A short essay on essays.* Oxford Open Learning. https://www.ool.co.uk/blog/a-short-essay-on-essays/. Accessed on June 12, 2023.

International Center for Academic Integrity [ICAI]. (2021). *The fundamental values of academic integrity* (3rd ed.). https://academicintegrity.org/images/pdfs/20019_ICAI-Fundamental-Values_R12.pdf. Accessed on February, 02 2024.

JISC. (2021). *Getting started with e-portfolios.* Jisc. https://beta.jisc.ac.uk/guides/getting-started-with-e-portfolios. Accessed on February 17, 2024.

Kyaw, A. (2023). *Report: Almost half of high school students use AI for schoolwork.* Diverse: Issues In Higher Education. https://www.diverseeducation.com/student-issues/article/15660259/report-almost-half-of-high-school-students-use-ai-for-schoolwork. Accessed on February 4, 2024.

Lopez, N. (2016). Microsoft is using AI to give Office spell-check on steroids and much more. *The Next Web.* https://thenextweb.com/news/microsoft-using-ai-give-office-spell-check-steroids-much. Accessed on November, 5 2023.

Luger, E. (2023). *What do we know and what should we do about…?* AI Saage Publications.

McDonald, S., & **Fotakopoulou, O.** (2023). Narrowing the digital divide in early Maths: How different modes of assessment influence young children's mathematical test scores. *Early Education & Development*, 1–18.

Moravec, H. (2009). Rise of the Robots – The Future of Artificial Intelligence. *Scientific American.* https://www.scientificamerican.com/article/rise-of-the-robots/. Accessed on January 27, 2024.

O'Sullivan, B., & **Cheng, L.** (2022). Lessons from the Chinese imperial examination system. *Language Testing in Asia, 12*, 52. https://doi.org/10.1186/s40468-022-00201-5

Open, A. I. (2024). *Sora: Creating video from text.* https://openai.com/sora. Accessed March 1, 2024.

Paul, T., Di Rezze, B., Rosenbaum, P., Cahill, P., Jiang, A., Kim, E., & **Campbell, W.** (2022). Perspectives of children and youth with disabilities and special needs regarding their experiences in inclusive education: A meta-aggregative review. *Frontiers in Education, 7.*

Perrigo, B. (2023). Exclusive: The $2 per hour workers who made ChatGPT safer. *TIME.* https://time.com/6247678/openai-chatgpt-kenya-workers/. Accessed on February 4, 2024.

Puentedura, R. R. (2013, May 29). SAMR: Moving from enhancement to transformation [Web log post] http://www.hippasus.com/rrpweblog/archives/000095.html. Accessed on January 27, 2024.

Ray, P. P. (2023). ChatGPT: A comprehensive review on background, applications, key challenges, bias, ethics, limitations and future scope. *Internet of Things and Cyber-Physical Systems, 3*, 121–154.

Rivers, C., & **Holland, A.** (2023). *How can generative AI intersect with Bloom's taxonomy?* THE Campus Learn, Share, Connect. https://www.timeshighereducation.com/campus/how-can-generative-ai-intersect-blooms-taxonomy. Accessed on February 11, 2024.

Squire, L. R., & **Dede, A. J. O.** (2015). Conscious and unconscious memory systems. *Cold Spring Harbor Perspectives in Biology, 7*(3), a021667.

Støle, H., Mangen, A., & **Schwippert, K.** (2020). Assessing children's reading comprehension on paper and screen: A mode-effect study. *Computers & Education.* 151, 103861.

Strait, A. (2023, January 10). *Twitter.* https://twitter.com/agstrait/status/1613849161362964488?lang=en Accessed on 04 February 2024.

Stray, C. (2001). The shift from oral to written examination: Cambridge and Oxford 1700–1900. *Assessment in Education: Principles, Policy & Practice, 8*(1), 33–50. https://doi.org/10.1080/09695940120033243.

Sweller, J. (1998). Cognitive load during problem solving: Effects on learning. *Cognitive Science*, 12, 257–285.

Tegamrk, M. (2018). *Life 3.0.* Penguin Books.

Tholfsen, M. (2022). *Introducing Reading Coach for personalized practice, and other major updates to Reading Progress.* Microsoft. https://techcommunity.microsoft.com/t5/education-blog/

introducing-reading-coach-for-personalized-practice-and-other/ba-p/3223533. Accessed on December 10, 2023.

Tran, K. (2023). *AI as the new electricity: Unleashing the power of data as the energy source.* https://www.linkedin.com/pulse/ai-new-electricity-unleashing-power-data-energy-source-kiet-tran-frm. Accessed on January 27, 2024.

Turing, A. (1950). Computing machinery and intelligence. In *Mind* (Vol. 49, pp. 433–460). Springer.

UCL. (2023). *Using AI tools in assessment.* Teaching & Learning. https://www.ucl.ac.uk/teaching-learning/generative-ai-hub/using-ai-tools-assessment. Accessed on February 11, 2024.

UCL. (2023). *Section 5: Level descriptors.* https://www.ucl.ac.uk/academic-manual/chapters/chapter-7-programme-and-module-approval-and-amendment-framework/section-5-level-descriptors#:~:text=Level%20Descriptors%20define%20the%20depth,or%20Module%20at%20that%20Level. Accessed on 25 February 2024.

UN. (n.d.). *United Nations Sustainable Development Goals. Ensure access to affordable, reliable, sustainable and modern energy.* https://www.un.org/sustainabledevelopment/energy/. Accessed on January 27, 2024.

Zarbin, M. A. (2020). Artificial intelligence: Quo Vadis? *Translational Vision Science & Technology, 9*(2), 1.

Prompt List

Prompt 1.1: Guidance for a neurodiverse student to be successful at university   17

Prompt 2.1: Study buddy/coach prompt   26

Prompt 2.2: Socratic study coach prompt   26

Prompt 2.3: Study prompt example   28

Prompt 2.4: Explain it to me like I am a 5-year-old   28

Prompt 2.5: Developing critical analysis   30

Prompt 2.6: Developing a critique based on student interests   31

Prompt 2.7: Starting an assignment   31

Prompt 2.8: Generating key search terms   31

Prompt 2.9: Document or text analysis prompt   32

Prompt 2.10: Sentence starters   33

Prompt 2.11: Time management prompt   34

Prompt 3.1: What is academic integrity and how is AI impacting it for my course?   41

Prompt 3.2: How to respond to a wrongful accusation of academic misconduct?   42

Prompt 3.3: How to future-proof your skillset   50

Prompt 4.1: Example of an AI image prompt developed in ChatGPT and then entered into DALL-E (9/11/23)   68

Prompt 5.1: Connecting session learning outcomes to assignment learning outcomes   81

Prompt 6.1: Deconstructing an essay title   100

Prompt 6.2: Understanding learning outcomes for an assignment   102

Prompt 6.3: Develop an essay plan and structure   105

Prompt 6.4: Action plan for an essay   110

Prompt 6.5: Sentence starters for an essay   115

Prompt 6.6: Generate a draft introduction   118

Prompt 6.7: Generate a draft conclusion   119

Prompt 7.1: Understanding learning outcomes for a presentation   130

Prompt 7.2: Action plan for a presentation   135

Prompt 7.3: Develop a presentation plan and structure   135

Prompt 8.1: Socratic-based prompt for revision   153

Prompt 8.2: Action plan for an exam   154

Prompt 8.3: Preparing for an exam   155

Prompt 9.1: Understanding learning outcomes for an e-portfolio   168

Prompt 9.2: Connecting learning outcomes to placement/work experience   170

Prompt 9.3: Connecting theory to practice in a reflection   175

Prompt 10.1: Understanding assignment feedback   190

Prompt 10.2: Analyse a marking rubric with an AI assistant   190

Index

A
Academia, AI's role in, 13–15
Academic integrity, 40–42, 44, 58
'Academic misconduct', 40
Academic-related assignments, 133
Accessibility tools, 16
Access study note, 78
Action planning, 49
   using AI assistant, 110
   using 'Magic ToDo' by goblin. tools, 109–110
'Adaptive teaching strategies', 96
Algorithms, 10
Analytical skills, 23, 29–31
Animations, 72
App.decktopus.com, 138
Apple, 61
Argument essay, 95
Arora, A., 15
Artificial intelligence, 7–8, 46
   application and interpretation in academia, 13
   assistants and content, 25, 46–47
   beginning your research, 113–114
   Bing's image creator, 68
   combatting writer's block with AI, 114
   contribute to equity, diversity and inclusion at university, 16–17
   controversy and limitations in development of ChatGPT, 12–13
   creating essay, 113
   deep AI, 68–69
   design function, 69
   editing, formatting and proofreading, 117–118
   ethical use of AI for exam involve, 152–153
   exam preparation phase, 153–154
   Gamma.app, 70–71
   generative AI and evolution of GPTs by open AI, 9–12
   grammarly, 65
   Hemingway editor, 65
   historical context and evolution of, 11
   image creation tools, 66–67
   image prompt components, 67, 67 (table)
   impacted academic integrity, 42–44
   inciteful, 114 (figure)
   integral role, 47
   Jenni.ai, 66
   literacy, 80
   magic media App in Canva, 69
   Microsoft PowerPoint, 69–70
   Moravec's paradox and landscape with, 15–16
   paperpal, 65–66
   preparation, 156–159
   presentation/slides tools, 69–72
   promoting academic integrity in relation to AI literacy, 44–45, 45 (figure)
   protecting privacy using, 48–49
   Quill Bot, 65
   research and write essay with, 109–111
   revision phase, 153
   rising sea of AI knowledge, 13
   role in academia, 13–15
   searching for literature or references with AI assistants or specific AI tools, 116
   sentence starters, 115
   study phase, 153
   take-home exam assignment, 156
   text-to-video model, 72
   Tome.app, 71–72
   tool functionality for video creation and editing, 73 (table)
   tools, 42, 44, 46–47, 58, 63–64, 77
   transcription tool, 83
   unpacking AI tool kit, 63
   used in assistive role, 47
   video creation tools, 72–73
   writing tools, 64
Artificial intelligence assistant/assisted, 33, 35, 42, 157, 184–185
   analyse recording of lecture or taught session, 84 (figure)
   approach to creating presentation, 135
   approaches to studying, 79

connecting theory and literature to e-portfolio entry using, 174–177
creating revision materials, 86–88
creating study notes during session, 82–83
creating study notes from digital content after session, 83–84
creating study notes from digital content before session, 81–82
detailed approach to action planning using, 110
flipping pyramid, 79–80
to help understand initial assignment feedback, 188–191
organising study notes, 84–86
output 2, 106–107
study notes, 80–81
Assessment E-portfolios, 164
Assessment process
  e-portfolios used in, 165
  essays used in, 96–97
  exams used in, 149–150
  presentations used in assessment process and feedback, 126–127
Award gap, 43

B
Back-and-forth interactions, 27
Bing.ai, 139
Bing's image creator, 68
Bloom's taxonomy, 44–45, 45 (figure), 51, 79–80, 80 (figure), 102
'Brain', 86
Burns, T., 78

C
Canva, magic media App in, 69
Case study-based questions, 149
Cause-and-effect essay, 95–96
ChatGPT, 12–13, 44, 68, 72
Chat PDF, 85
Cheng, L., 146
'Children', 99–100
Child poverty in England, 136–138
Claude.ai, 158
Closed-book exam, 151
Closed exams, 147
Cloud-based services, 66
Cognitive Load Theory, 29
Cognitive science, 26
Combatting writer's block with AI, 114
Concept maps, 78
Consent, 49
Construction, 100–101
Constructive alignment, 155
Constructive criticism, 126

Cornell notes, 78
Coronavirus disease 2019 (COVID-19), 123
Courage, 44
Critical thinking, 23, 29–31

D
DALL-E, 68
Data
  analysis, 47
  security, 49
Deconstruction, 99–100
Deep AI, 68–69
Deep learning techniques, 10, 72
Definition essay, 96
de Montaigne, M., 95
'Designer' function, 69
'Detailed action plan', 110
Developmental E-portfolios, 164
Digital approach, 77–78
Digital content, 82
  creating study notes from digital content after session, 83–84
  creating study notes from digital content before session, 81–82, 82 (figure)
Digitally available content, 81
Digital notes and approach, 78
Discussion essay, 95

E
Eaton, S., 42, 43 (figure)
'Edit' mode, 65
Editing, 34, 117–118, 117 (figure)
'Educational technology', 103
Electricity, 8–9
Electromagnetism, 9
Electronic portfolio (e-portfolios), 163–165
  action plan, 172 (table)
  assignment overview, 167
  checklist to begin assignment, 166
  connecting theory and literature to e-portfolio entry using AI assistant, 174
  content requirements, 168
  e-portfolios used in assessment process, 165
  ethical use of GAI in e-portfolio involve, 169–170
  GAI permitted in final assignment, 169
  image-based entry, 177
  learning outcomes, 168–169
  learning outcomes from, 170–173
  seven-step checklist to completing, 166 (table)
  submission details, 167
  submission process, 167–168
  text-based entry, 174–177
  time management, 173–174
  tools and software, 166
  understanding assessment format, 167

Index

understanding e-portfolio assignment brief, 167
England, child poverty in, 136–138
Essays, 94–96
   action plan checklist, 112 (figure)
   AI-assisted approach to creating essay, 113–119
   balance of AI input, 108 (figure)
   checklist to begin assignment, 97
   connecting learning outcomes with assessment format and taught content, 104–107
   detailed approach to action planning using AI assistant, 110
   developing essay plan and structure, 105
   developing essay title, 101
   essay prompt with Generative Artificial Intelligence, 105 (figure)
   essay-based questions, 148
   essay-writing process, 94
   essays used in assessment process, 96–97
   example of essay title, 101
   fixed essay title, 99–100, 99 (figure)
   general approach to action planning using 'Magic ToDo' by goblin.tools, 109–110
   learning outcome for assignment, 102 (figure)
   self-expression and human creativity, 108 (figure)
   seven-step checklist, 97
   time management, 109–112
   two types of, 95 (figure)
   understanding assessment format, 99–101
   understanding learning outcomes, 104–107
   use of GAI permitted in final assignment, 107–109
   walk-through example, 113–119
   writing, 94
Ethical transparency, 58
Ethics, 40
Examinations, 146
Exams, 146–147, 149
   approach, 153
   case study-based questions, 149
   checklist to begin assignment, 150
   closed exams, 147
   content requirements, 152
   essay-based questions, 148
   ethical use of AI for exam involve, 152–154
   exam process, 151
   exams used in assessment process, 149–150
   familiarisation with learning outcomes, 155
   GAI permitted in final exam, 152
   multiple-choice questions, 149
   open-book exams, 147–148
   overview, 151
   preparation phase, 153–154
   preparing for, 154
   PROMPT-assisted preparation for, 155
   restricted exams, 147
   short answer-based questions, 148–149
   submission details, 151
   take-home exams, 148
   time management, 154
   types of, 147
   typical question types in, 148
   understanding assessment format, 150
   understanding exam preparation and strategy, 150–151
   walk-through example, 156
Extended narrative comment, 187, 189–190
External resources, 147

F

Face-to-face presentation, 125
Factual essay, 96
Fail, 186
Fairness, 40
Feedback, 184
   using AI assistants to help understand initial assignment feedback, 188–189
   assessment to assessment process, 188 (figure)
   important, 187–188
   initial feedback, 189–190
   interpreting feedback across assignments, 191–192
   rubric-based feedback, 190–191
   tracking and mapping feedback, 191 (table)
   types of grades used at universities, 186
   types of summative related feedback used at universities, 186–187
   UCL's guidance on level descriptors, 185 (table)
   understanding grades and feedback mean at university, 185–186
   university grades and, 185
Fido, D., 44
Fillers, 70
Flashcards, 79
Formative task, revising for, 87
Formatting, 117–118, 117 (figure)
Framework for Higher Education Qualifications (FHEQ), 185
Franklin, B., 8
'Free AI transcription tools', 81
Freemium
   access, 59
   models, 60
   version, 65
Furuta, A., 147

G

Gamma.app, 70–71, 138–139, 139 (figure)
   content analysis of first draft using, 139–140

gamma presentation content analysis, 140 (table)
Gemini.ai, 172
'Generate', 70
Generative adversarial networks, 10
Generative artificial intelligence (GAI), 2–3, 9–11, 23, 25, 30, 58, 76–77, 79, 87, 152
  academic integrity, 40–41
  advantages and disadvantages of free access and paid access to AI tool, 60 (table)
  advantages and disadvantages of using account to access AI tool, 59 (table)
  AI image creation tools, 66–69
  AI presentation/slides tools, 69–72
  AI tools, assistants and content, 46–47
  AI video creation tools, 72–73
  AI writing tools, 64–66
  AI-assisted study, 35–36
  AI impacted academic integrity, 42–44
  based presentation tools, 137
  critical thinking and analytical skills, 29–31
  developing plan and structure with, 135
  end scenario, 27–29
  enhancing learning, comprehension and application independently, 25–27
  in essay writing, 94
  ethical use of GAI in e-portfolio involve, 169–170
  ethical use of GAI in presentation, 133
  and evolution of GPTs by open AI, 11–12
  free or fee, 59–60
  future-proof your skillset, 49–50
  to help with writing essay, 108–109
  models, 31
  needs and studying, 25 (table)
  novice or pro, 61–62
  officially vetted vs. wild west, 61
  permitted in final assignment, 133, 169
  permitted in final exam, 152
  permitted use in final assignment, 107–109
  promoting academic integrity in relation to Bloom's Taxonomy and AI literacy, 44–45
  prompting and prompting frameworks, 62–63
  protecting privacy using AI tools, 48–49
  safeguarding concerns for Jamie, 27
  searching for literature and writing assistance, 31–34
  to sign-up or not to sign-up, 59
  skills to prioritise, 50
  start scenario, 27
  study buddy AI assistant, 23–25
  study guide on using, 1–2
  time management and studying efficiently, 34–35
  tools, 146, 185
  University students face, 42–44
  unpacking AI tool kit, 63–64
  used in writing, 2–3
Generative pre-trained transformer (GPT), 10, 15
  generative AI and evolution of GPTs by open AI, 11–12
  GPT development, 12 (table)
Gmail account, 59
Goblin.tools, general approach to action planning using 'Magic ToDo' by, 109–110
Google, 61
Grade Point Average (GPA), 186
Grades, 184
  using AI assistants to help understand initial assignment feedback, 188–189
  assessment to assessment process, 188 (figure)
  feedback important, 187–188
  initial feedback, 189–190
  interpreting feedback across assignments, 191–192
  points, 186
  rubric-based feedback, 190–191
  tracking and mapping feedback, 191 (table)
  types of grades used at universities, 186
  types of summative related feedback used at universities, 186–187
  UCL's guidance on level descriptors, 185 (table)
  understanding grades and feedback mean at university, 185–186
  university grades and feedback, 185
Grammarly, freemium version of, 65
Group presentations, 124, 124 (table)

H

Hamano-Bunce, D., 82
Handwritten approach, 77–78
Harper, C., 44
Hemingway App, 65
Hemingway editor, 65
Higher education
  assessments, 94
  environment, 51
  institutions, 48
Higher-level essays, 94
Higher-order thinking skills, 79
Holland, A., 44, 79
Honesty, 40
Hulme, D., 95
Humata, 86

I

Image-based entry, 177
Inciteful, 60
'Inclusivity and diversity in education', 101
Individual presentations, 124, 124 (table)
Initial feedback, 189–190
Interactive presentation, 125–126

Index

Intermediate approach, 86
International Centre for Academic Integrity (ICAI), 41

J
Jamie, safeguarding concerns for, 27
Jenni.ai, 66

K
Kasparov, G., 11

L
Landscape, 13
  with AI, 15–16
  of human competence, 15
Large Language Models (LLMs), 9, 42, 67, 81, 87, 138
Lateral.io, 86
'Learning', 15
  development, 14
  process, 23
Learning management systems (LMS), 35, 77
Learning outcomes (LOs), 94, 98, 130, 168
  connecting LOs with assessment format and taught content, 104–107
  from e-portfolio, 170
  example of, 101, 170–173
  understanding, 101–104, 129–133
Letter grades, 186
Level descriptors, 185
'Load shedding', 9
Locke, J., 95
'Logic theorist', 11
Lower-order thinking skills, 79
Luger, E., 10, 12

M
Machine learning algorithms, 9–10
Magic media App in Canva, 69
'Magic ToDo' by goblin. tools, general approach to action planning using, 109–110
McCarthy, J., 8
Media, 167
Memory systems, 26
Microsoft, 61, 68, 70, 125
Microsoft PowerPoint, 69–70
Mills, J., 9
Mindmaps, 78
Monitoring tools, 16
Moravec's landscape, 15
Moravec's paradox with AI, 15–16
Motivation, 184
Multiple-choice questions, 149
Multiple choice-style exams, 149
Multiple PDF document reader, 86

N
Narrative comment, 186, 189–190
Natural language processing, 10
Neural networks, 9–10
Neuro-typical students, 23
Newell, A., 11
Non-digital tools, 78
Non-neurotypical students, 23
Note-taking, 78
Novice approach, 61–62

O
Online
  graphic design tool, 69
  home exams, 151
  presentation, 125
  version, 65
On script feedback, 187
OpenAI, 11–12, 68, 72
Open-book exams, 147–148
Oral assessment, 123
Organise note, 78
Organising study notes, 84–85
  multiple PDF document reader, 86
  single PDF document reader, 85
  tools that allow for analysis and concept creation, 86
O'Sullivan, B., 146

P
Paperpal tool, 65–66
Paraphraser tool, 65
Paraphrasing, 108
Pass, 186
Pattern notes, 78
Pattern recognition, 47
Paul, T., 96
Percentages, 186
Portfolio presentation, 126
Poster presentation, 125
Post-presentation feedback for presentations, 126
Premium version, 65
Pre-recorded presentation, 125
Presentations, 123–124
  app.decktopus. com, 138
  assignment focus/selection, 129
  assignment overview, 128
  checklist to begin assignment, 127
  content analysis of first draft using Gamma. app, 139–140
  content analysis of first draft using Tome. app, 141–142
  content requirements, 129
  creating presentation content with presentation AI assistants, 142

creating presentation with key phrase or term, 137
creating presentation with structure, 138
different types of, 125–126
ethical use of generative AI in, 133
example, 136
gamma.app, 138–139
generative AI permitted in final assignment, 133
generative AI-based presentation tools, 137
individual or group presentations, 124
learning outcomes, 129
presentation-based assessments, 123, 128
seven-step checklist to beginning, 127, 127 (table)
submission details, 128
submission process, 128
time management, 133–135
tome.app, 140–141
understanding assessment format, 127
understanding learning outcomes, 129–133
understanding presentation assignment brief, 127–128
used in assessment process and feedback, 126–127
walk-through example, 135
Pre-trained models, 10
Prioritise, skills to, 50
Privacy, 48
'Pro' approach, 61–62
Problem-solution essays, 95
Process E-portfolios, 164
Professional E-portfolios, 165
'Prompting', 62
  frameworks, 62–63
  getting started with, 63 (figure)
  prompt frameworks, 63 (table)
Promoting academic integrity in relation to Bloom's Taxonomy and AI literacy, 44–45, 45 (figure)
Proofreading, 117–118, 117 (figure)

Q
Quality Assurance Agency (QAA), 185
Quill Bot, 65
Quivr.app, 86

R
Ray, P. P., 13
Real-time feedback, 64, 70
Reflective E-portfolios, 164–165
Reflective essay, 96
Responsibility, 40
Restricted exams, 147
Review essay, 96
Revision methods, 79

Revision phase, 153
'Rising sea' of AI technology, 13
Rivers, C., 44, 79
Rubric-analytic focused feedback, 187
Rubric-based feedback, 190–191
Rubric-checklist focused feedback, 187
Rubric-learning outcome focused feedback, 187

S
SAMR model, 13, 100
Samuel, A., 10
Sanctioned tools, 48
Shaw, C., 11
Short answer-based questions, 148–149
Showcase E-portfolios, 164
Simon, H., 11
Sinfield, S., 78
Single PDF document reader, 85
Skillset, future-proof your, 49–50
Skills to prioritise, 50
Solution to requirement of linking, 59
Sora (text-to-video model), 72
Stereotypical image, 77
Store note, 78
Student learning, 77, 79
Studying
  creating revision materials, 79
  creating study notes, 77–78
  organise, store and access study notes, 78
  traditional approaches to, 77
Study phase, 153
Summative assessment, revising for, 88
Summative-based exams, 149
Summative related feedback used at universities, types of, 186–187
Sweller, J., 29

T
Take-home exams, 148, 151–152
Task prioritization, 34
Taught content, recapping on, 87
Technology, 58
Tegmark, M., 13
Testing algorithms, 10
Text-based assistants, 62
Text-based entry, 174–177
Text-to-image generator, 68
'Text transform', 70
Tome.app, 71–72, 140–141, 141 (figure)
  analysis of first draft using, 141–142
  creating presentation content with presentation AI assistants, 142
  tome presentation content analysis, 141 (table)
Traditional approaches to studying, 77–79
Traditional face-to-face presentations, 123

Traditional sense, 123
Tran, K., 8
Transcription tool, 81
Turing, A., 8

U
United Nation's Sustainable Development Goal, 8
University
   grades and feedback, 185
   students face, 42–44, 49
   types of grades used at, 186
   types of summative related feedback used at, 186–187
   understanding grades and feedback mean at, 185–186
University College London's guidance (UCL guidance), 46

V
Verbal-based assessments, 123
Verbal delivery, 129
Virtual Learning Environment (VLE), 80, 128, 166, 168

W
Western colonialism, 147
Workshop presentation, 126
Write mode, 65
Writing, 34, 118

Y
YouTube, 62

Z
Zoom, 125